SAFE HAVEN

SAFE HAVEN

THE POSSIBILITY OF SANCTUARY IN AN UNSAFE WORLD

LARRY GAUDET

RANDOM HOUSE CANADA

Copyright © 2007 Larry Gaudet

All rights reserved under International and Pan-American Copyright Conventions. No part of this book may be reproduced in any form or by any electronic or mechanical means, including information storage and retrieval systems, without permission in writing from the publisher, except by a reviewer, who may quote brief passages in a review. Published in 2007 by Random House Canada, a division of Random House of Canada Limited. Distributed in Canada by Random House of Canada Limited.

Random House Canada and colophon are trademarks.

www.randomhouse.ca

LIBRARY AND ARCHIVES CANADA CATALOGUING IN PUBLICATION

Gaudet, Larry
Safe haven : the possibility of sanctuary in an unsafe world / Larry Gaudet.

ISBN 978-0-679-31383-0

1. Security (Psychology) 2. Refuge—Psychological aspects.
3. Gaudet, Larry. 4. Gaudet, Larry—Travel. I. Title.

PS8563.A824Z475 2007   C818'.5403   C2007-901538-7

Lyrics from "O Marie" by Daniel Lanois reprinted with permission from Daniel Lanois. Lyrics from "Bud the Spud" reprinted by permission, copyright Crown Vetch Music (a division of Stompin' Tom Ltd.). Quotations from "The Idea of North" used by permission of the Estate of Glenn Gould and the Canadian Broadcasting Corporation.

Jacket and text design: Leah Springate

Printed and bound in the United States of America

10 9 8 7 6 5 4 3 2 1

For Theo, Jackson and Alison

James and Donna

Susan, May, Fran and Reg

Vivian and Stan and their family

My friends

And in memory of my parents, Vera and Gerry

It still strikes me as strange that the case histories I write should read like short stories and that, as one might say, they lack the serious stamp of science. I must console myself with the reflection that the nature of the subject is evidently responsible for this, rather than any preference of my own.

—SIGMUND FREUD

PART I

CRITICAL INCIDENT

1.1

SANCTUARY IN THE FOG (Ghosting)

Foggy Cove, June 2006

IN MY TRAVELS, I've developed a fondness for older neighbourhoods that celebrate the diffuse and unseen, the spooky
both planned and improvised. The French Quarter. The
Dorobanti in Bucharest. Venice. Vieux-Montréal. Even
when I'm moving inside a tourist throng, I'm still the willing pawn on a grid of haunting streets and alleys, soaking
up the orchestrated melancholia in the shadows and whispers between cobblestone and gable. I'm attracted to the
gestures that keep strangers on the outside, flat-footed
before the imposing facade, or too intimidated to knock on
the towering bronze doors. More than once I've peered
through wrought-iron gates into courtyards obscured by
foliage and lattice, imagining a weathered marble shrine or a
caged exotic bird talking to itself in complete sentences. I've
studied half-hidden entrances that seduce the eye only to
repel it, leaving me to wonder: Who's in there? What are
they doing? Why am I out here?

Whether I'm on the outside looking in, or the inside
looking out, I'm in love with mystery itself, the idea that
within everything and everyone there are hidden meanings,
and conflicting meanings, too, and things that just never
add up, no matter how many clues to the puzzle you have. I

don't know exactly what triggered my obsession to buy land and build a home in Foggy Cove. The mystery still beguiles and indeed engulfs me, not just as a mind game, but as a physical force that shapes life here. A seaside village in southeastern Nova Scotia along the North Atlantic coast, Foggy Cove is often shrouded in the ambiguous conditions of coastal fog, the mythic substance of ghosts, the inspiration for a thousand clichés on the human tendency to orient toward inward horizons when there's nowhere else to gaze. And that's just what I'm doing this morning as I lie awake in bed.

Here, in our barn by the sea, we're a nuclear family enclosed within itself, expecting summer to arrive any day now and finally warm things up. The fire went out hours ago; it's chilly in our loft bedroom. I'm assuming (but can't yet verify) that small dramas are unfolding outdoors in the fog: spiderwebs thickened to visibility by heavy dew; an intrepid family of deer in the field, munching on clover; a trio of blue jays in a fight at the bird feeder. Someone is likely walking a dog along the beach or the cliffs, intending to pick up the mail on the way back, having determined that this time the dog will not escape into the house before its muddied belly gets rinsed with the hose and dried in the sun, should the sun ever appear again, which seems very unlikely right now.

Everyone else in our house is asleep, oblivious to the clouds on the ground around us, the air uniformly congested with condensation made from heat rising off the land, the evaporating water seeking a home in the sky but temporarily manifest as fog in our midst. Water can't be stopped. It goes where it needs to, when it's tired of hanging around, creating fog blindness. Fog reminds me that our bodies are nearly all water. Maybe walking through fog, as so many of us who live here like to do, breathing it in deeply, speaks to an unconscious desire to connect with our distant amphibian past when we were gilled water creatures in search of land, backbone, lungs, a down comforter like the one covering me now. Through the loft windows I can't even make out the silhouette of our apple trees down below the house, only fifty feet away. The world outside appears like the one behind my eyelids: a shimmering grey surface. So why even make the effort to keep my eyes open? I dig deeper into the comforter, also conscious of the soft pyjama flannel on my skin. Cozy bliss. As womb-like as it gets. Why move? Ever again . . .

Still, as much as I love fog, it has taken me a few years to learn how to gaze with unclenched teeth and unsweating palms into the visual nothingness that greets me here on so many mornings and can muck up the view for days on end. As a cataract over my watchable world, fog channels the hungry eye through veils in the air that come and go, and always come again, softening edges, distorting depth and sound, hiding things. I've observed people vacationing in our village for the first time who, in their experience of persistent fog, present symptoms of a panic attack, an anxiety disorder. It's as if they see a conspiracy behind the weather: something or someone is out to get them from behind the wall of meteorological vagueness. Or worse: maybe there's nothing there at all. A foggy day disarms the defence mechanisms that provide immunity from the risks of prolonged self-awareness, and that can be disquieting. I personally don't know many people who go on vacation for the purpose of tunnelling into the darker corners or less travelled pathways of their psyche.

Alison's feet seek out mine as she turns toward me. Cold feet. I thought she'd got into bed with heavy socks on, but she seems to have lost them in the night. The message encrypted in her toes is established bedroom code in our house: I'm supposed to get up and start a fire. But in this dialogue between feet, I respond sullenly. I have no intention of getting up yet. I'm wiped. As she is. As everyone is. We arrived in Halifax last night after a two-hour flight from Toronto, then we drove two more hours in rainy darkness and arrived in time for dinner at Alison's parents' house next door. The evening featured our two young boys acting out the part of runaway-train engines, chugging and tooting around the furniture. Only deep dishes of ice cream curtailed the meltdown caused by a derailment after four-year-old Theo missed a signal and collided with Jackson, his six-year-old brother. The incident happened in a quadrant where the invisible tracks weren't supposed to intersect. Back at our place, in the final minutes before bedtime, it seemed unwise to insist that the boys, after such a long day of travelling, be required to wash the vanilla streaks off their faces. They're sleeping everything off, and good for them.

Ignoring the prodding of my wife's toes, I close my eyes and try to recapture that luxurious feeling that comes with being sheltered in a space of one's own making. I am protected here, and happy doing the protecting, as a father, husband, neighbour, alert to my good fortune, listening for any source of danger, no matter how insanely remote the threat. My vigilance scares me. I'd sleep with an axe, stick pins in voodoo dolls or clench prayer beads if I knew it would keep us safe here or anywhere else.

The foghorn sounds again: an extended brooding note, like a million owls in symphonic lockstep.

I love the sounds of nature. Pheasants squawking. The thrum of hummingbird wings. The wind teasing out ditties from within leaves and branches. The acoustical variations that result from collisions of tidal water and land mass. But foghorn music resonates deeper with me. It feels like nature invested with a human spirit. It gives meaning to fog, not only protecting ships from being wrecked on shoals, but assuring those of us onshore that there's always something or someone out there: we are not alone. The foghorns in our vicinity are positioned on remote islands and headlands, and echo fantastically. Sonic fragments bounce here and there and overlap one another, like the distortion of an electric guitar tweaked by a reverb pedal. The foghorn functions like a heart, thumping for an essential purpose, reassuringly steady. It's a voice like many voices in Foggy Cove: an echo with distant origins. Or possibly a homing device for those who have fled here for one reason or another. Sometimes, however, there's *another* voice in the mix, similar to a foghorn. It's a sound with more grit, lower on the scale, hollow and uneven, unpredictable, like an injured monster moaning in its lair. A monster that can't carry a tune. This sound, I've been told, is produced by tides swirling into crevices on the headlands. But no one around here speaks authoritatively to that claim. It's Mother Earth speaking, absolutely—too eerie for my liking. I feel I'm being stalked, not soothed, by the incomprehensibly large forces all around me.

"Honey, I'm freezing." Alison is finally drawn to words.

I don't even pretend to snore. A dead giveaway of wakefulness.

She's layered up in fleece and flannel, an elaborate getup she dons each night here with the seriousness of a high priestess, in the belief that more is better when it comes to producing body heat.

"Larry?" She shrugs her body into mine.

When I make no response, she turns away in a mini-huff. With her back to me, the silence is too pregnant. She's calling my bluff, my extreme stillness alerting her to the possum act. There's no way I can win at this. I'm going to have to get up and make a new fire. Of course, I could simply turn up the electric baseboard heaters—but that would be the triumph of sense over sensibility. I give up the game.

"Could you put the water on for the coffee?" she asks.

Last night we went to bed listening to the foghorn, the rain patter on the roof, the wind and whitecaps scouring the cliffs. The wood stove murmured with high-tech efficiency, the incineration of old maple making the place all toasty while the greenhouse gases escaped into the blustery night. As the fire created a torment of shadows, I lay there drowsily content. In my final seconds of wakefulness, my thoughts were of the eternal tomorrow resident in my imagination: waking up to a calm blue sea, a temperate summer morning, the beaches fattened up with sand returned from its winter home in the deep waters of the bay, the air peaty with seaweed, the army of tourists absent for a while longer and nothing on the schedule but chopping firewood or watching our boys invest their toy bulldozers with the power to regrade the landscape.

But now morning is here again, and with it the burden of clarity.

Two years ago, our family embarked on an adventure in Nova Scotia. That's not quite true. We were dragged by me into a rural existence in a remote village by the sea, despite palpable reluctance in strategic decision-making quarters, notably Alison's. This move was instigated by my untested fantasies about the merits of solitude, if not total isolation from the big bad world. The idea was to vacate our condominium in downtown Toronto, leave our lives and friends behind for a year and move to the cottage we had recently built in Nova Scotia, near the great heritage town of Lunenburg, ninety kilometres south of Halifax.

We made it through the year in Nova Scotia in one familial piece, and we've returned again for the summer, not as residents but as seasonal visitors. There was much about our year in Nova Scotia that surprised me. Much that confused and, at times, unhinged me. There were many days I felt fragmented, in psychological disarray, standing outside my body looking in, unable to concentrate, frozen by interior storms that seemed to come out of nowhere. There were beautiful moments, as was expected for the sticker price. But who remembers those with the same vividness?

When we decided to buy land here, Alison's parents, Stan and Vivian, needed a retirement home. So we went fifty-fifty on a property and created two deeds to reflect the division of ownership. There were only three homes on the drumlin hill that winds lazily through the Foggy Cove basin; now there are fifteen, including our two places. In theory, we'd moved to paradise, our property located in a 250-year-old fishing and farming village (a series of villages, actually) of weathered capes and ancient barns, a good number of which have either been restored or built fairly recently, in tasteful deference to the muse of heritage preservation. Our home, a grey-cedar-shingled structure, is well anchored in an old sheep pasture at the end of a gravel road that meanders along the contours of the drumlin ridge toward the coast; it pretends to be a barn but doesn't entirely succeed because of the immodest wall of sea-facing windows, the antithesis of blunt Nova Scotian thriftiness. We have captured, to borrow from the jargon of real-estate agents, the boldest ocean views. From inside, our place seems like one big window, an instrument for viewing, floating high on the lot, boatlike. We're behind and above wetlands of mature alders and waves of dune grass that flow to the beach, flanked by two imposing headlands of dark spruce that jut far out into the sea, creating a protected bay where, in the warmer months, and in many colder ones, you can hear the waves collapsing in deep sand, or watch lobster boats groaning along, in a diesel funk, their trap bunches plopping off the stern. In good weather, when the windows are open in the great room, the screens in place, it seems we're living in a cavernous, bugless porch. And the windows go way up too, with huge transoms topping the double-hungs across a thirty-foot facade that's oriented northeast toward the ocean. The effect is passive-aggressive solar: all the light you would ever need, theoretically, although fog undermines that theory.

We designed the house ourselves. It was meant to be a simple structure: a gabled barn, insulated for year-round use. We hand-drew the floor plan and elevations. Our builder quietly corrected our errors, added new ideas and created the working plans. Recalling the ambition in that first drawing is always embarrassing. We didn't know the first thing about how a house should be built. It's mostly wood, this place. Framed, nailed, sanded, primed and painted by human hands. An ecologically sensitive architect would cringe at the waste in stud-frame construction, the anachronism of shingles, pine floors, wood trim. The suggestion would be to source out prefab structural forms, holistically manufactured metal hybrids for the beams and window sashes, straw bale insulation, more green design strategies in general. There'd be talk of photovoltaic panels, chemical toilets, micro-windmills and engineered floors made from recycled radioactive waste that magically looks like three-hundred-year-old oak. In hindsight, we didn't exactly hit the high points of ecological responsibility during construction. There were mounds of debris, now in a landfill. But I've conveniently come to terms with my horror. Amazing what tricks the mind can perform once the garbage bins are hauled away. We had a few good ideas, though, like insisting on the wooden storm doors that make the place look like a real barn. Made from V-grooved pine, they're painted a deep molten red, a colour they used to call

bull's blood around here. As the story goes, barn paint was
once tinted with cattle blood, when people weren't so afflu-
ent, when paint chips were things that fell to the floor many
years after the walls were painted, and not something you
picked up at the design store. We selected a subtle grey-
green for the cabinetry, also made from V-grooved pine, and
it was amusing to hear the builders, their contempt for
designer talk undisguised, openly teasing us by saying how
good the shelves looked after that second coat of Monroe
Bisque.

In the two years since the two homes in our extended
family were completed, the hayfield has been in recovery
from a large scar created by a long septic field that probably
has enough leaching ability to process the waste water of a
small city. But by the end of last summer, new growth
started to colonize the field from a mongrel seed assortment
we planted—called highway mix. We watered it twice a day,
fanatically, relying on six sprinklers and hundreds of feet of
green hose, which I often turned on without checking the
weather reports, being afflicted with a suburbanite's crazed
expectation for immediate, uniformly picturesque results.
This year, with the seed fully taken, having grown through
the winter nourished by the five hundred pounds of crushed
limestone that I spread by hand last fall—a process that
ended with me dusted beige—the field looks much more
natural, but the truckloads of topsoil were spread too uniformly. I need to introduce irregularity into the landscap-
ing, an idea that causes some villagers to look at me
strangely when I mention it.

So this is where we'd arrived: a personal sanctuary, as I
had ideally imagined it, constructed as an escape hatch from
urban stress and corporate disaffection, but also as an
emblem of my belief in solitude as a creative means of re-
juvenation. In Foggy Cove, I would finally unlock the code to

my untapped human potential, and transcend the meaner forces that inhibit awareness and sensitivity and weaken family bonds. This was a powerful incentive to get the hell out of town. But during the sabbatical, all too often I was immune to Foggy Cove's seductions. In my skeptical moments, what I saw out of our enormous windows was something akin to a satellite picture from low orbit, the weather transfigured from an immediate drama into a grainy smear of continental currents—a schematic—above abstractions of topography, as if I were peering at an ultrasound image on a swatch of thermal paper. My assessment of the monumental Atlantic was also frequently problematic: a flat blue form contained by land. The ocean wasn't *oceanic* to me, not all the time, perhaps because I had viewed it a fair number of times from miles up in the sky, on overnight flights between Halifax and London.

At night, on my walks around the village, I would often track planes that appeared as blinking disturbances among the stars, wondering: Why can't I fit in fluidly here? Why can't I enjoy the moment for what it is?

Once the fire is cranked, the house heats up fast, nearly a sauna, the big transom windows sweating. The fog has thinned for the moment into a gauzy mist enlivened by an undercoat of green. Temperature in the low teens, Celsius. Hard to believe it's late June, supposedly the longest days of the year. Our view reaches through the fog across the marsh to the beach dunes in the distance, the limit of our visual world. There's no ocean in sight today, not yet, and so there's still psychic containment. We all feel it, I think. Alison and I cling to mugs of strong coffee that anchor us to the old pine table as the boys create a racket over their breakfast. Train noises in steam engine and diesel tonalities.

Simulations of the beep-beep warnings of forklifts in reverse gear. Mauled fragments of nursery rhymes. Verbal flatulence, also known as raspberries. All of which cause cereal to sputter from little mouths and gobs of scrambled eggs to fall to the floor. Theo's pyjama top is a fluid extension of the red bean-and-egg palette on his face. The mess does little to diminish the presence of his large brown eyes, which evoke twin basketballs in my mind. All children, in my experience and regardless of contrary evidence, have large eyes and lengthy lashes, if you look closely or sympathetically enough. Jackson, too, is all eyes, which are blue like his mother's, luminous and intense, conveying a take-no-prisoners ferocity that I want to believe comes from me. The boys keep mangling their breakfast and berating each other until Alison steps in and asks for littler voices, boys, use your inside voices.

My wife mostly favours the subterranean approach to conflict management. She listens very carefully to children and pets but also to the loudmouths at parties who spot the easy mark and exploit her courtesy in withstanding stupidity without a frown. Lord, I've done that to her myself on many occasions. But something wound tight also lurks in Alison, the voice of maternal command-and-control. Despite being moved to tears by the symbolism and fabrics in the new Prada collection, despite being a lover of art from the Italian Renaissance, she's developed a dispatcher's aggressiveness in managing the circumstances of three boys, if you include the husband. I do not mess with her on mornings like this.

As I sit glumly staring into my coffee, Alison coaches Jackson and Theo in the proper use of a spoon. She's been going nonstop since she got up, and in the unwritten but well-kept ledger of domestic accountabilities, it's obvious that making the fire alone won't suffice as my contribution.

It will surely fall to me to accompany the boys into the field, into their sandbox, so that they can happily turn into teeth-chattering mud balls. Perhaps if I had made the oatmeal or got the boys dressed, there might be an argument for going fifty-fifty on the outdoor assignment, but I've missed that opportunity. Alison turns her attention to me, silently considering the trail of bark and wood bits leading from the basement to the wood stove over to the breakfast table and up my pyjamas.

"I'll clean it up," I say as I stand up, shuffling toward the broom and dustpan next to the stove. It has started to rain, the wind picking up.

As I sweep the floor, Alison vanishes into the hallway and soon returns with the boys' rain gear and fleece jackets, tossing the pile on the floor. She then retires to the kitchen; next comes the noise of the coffee grinder followed by the clang of dishes entering the dishwasher.

"You guys wanna go outside?" I'm half hopeful they'll say no.

Jackson shouts, "Yay!"

Theo seconds the motion.

"Then finish your breakfast."

"And then wash your face and hands," comes their mother's voice, predictably.

All three of us in the sandbox. The boys are constructing a highway and train-track system for their fleet of toy vehicles, oblivious to the rain and wind. Ocean is now visible for the first time today, a bland grey expanse the same colour as the cloud blanket. Between these grey borders of sky and water, there's a band of purple, a bruiselike atmospheric effect near the horizon.

The sandbox is constructed with massive hemlock logs.

It took two men one full working day to build it and popu-
late the interior with a load of sand that had nearly filled a
real dump truck. The sandbox is the boys' sovereign territory, and I'm always cautious around it, careful not to harm
a work-in-progress that, to a parental eye, often looks
merely like a safety hazard.

All children are poets or visionaries, if you listen to them.

"So, who's in the sandbox right now?" I ask.

"Bami and Baloan," says Theo.

"I'm Baloan," says Jackson.

"I'm Poop," shouts Theo.

"No you're not, Theo," Jackson admonishes. "You're
Bami."

"I'm Bami!" Theo chortles.

"And where is Stain?"

"Stain is dead." Theo reports this.

"He was killed by a bad man," Jackson adds, pausing in
his work.

Bami, Baloan, the now-murdered Stain, along with
Bomit, Jose, Fatigué (pronounced as the French word for
tired) and Poop, the new guy on the block, are all characters
in the boys' imaginary world. I've been honoured to contribute to their pantheon, inventing Jose, the friendly monster (a Hispanic-American male monster, it seems, inspired
by the Tasmanian Devil of Warner Brothers cartoon fame),
a super-mouse capable of shrinking or expanding to any
size, a protector of the boys from other monsters not welcome in the household. In the sandbox, there are houses,
invisible to the eye, where these imaginary characters live.

"So what do these houses look like?" I ask. "Are they
built?"

Jackson wrinkles his face, as if I'd questioned something
as obvious as the difference between night and day. He
keeps digging with a trowel. He's tall for his age, wiry, with

a mop of curls that started out blond in the manner of his fair mother but are now brown. A good-natured boy but operatic in his disappointments, and given to conspiracy theory. His sweetest quality (which he'll be taught to unsweeten later in life, I know) is a lack of deviousness in manipulating others. On balance, Jackson plainly tells you what he wants, and if he doesn't get it, he reacts with a sulky resistance that evaporates the instant he's distracted by any fun alternative. A resourceful boy, never bored in his own or his brother's company, at least not yet.

Theo, too, ignores my inquiries about the houses. He's escaped his rubber boots and is marching around the wet sand in mismatched socks, shouting, "I am a robot!" At any second, he's going to claim to be too hot and strip off the rain jacket and fleece, too. Testing limits, always, but with a smile. A talented flirt. Whenever he detects disapproval in me, the first words out of his mouth are, "Am I a cutie?" Or "Do you love me, Daddy?" As his grandmother says, he's always working the room.

Today for some reason I keep pestering the boys to describe the houses in which their imaginary friends live. Maybe I'm doing this because I'm grumpy at being out in the rain, or perhaps it's a petty rebellion arising from my low status on the work site—mainly, I'm a digger of sand— compared to the design responsibilities assumed by Jackson the architect and Theo his loyal intern.

"Daddy, the houses are just there," Jackson says, exasperated.

"What do you mean, *just there?*"

"You don't have to see them."

"I don't?"

"No, Daddy."

"But how do you get inside if you can't see them?"

He thinks for a long minute. "You just go in."

"Just like that?"

"The houses have doors, Daddy."

"And you just walk in through the doors."

"You walk in," Theo adds, as if all this is completely obvious.

"Okay," I reply, satisfied enough.

I rather like the idea that a home exists if you believe it does, and that the process of its construction has more to do with what's going on in your head than the evidence on the ground. As we work together to build the highways around these invisible homes, I'll walk through any door the boys say is open, even if they have to lead me there by the nose.

For the longest time I've been intrigued by the many possible meanings of the word sanctuary. My objective with this book was to explore sanctuary as an idea or concept with a diverse historical legacy and enduring cultural importance around the world, anchoring the whole business with my present-tense journey to create a sanctuary or home for my family in Nova Scotia.

I saw this as the literary equivalent to reality television.

Perhaps I had visions of myself as a solitary figure at a desk, intellectually composed, surrounded by hefty books, illustrated manuscripts, studying great philosophers and the archetypal forms and rituals of sanctuary in its religious, political and contemplative dimensions, like an archaeologist intent on making original connections between past and present. Nearly everyone to whom I mentioned the project would affect a faraway look, a signal of agreement that profound things could be achieved. I didn't anticipate that this creative work—undertaken mainly within my sanctuary by the sea—would be, at its core, an occasion to explain my own condition to myself with more clarity than

I'd ever desired. Acquiring self-knowledge is useful but also presents challenges if you're unprepared for it.

Entering the sanctuary, you must be prepared for the confusion and panic that come with confronting who you are, or might be. Who you could have been. And that can be a little risky. How was I to know that I would see ghosts from my own life that I thought were long dead and buried?

I have a hunch that most of us know the sensation of ghostly forces roaming around inside us. Sometimes these forces manifest in positive ways—as hunger for passion and adventure, as a search for love or friendship—and thus bring us closer to others and in touch with the better part of our nature. Sometimes, though, we're at the mercy of unresolved tensions that seem vengefully intent on bringing out the worst in us, spiriting us toward rootlessness even when we're anchored down. Before I moved to Foggy Cove, it never occurred to me that what we all may need sometimes is sanctuary from who we've become.

Sanctuary is a beautiful word, evocative of so much: protection, safety, contemplation, solitude. But it's also easily exploited, not just by the vulnerable and the dispossessed or the mystically inclined but by the powerful. In documents used by public companies for financial reporting, there's typically a paragraph in small print in the opening pages, a legal convention known as *safe harbour*. This claim of safe harbour is for protection from investor litigation in the event the company's rosily conjectured future remains unprofitably fictional.

The dictionary definition of sanctuary, which showcases the Latin root of the word *sanctus,* meaning holy, is not much help. The history of holy—of sacred thought, of God itself, or the gods—could mean anything, and certainly it means many things to many people. Perfect: not only am I unqualified to write this book, nobody else is either, the subject being effectively a thousand angels on each of a billion pins. In her bestseller *A History of God*, the religious-affairs writer Karen Armstrong bravely attempted a comparative study of the evolution of the monotheistic religions—Christianity, Judaism, Islam. She tried to keep things simple for the non-specialist, but the book is lengthy and exhausting for the many millions of us who do not want to become theologians. As Armstrong concedes, "All talk about God staggers under impossible difficulties." So it is with sanctuary.

The story of sanctuary will always be a work-in-progress, an educational Venice, monstrously beautiful to behold. You could spend a lifetime sauntering its alleys and gliding its canals, and then vanish while hopelessly trying to summarize the grand plan. No single specialty among the myth-creating professions—history, theology, anthropology, archaeology, philosophy, film, branding, propaganda, journalism—can explore the connotations of the sanctuary principle without adopting the multi-disciplinary voice. Stepping into sanctuary as subject matter, you're instantly adrift in the grand history of protection—or shelter—from everything that intimidates or scares us: the elements, the gods, our own ignorance and violent tendencies, but also our enemies whoever they happen to be, the tribe over the hill, the witch in the Salem housewife, the stalkers, the homeless, the meat-eaters, perfume-sprayers, fur-wearers, the literal refugees climbing off their rafts on our shores, or falling from the landing gear at ten thousand feet, or the people three blocks over with a postal code ignored by the direct marketers of luxury goods.

Popular historians skilled at speaking to a broad audience might be inclined to explore sanctuary as a fusion of architecture, religion and ethics. Such an approach could produce a plausible narrative about the steady stream of progress and innovation over thousands of years in the methodologies and rituals that humans adopt and the edifices we build to protect and worship whatever is most deserving of protection— of shelter. We shelter a lot of things: ourselves, but also animals, plants, food, the fruits of contemplation, knowledge, belief systems, cultural memory and artifacts, truth, lies, the daily rituals that give life meaning.

I like the notion of sanctuary as a permanent stream of creativity, a symbol for the human capacity to rise above murder and tribal venality as its prime organizing principle. But the word also describes creativity in *not* rising above murder and venality, because there are the anti-sanctuary sanctuaries: concentration camps, ghettos, slums, detention centres, holding cells, demilitarized zones, the old walls between East and West and the new one between Palestinians and Jews.

Sanctuary, to me, is the sound of doors opening and then slamming shut: opening to a new need for protection, and closing to protect those lucky enough to be on the inside, keeping others out. Throw a dart at any embattled or emerging belief, economic sector or outlaw desire and you'll hit an innovation in the sanctuary principle, and sometimes a degradation. Everywhere we look there's evidence: refugee camps, women's shelters, safe houses, suicide cults, witness protection programs, panic rooms, private clubs, password-enabled chat groups, foster homes, wild animal preserves, orphanages, hospices, ecological protection regions, gated communities, gay zones, think-tanks, celebrity colonies, Malibu, Monaco, brothel nations, tourist meccas, Mecca, tax havens, bohemian outposts. And let's not forget the plutocratic prerogative to buy an island or a mountain or a prairie and turn your back on everything and everyone, as did William Randolph Hearst, Aristotle Onassis, James Goldsmith, Ted Turner, Marlon Brando.

But sanctuary is a story that belongs to everyone, regardless of our station in life, as the ultimate human fable in the search for home. So many adventures in the epic stories— from Homer's *Odyssey* to James Joyce's *Ulysses,* from Günter Grass's stunted drummer boy in *The Tin Drum* to John Irving's version of the same in *A Prayer for Owen Meany*— involve a vision of home, the safe harbour, often under attack from within (or without), followed by the journeys launched and battles fought to conquer the enemy, concluding with the return to the sanctuary, wiser for the experience, or maybe no wiser at all.

Home. A myth that launched ten million books. Including this one.

Forgive the assumptions I'm about to make. I'm sure they say much more about me than you.

You have a dream of sanctuary too.

It's possible that today you don't know where your personal retreat is located, or what it looks like. But it's only a matter of time before you, like me, have a dirty little secret: the time you spend at vacation property websites, clicking into thumbnail images and virtual reality tours, searching for a virgin slice of septic-approved acreage on which you will, finally, build a place to spend quality time with a calmer, more enlightened, healthier version of yourself.

If you live, as I do, in Canada, on the northern margins of North America, you may envision the classic getaway to be somewhere rather warmer in winter, an island in the Caribbean, a hedonistic shrine cooked up from images we've all seen in the airline magazines in the seat pouch: a thatched-roof hut near a sandy beach, within a strand of coconut trees (a charmingly fragile affront to the inevitability of storm surges), a hammock for your afternoon nap, lulled to sleep by rum punch, the ocean babbling at low tide, a guide to wealth management tented over your gently heaving belly. It's a lovely vision, but the reality for many who go south isn't so privileged. The Florida economy depends on millions of retirees from the north crammed into condos, trailer homes and budget motels rented for the winter on a pensioner's budget, offering amenities such as a nurse on call, a nearby public golf course with a snoozing alligator in the sand trap and clam dinners at a suburban mall on Saturday night.

But sun and beaches aren't part of everyone's dream grammar, even here in Canada. With the threat of climate change and global warming, living near a beach, especially in hurricane season, has lost some of its allure. Many also detest the cattle-car nature of charter air travel, the prospect of beggars and touts outside the gated beach community, the gastrointestinal turbulence from eating spicy island food. And so they look closer to home. I know people who have spent years searching for a farm that reminds them of the land that their grandparents abandoned because of the rocks, hard winters, thin topsoil. Their nirvana is a view over snowy fields after the old barn is turned into a studio, plate glass from floor to gable, ideal for making crafts, writing software or nurturing the solemn belief that the acreage must be loved, in all seasons, under all conditions, good or bad.

There are as many visions of sanctuary-as-escape as there are people. Over the years I've stoked many conversations by asking, "What does sanctuary mean to you?" When I'm talking to an adult familiar with the stress of modern life—the existential frisson of calculating long-term mortgage interest, a punishing career pace, the used condoms found in the lane behind the house—the response is often a dreamy silence. And then comes the narrative deluge, the detailed monologues of personal redemption through escape, the riffing on the virtues of privacy and solitude from what we might call real life.

I'm really talking about myself here. But admit it: on some days you feel a need for a heightened level of protection from whatever life you've made for yourself, the desire to have more control over what comes into your presence, and what goes out. And you have likely muttered, at least once, after dodging a panhandler's palm or the telemarketer's call, *I'm outta here.* So many of us, myself included, also wish to function on an exalted plane of connectedness to the part of us that wonders where we come from, and where we go, if we go anywhere, after we die.

Where, in fact, did Stain go? A question for the ages.

An adult without an elaborate escape fantasy—is this possible? Unlikely. But some people are so downtrodden, so overburdened by misfortune, that sanctuary can only really be about stealing food or clothing for the kids, begging for booze, copping a handful of red pills, feeling grateful for the blanket and a bunk at the shelter, marvelling at the cleanliness of the bandages handed out by the social worker. The very rich and super-powerful marvel at other things, and may already live in the throes of their sanctuary fantasy, engaged in volunteer work and heart-friendly recreation in a tax-optimized version of the gated community, surrounded by people of similar financial worth, buying attack dogs and new lasers for the perimeter. Because life is short, mean, brutish and requires advisers who speak in the logic of particle physics to explain why no matter how much money you have today, you need more tomorrow.

Sanctuary is as much about indulging fear or manifesting paranoia as it is about chasing solitude. An old friend of mine, while going through a very rough patch in the dating wars that involved fending off a stalker, confessed that he'd once had a dream in which he won the lottery, retired, then hired a troupe of sexy women in their twenties as security guards, equally capable with massage oil as with a machine gun. This isn't so implausible: billionaires, dictators and potentates have been known to live like this. But it makes you wonder what you'd do if money were no object. Perhaps it's better not to know.

The early education experts say that one stage of mental development in children involves them acquiring awareness of shifts in their body temperature and realizing that being wet and cold is uncomfortable. Only after I had got the boys out of the sandbox and into the house, which involved a twenty-minute argument as the rain poured down upon us, did they accept that they were chilled. As usual, they then began questioning why I hadn't brought them in earlier.

Stripped naked and bundled into colourful beach towels, the boys huddle together on the sofa, clamouring for hot chocolate and scones as their mother comes down from the loft, a laptop under her arm. Alison scrutinizes the pile of wet clothes on the floor and knows instantly that Theo's red fleece isn't there but outdoors somewhere because of my failings as a parent. A few words are exchanged. As I start putting on my rain gear again, the fog momentarily dissipates and enables me to see the fleece soggily inert on the ground near the sandbox. I announce the discovery and the boys immediately clamber up on the pine table to confirm the sighting, dropping their towels in the process. It's as if I said there was a battleship or circus elephant out there.

I march outside in rubber boots and a black toque—but coatless. I can see my breath but not much more: the fog is thick again, a wall of grey, constipated in its movements. The ocean roar is present, and since I can't see the surf, it sounds louder than it normally does.

Wind swoops down from the hill behind me, and for an instant I have a clear view back to the house. The boys are still watching me from up on the pine table. Alison hovers between them, a coffee mug the size of a grapefruit in her hand. Jackson and Theo are as safe here as they're ever going to be in life, but they still seem so defenceless from where I stand, much like the deer in our midst, vulnerable creatures on the fringes of changes they don't understand, which keep them on high alert, suspicious of sudden movements, unusual noises.

I retrieve Theo's fleece just as the fog thickens up again. My clothes have dampened fast. I've been out here three minutes and I'm frozen.

An engine drones overhead. Perhaps it's the sea rescue helicopter, flying up and down the coastline above the fog, waiting for enough visual clarity to descend. I wonder whether a ship went down in the night or someone fell overboard. Perhaps it's a training run, or surveillance on suspected drug smugglers or lobster poachers. But I see nothing at all to confirm any suspicions.

The foghorn. Again and again.

The next day we're given a reprieve: visible sun and blue sky for hours at a time. It's the kind of day where Alison and I negotiate with each other for time away from the kids for some exercise. My strategy is to remind her that my survival in the long term requires cardio fitness to ward off heart disease. This is no joking matter. Strokes took both my parents, my mother at forty-five, my father in his mid-sixties. Alison's strategy is to remind me that unless I want her to blimp out and thus cease to look like the girl I married, she needs to get her daily run in. As the day progresses, disease prevention gains the upper hand over weight control. This was never in doubt; Alison is slim.

It's late afternoon when I start my hike, warm but not blistering hot, the light softening toward the hues of dusk.

The tourist season hasn't kicked into gear yet. There are no crowds at the beach, only a few local residents stopping by for a walk after work, men and women who already have farmer's tans, looking like human versions of Neapolitan ice cream: chocolate arms, pink faces, white legs. No boogie boarders or surfers in sight. No one in wetsuits.

On the beach I meet one of the carpenters who built our house. He has recently returned from a family vacation driving to Boston via Maine and back. In the car for a week. They found the whole experience a nightmare of traffic and expense they won't repeat. He says they're going to Disneyland next year, or Disney World. Some Disney place, somewhere.

I resume walking down the crescent beach away from the village, away from everything—buildings, roads, utility poles, people. I'm heading toward the southern boundary of Foggy Cove, the estuary of a large river that cleaves the coastline. There, on the back side of a high drumlin, a place inaccessible to all but the most determined hikers, is a hidden valley. Soon I'm clambering up dunes of rocks and pebbles, a naturally forming sea wall that encloses a lagoon below the drumlin. From there I tiptoe through marsh, traversing a path made walkable by large flat stones and the occasional two-by-six board. I emerge through trees at the bottom of a cleared field and begin the climb. At the drumlin ridge, I can see the hidden valley below.

This is where the ghost village is. Four-hundred-year-old ruins.

And among those ruins, which are mainly excavated stone foundations, there are fantastic structures more recently built that look and feel less like buildings than like monumental sculptures, wild experiments in wood-frame construction. These additions come from the epic laboratory of Brian MacKay-Lyons, an architect of some considerable international reputation, who is a Nova Scotian born and bred. In his late forties, he runs an architectural practice in Halifax while also serving as a professor of architecture at Dalhousie University. Brian and his wife, Marilyn, own this landscape of ruins, purchased in chunks going back to when they were a few years out of university. For two weeks every year, Brian holds a kind of summer school here for architectural students who come from around the world to work with him. Under the direction of Brian and his colleagues—architects, carpenters, builders—the interns help to design and build a new structure, a collaborative act that someone once described as large-scale guerilla carpentry.

I descend into the valley to wander around. There are students here today doing a group sketching exercise, many sitting on rocks or tree stumps in the field, lost in thought. I deeply envy them.

The newer structures on the property are sizable statements. Some are extreme ruminations on the barn or shed form, and others conceptually amputated from the skeleton of a schooner, or the belly of a fish factory. Yet others are just plain hard to figure: beautiful abstractions made out of complicated joints and framed platforms used as walls, floors and a variety of roofing configurations that create shapes open to the elements and yet sheltering too. They all have qualities I've seen in Brian's work for his clients, a soulful amalgam of modern design sensibility and a much older, distinctly Nova Scotian building style.

These structures in the hidden valley are as much artistic as architectural—but of course that distinction is silly. Whatever Brian and his colleagues have created—and regardless what you call it—it's a vehicle for a conversation between past and present: a shrine where the ghosts of Foggy Cove have a home. Amid the large-scale experimentations and eloquent manipulations of wood, there are the deep stone foundations of houses built by those who were among the first French settlers to land in North America. The Acadians. We are not far from where Samuel de Champlain paused in his travels to winter at the mouth of the LaHave River, which he named The Haven.

I'm an Acadian, but until recently I haven't been particularly diligent in researching my heritage. I've usually looked sideways at recreational genealogists who spend their summer holidays at jamborees with other trailer-hitch comrades from the lost country of Acadia. I've never dressed in eighteenth-century costumes for fun, or participated in battle recreations, or used the old recipes to cook something up from fried potatoes, duck grease and spruce sap. These manifestations of nostalgia never spoke to me. But in this ghost village—named so by Brian—I never tire of looking at my ancestral past come imaginatively to life.

I see Brian walking toward me, aided by a large wooden staff. One day I must ask him about the business of the staff. That this is his domain is evident in every purposeful step he takes. He's an athletic, stocky presence, with a wide face, intense blue eyes. In his work clothes, he looks like a prosperous farmer or fisherman, a hands-on guy, someone connected to every apple tree in the orchard planted here by the early settlers. Someone who can drive a tractor through his land blindfolded, bushwhack stumps and boulders, fence a pasture on his own. In town, when I've come across him dressed in, say, a black turtleneck, or at the wheel of a black Volvo suv, the impression is of ruggedness only barely contained by the mannerisms of professionalism and the academy. I sense that his natural exuberance has been forged into something harder—a mature, taciturn intensity—from many battles over decades to raise his buildings on the streets and fields and cliffs, the mythic disturbances on the landscape that speak to the old but feel radically new.

"How are you," he says. Eyes hidden behind shades. No question mark in his voice. At first I'm not sure he recognizes me.

"Not too bad."

"Fine day to be out here, Larry."

And so we continue, saying nothing or nothing much.

In Brian's voice I hear a lilting syntax born from some shotgun marriage of Acadian and Irish. He has an oblique way of coming around to things, a diplomatic folksiness I'm disposed to associate with country people, who know all things need not be revealed just because a stranger asks a question. I'm a knowledgeable fan of his work, and I've let that be known. I often visit the sites of his buildings when I have a free moment, and introduce his work to others when they visit us here.

"Tell me something, Brian," I say once the small talk dies out. "What would the Acadians make of this program of yours out here?"

He chuckles. "Acadians now or Acadians then?"

"Doesn't matter."

He tilts his head, as if evaluating me: "I've learned the hard way that some people view architects as villains. Destroyers, not builders."

"That being said . . ."

"I'm not sure everyone wants to see their past turned into something else. Used as a source of someone else's passion or creativity. I'd hope they would see something of themselves. Something they'd be proud of. But I'm not in their boots."

"It's an intense place." Then I add, somewhat obsequiously, "I like that line of yours I read somewhere . . . about 'compression over ruin focuses the energy of the valley and the sea.'"

I have to wait for his reaction.

"These are the bones of a village at the edge of the world," he says. "I could spend the rest of my life building here. There's so much buried here, one has to be careful. And not just the Acadian past, but those who came after, the Germans, the Swiss, the life of the 1750s. A little farming and fishing village. You have stone foundations from dozens of buildings. From an extended family structure. Three houses. Each with massive stone chimneys, next to three barns, six wells, three chicken houses, fish sheds. Countless buildings. And when you put together the plan, you realize there's a kind of classical order at work. Why did they take the trouble to align their houses, hearths and wells on a north-south axis?"

"I haven't a clue."

"All we have are clues. Consciously or unconsciously, they put themselves into the path of a building tradition that outlives a particular time and place. I'm thinking they wanted to be remembered long after they were turned to ashes."

"So you have to be careful not to disrupt that."

"Up to a point. We have a story to send to the future too."

And that story is being created without compromise. Brian's commissions in Foggy Cove have produced houses that have disturbed and upset as many people as they have elevated and pleased. But if there are architectural critics and heritage preservers in this area a hundred or two hundred years from now, I believe they'll be lobbying governments and private patrons to save Brian's buildings as an important link to their cultural past. His work, as I see it, developed from heaving the past forward and keeping it meaningful and energetic to a contemporary eye. His approach is enlivened by the idea that within the history, traditions and geography of a place, you'll find the practical and imaginative tools to be inventive. I believe what disturbs his critics most is his unconcealed ambition to reinvent architectural traditions that people have come to expect from coastal Nova Scotia—like the shingled Cape Cod house, gabled and with dormers. Local people are uneasy, confused and sometimes angered by what they probably view as flagrant or boastful experiments with their building traditions. These complaints sound to me like insecurity speaking, the question of the moment being, How can structures inspired by a barn or fishing shack be worthy of a big fat book published by Princeton Architectural Press? There's also some haughty disdain expressed at cocktail parties by well-heeled newcomers, the seasonal habitués, who question Brian's presumption that brilliance need not originate in the centres of fashion. Some get over being disturbed, and eventually become fans. They discover that disturbing things can be good, they just take some getting used to.

"Look around you," he says, waving his staff at the ghost village. "Then walk around."

"I'm always doing that."

"I mean, truly look at each of the buildings from different points of view on the land. The whole relationship in all its aspects."

"In what sense?" He has me confused.

"What really thrills me is the little journeys from one place to the next, across one field here, or a colonnade there, around this gable or through that garden or courtyard. Even with slight shifts in perspective, the world becomes a different place."

Then he's gone into the valley, his back to the sea, walking on memories under his feet.

Recently I read the so-called definitive novel—a mythically creative saga—about my ancestral family's expulsion from Atlantic Canada in the mid-1700s. *Pélagie: The Return to a Homeland* was written by Antonine Maillet of New Brunswick. In 1979, it was awarded France's Prix Goncourt. The novel concerns a group of refugees, an extended family, called the children of the cart, deported Acadians trying to make their way home from the swampy Carolinas in the bed of an ox cart driven by the mother figure, Pélagie. The novel doesn't feel like it belongs to the historic novel genre as it is usually manifest in Canadian literature. It's less a story about trees and survival in the Gothic bush and more a sustained hallucination, something out of Gabriel García Márquez, a magical but dangerous journey led by a woman infused with a redemptive capacity to dream and persevere. It's a story that says that risks, all risks, are worthy when the search is for home, for belonging.

The kids are asleep, and we're nearly there too. I've dozed off twice tonight while reading.

In this house I intend to expire painlessly in my sleep, decades from now, having lived happily ever after among my family and favourite things, breathing pure air and golden sunshine, and fog too, my last will and testament under the pillow, a small trust fund for the grandchildren, a bequest to the local conservation group if it names a coastal trail after me.

It really is safe here. We're not among the families destroyed at train stations, in freight cars, in holding pens.

We're not among the hopeful on makeshift rafts, drifting to freedom, sinking on the horizon edge. We do not answer to the description of boat people, tsunami victims, homeless persons, holocaust survivors, endangered species. We've never begged for entry into safe havens protected by soft blue flags, not steel. Our children aren't on the road, in the air, in orphaned transition, cauterizing wounds even before they appear.

We all have nightmares.

How many live them?

There are bruises under the skin of this book, as there are, or should be, in every book worth reading, or in every life worth living. The injuries aren't life-threatening, but sometimes they do produce reflections on mortality that are more disturbing to me than they used to be.

Those who really do experience terrible things, such as a long fight against illness, know all too well that the illusion of invincibility is a wonderful contrivance of our psychological design. It's a depreciating asset, though, strongest in youth but yielding paltry returns in the later years. Still, many of us assume that our dreams are born and nurtured under blue skies, and that we'll live forever. For one reason or another, I'm experiencing more dark moments of late, an eclipse of the light that used to greet me on mornings when the future seemed the place to live, not the present. I want to step back in time but can't, and so I muddle along, just like everyone else. I suppose this is what it means to grow up.

This story of sanctuary begins in fog, and that's where it will end. For who am I to presume that arriving at a sunny conclusion is inevitable? At best, lucidity is cyclical, and wisdom not so much a destination as an unexpected interlude along the path, or for me it is: a moment when the jungle gives way to the river view, or the steep mountain trail opens upon a plateau, inviting consideration of the huts and smoking chimneys in the valley. So let us not belabour here the scary opaqueness in arrivals and departures, the lies we tell ourselves about how we got here, or where we're going after it's all over. Let's enjoy the journey itself, the sweet panic between the beginning and the end.

ISOLATION BY THE SEA (Critical Incident)

DURING OUR YEAR IN FOGGY COVE, I kept a daily journal, the intent being to write down ideas for this book. I
soon lost my way in the vastness of the subject. The more
I researched, say, the history of temple architecture or political asylum, the more lost I felt. I only started to find my
bearings when I considered the domestic story: the task of
creating a sanctuary for our family. But I was unprepared
for what surfaced in documenting our existence by the sea.
I began to realize that I'd imposed conditions upon my family with the potential not only to isolate us from the world—
but from one another.

Foggy Cove, May 2005

Days and nights of rain that could have numbered a biblical forty—and feel like a hundred—but probably don't
exceed twenty, a deluge that's as detrimental to household
psychology as it is to the local ecology. As the marsh swells
from rain, including runoff streaming down every available slope and culvert inserted into the amphitheatre of
hills around the village, I finally understand that our property borders on a very large natural sponge. I can now
visualize why it's possible to get fresh drinking water from
a shallow well, not just from the deep wells drilled through

the aquifer; although, let it be said, the runoff from the hills has probably acquired fertilizer residue from the manicured lawns (and there are a few of those) that appear spray-painted a shiny green.

When I started looking to buy property in Nova Scotia, proximity to a marsh wasn't high on the list of must-haves. But in this season of rain, I've fallen in love with the bog. The swamp. Home to cranberries, yes, but also to mosquitoes, mud and slithery-looking bog creatures. A bobcat too. During the rains, I view the marsh as more or less showing off, absorbing water and bulking up as if it has been secretly taking performance-enhancing steroids. The marsh may not be a picnic locale, or the route of choice down to the beach, but it is something marvellous to behold under aquatic stress. The water level keeps rising above the vast plane of greenery, causing small ponds to expand and overflow into tributaries between them. From a marsh, in essence, a temporary lake is taking shape before my eyes: everything's flooded, including the road along the beach that connects the village to the Wreck Point headland. The road remains submerged for weeks. The folks who live on the surrounding dunes and on Wreck Point have little choice but to commute across the road in hip waders, or in trucks that have significant ground clearance. One morning a friend tries to drive through in a small sports car, only to be rebuffed by water reaching the windshield over the engine bonnet. I watch this unfold from the house, half expecting him to turn up the hydroplaning function to levitate across the marsh, but instead he reverses away, very fortunate not to stall. An hour later he trudges up to our place, soaked, in his business suit. We call a cab to take him to the airport. He's supposed to come back in a week, but he stays away a month.

At times the rain stops for a few hours, or as long as a day. When these interludes occur at night, I step out on the deck and listen for the symphonic keening of frogs in the marsh. But, honestly, how much delight can one take in atonal frog music when life in the house is becoming less happy as each rainy day turns into another? The kids are cranky, and Alison and I are nursing our own resentments. I'm losing chunks of my mind in the basement office, gloomily wishing for sunshine and for less family disgruntlement at the terms of their confinement in Foggy Cove. On two occasions during the siege, I impatiently observe the runoff sluicing down our hill, messing up the soil packed around my shale step path below the house and washing away the shallow roots of the ground cover planted last fall. Twice I go outside and pointlessly shovel up soil that has oozed away to repack the steps, like a child making mud pies. The area will have to be re-landscaped when the rain stops and stabilized with slabs of nursery sod. But my problems are minor compared to the situation near the beach. The runoff has pushed through the marsh toward the back side of the beachfront houses. If the rains continue, I wonder, will the beach be destroyed from *behind*? These houses are being attacked from water at both ends, protected only by the most fragile element: a sliver of high dune.

Willie Cornwall and I are out in the rain one afternoon shooting images for a laptop slideshow he's assembling for an upcoming meeting with the Nova Scotia minister of natural resources. As a board member of the local conservancy, he's lobbying for more restrictions on residential development in the marsh. A retired teacher, Willie is a robust man in his fifties, an unofficial powerbroker and political operative in Foggy Cove. He has the hands of a boxer but a fine touch with email and on the electric bass. At parties, the two of us have been known to trade air guitar riffs and sing harmonies on old blues tunes we love. Raised in New York, he went to college at Penn State, and then came here with his wife, Barb, in the early 1970s. They never went back. They bought and restored an old farm inland, where they raised two boys, before building a home in Foggy Cove along our road. Barb worked as a registered hospital nurse and does a lot of community work, helping to set up medical clinics and the like. Willie is entrepreneurial, financially savvy. He invested in Dell and Microsoft stock early on, and for years he bought, sold and traded land with an empire-builder's madness while he taught high school.

Willie's belief, which I share, is that Nova Scotia lacks progressive coastal management regulations to protect the beaches and marshes, and is generally reactionary on ecological matters. But all isn't lost yet in Foggy Cove. Seven or eight years before we got here, the provincial government slapped a building freeze on the dune beach as homes started to invade the most photogenic vista. And there were lawsuits and court cases, which resulted in bad feelings that even wildly rising real-estate prices haven't healed. There have been grapevine reports that the development freeze may be lifted or modified. But this isn't something I want to hear; development in the marsh is ill-advised because it's a natural flood plain. Willie and others in the community tell me that some influential people—landowners with properties in the protected zone, mainly—want the development freeze lifted. For that reason, the conservancy has been lobbying in Halifax to take action to mitigate the worst effects of aggressive violations of the beaches and marshlands. Some victories have been won over time. But there's a feeling among the ecologically minded that you can't trust a government that has no legislated controls in place, and seems to run by ministerial fiat: the whim of whoever is in power. This time the minister himself is a former real-estate developer.

"People get strange near ocean," Willie says above the racket of wind and rain. "They get the Hollywood dream.

The big house on the beach. They must see the nightmares on TV. The houses in California falling from cliffs into the ocean. Tsunami. And still they come. And build."

"I know what you mean," I shout back. "The village where my mother was born is all underwater. All that's left of the old buildings, the lobster cannery, the general store—all I have are some old pictures."

"Is that right?"

"And they had to move a whole bunch of houses inland, maybe twenty years ago. And now they likely have to move them again. All the high dunes are gone, and now there's nothing to stop the water."

"The dunes were likely wrecked by the homes in the first place."

We are up on the ridge of our hill. From there we take in the bloated condition of the marsh, and the flooding across the road. Even with our rain gear, we're getting wet, cold. Rivulets of rain pour off our noses. Willie points to the part of the marsh where the giant beaver hutch is now only barely visible in the rising water.

"I gave a lot of thought to buying land right on the beach," I say. "I was afraid of the dunes retreating, and hurricane damage. But I never even gave a second thought to the ecological danger to the marsh. I didn't give a damn. Marsh was nothing to me, honestly."

There's a full cast of characters around here. At one extreme, there are people, very few, admittedly, who wouldn't object to a Trump Casino or Club Med on the beach. There are still some property developers in the area for whom a marsh is a dirty bog, something to be drained and paved over. Opposing them are the viewplane advocates, who argue that vistas should stay exactly as they are, no more building, not near the beach or in the wetlands. The eco-progressive residents desire that Foggy Cove retain a "communal" aspect; people should pretty much be allowed to walk anywhere they want, at any time, but especially to the beach. Some property owners appear to prefer restrictions on informal rights-of-way because of liability and privacy fears; some also worry that a long-standing path might turn into something that limits their property rights, hurting the value of their land. And then there are the gaters, few daring to be open about their bias, believing time is on their side as long as enough rich people move in and kick the lower-income types out.

Where do I stand?

I want Foggy Cove to remain beautiful, and welcoming, whatever that means. Like most sane people, I know that too much development in the marsh and on the beach isn't a great idea, and certainly not in the interest of those already here. I believe the coastline should be open to walking by all, for all time, and the beaches easily accessible, always. But do I want tourist crowds having barbecues or parking their RVs behind the dunes? Do I want our beaches to have overnight camping facilities?

I believe we should be mindful of the intimidation we cause by posting Private Road signs in the village or on community paths across our properties. But I certainly don't want a daily fleet of strange cars blasting up and down our road. I have young kids. I even want speed bumps to slow everything down, no matter how lame that sounds. Yet, I don't want to see Foggy Cove turned into a gated suburb or a boutique hotel environment available only to the wealthy. I believe in respect for what remains of the so-called natural environment—or perhaps I just want Foggy Cove to look like my Foggy Cove forever. But who am I? A newcomer, an invader myself.

My beliefs are contradictory.

I fear self-interest disguised by arguments about the public good on the one hand, and property rights on the other.

It's also conventional wisdom around here that agriculture doesn't fit in the mix any more. The land is too valuable for mere food production. Food can be sourced anywhere, right? That's why we have 747s, free trade, refrigerated trucks, superstores. That's why every Thursday morning in the summer we drive a forty-kilometre round trip into town in our fossil-fuelled vehicles to shop at the organic market with stalls of lovely meat and fresh produce brought there from farms in the interior and marketed by New Age farmers just about to come mentally unglued and city-bound again after the brutalizing, financially unattractive work of actually operating a farm and slaughtering livestock and picking greens and garlic in bad weather. Serious agriculture in Foggy Cove? No way. Oh, we love the idea of looking at cows and sheep in the pastures. On our hill, we have a perfect situation: a farmer grazes a small flock of sheep. But a real farm? No, we don't want that. No one wants cows near streams and ponds or runoff sources. What if E. coli were to make it into the proliferating number of drilled wells? The cows have to be raised somewhere else, to protect us. Cows don't have human rights; they're cows. Makes perfect sense to everyone. The pungent smell of cow shit in the breeze? That's for novelists to write about.

One morning Alison summarily evicts the men in her life so she can have a mental health moment in the form of a top-to-bottom vacuum cleaning of the house, several loads of laundry and perhaps a short nap in silence.

The rainy-day destination of choice: the railway museum near Porter Cove. The boys and I frequently spend an hour or two lost in this elaborate model train world, the sets being miniature recreations of the big towns in Lunenburg County as they might have looked in the golden era of trains fifty or sixty years ago.

"We'll be back before dinner," I say to Alison as we go out the door.

No spousal response.

We run to the car in the rain. I manage a rapid-fire installation of the boys into their car seats. With parental sleight-of-mind, I refuse to register the fetid presence of organic debris in the back seat: raisins, apple cores, grapes, wet socks, crumbs, trail mix. By now only a soiled diaper can get my attention.

"What's best about the railway museum?" I say as we set off.

"Trains," Jackson responds blandly.

"Yes, but what about the trains do we like the most?"

"That the trains are there, Daddy."

The boys start making steam-engine sounds, giddy at their escape from too much time indoors. The failing climate-control system in the old Mazda is unable to completely rid the windshield of interior condensation; as a consequence, I'm required to drive with the windows open, the rain in my face. I'm hungry. I look around: a chunk of vegetarian sushi roll on the front seat, a pickled radish number and a smidge of wasabi. Bought yesterday at the superstore. Still edible. I swallow it. Then I open the glove compartment: a single wheat cracker, no visible fungus. Swallowed.

As I drive along the coves, I come across flood warning signs, which I ignore, hurling the car into fender-deep waters.

No stalls, no rerouted roads; not bad so far.

"Can we build a model train at home one day?" Jackson says.

"Well, that's a good question, Jackson."

Theo saves me. "Do you like steam engines, Daddy?"

That question I will answer. "I love all kinds of trains, Theo. Daddy used to go on trains all the time as a little boy. All those trips from Montreal to Halifax. And then the train would be put on a big boat and taken over to Prince Edward Island, where my mummy and daddy were born."

"The passenger car went on the boat?" Jackson asks.

"Yes."

"Oh."

"I went on a train from Montreal," Theo says.

"That's right. From Montreal to Toronto and back. Remember? Daddy has been on that train so many times. So, so many times."

"Daddy?"

"Yes, Jackson."

"Is it going to rain forever?"

"No."

"Is it raining in Toronto?"

"I think it's raining even harder there. Actually, it's snowing."

"No!" they both shout. They know snow doesn't come in May.

Jackson: "Is the rain infinite, Daddy?"

"Infinite," I say, stunned.

"You know, when things go on forever," he explains.

The sabbatical looked good on paper, sitcom simple. I'm a writer on a book-writing sabbatical. Alison's career as a fashion designer is on hold while she takes on the tougher assignment of full-time mother and chief domestic officer. We plausibly slotted ourselves into the back-to-the-land, bohemian-artsy-sensitive category: earnest refugees from urban excitement and bourgeois expense, the kind of clog-wearing characters often seen in contemporary sanctuary-porn storylines.

You know what I'm referring to—

Books and movies that seductively idealize life in the boonies.

The comic adventures of the couple restoring a country home during a zany year in Provence or Napa or Tuscany.

The journeys of do-it-yourself aesthetes, the white-collar men happy to trade their laptop for hammers and overalls on weekends, who rekindle their marriages and discover parenthood, or lower their cholesterol while building a cabin in the woods—if not with their own hands then certainly with their own money—invariably serving as the apprentice (and lunch-box carrier) to the experienced local carpenter, the quiet, trustworthy man in possession of blue-collar integrity.

In travel writing, sanctuary porn is a time-honoured muse in the expression of achingly beautiful thoughts.

Think of the intrepid backpacker in search of transcendent moments at the great temple, observing beggar children chanting from sacred texts, or discovering that the monk guiding him through the snake-infested valley has a great sense of humour and can recite poetry in Sanskrit and then translate it into French or English.

Or the cosmopolitan traveller escaping the indignity of a high-society life in Paris and New York, perhaps to climb Everest on the back of a sherpa.

There must be a million books that take the reader to an ancient walled city or mountain teahouse or grotto approached through the mist. Books in which midnight offerings are made to the gods, requiring a small wooden boat to be set adrift in a stream on which petals float, the mast aglow with a flaming candle, the cargo a calligraphied message to a dead lover and lute music coming from a nearby temple.

An old red Mazda bashing through coastal flood waters, the passengers yelling at the driver to drive superfast through the big puddles, creating waves in the air that spray over ditches and mailboxes, frightening rodents huddled in the tall grass because it's no longer dry or safe enough for them to take refuge in the culvert.

The train museum is housed in a metal barn. The entrance, with theatrical support from authentic railway relics and signage, was built to look exactly like the ticketing booth at an old-fashioned train station—lots of varnished wood, brass fittings, the smell of a long-gone era.

Behind the counter in the ticketing office, Wally Mclean, a heavy-set, middle-aged man in a striped engineer's cap, greets the boys by name.

"Theo, where do you want to go today?" Wally gently inquires as he sorts through a chapbook of "train tickets" we buy to enter the museum. Theo is allowed in free, a museum policy for those under five, but of course he wants his own ticket.

Theo steps up to the counter with the vertical assistance of the vintage Canadian National stepstool, all polished metal except for the rubber surface matting. Once elevated, he looks at the scheduling information on the blackboard. It names places from a forgotten Canada—railway towns in northern Ontario, on the prairies and Maritime outports consigned to irrelevance by vehicular blacktop.

"I want to go to Churchill in Manitoba," he says.

Wally's eyes widen, then he looks at me.

"Daddy's been to Churchill," Jackson volunteers.

I told the boys I'd once gone up to the subarctic by train.

"Well, well," Wally says in a ho-ho Santa voice. "We can get you to Churchill by way of Portage la Prairie and then Brandon and up through Saskatchewan, then up and over to Hudson Bay."

"Okay," Theo says, made glum by the complexity of it all.

"Jackson, your turn," Wally says.

I lift Theo from the stepstool and usher Jackson toward it.

"Dad, I don't need the stepstool."

The towns are connected by sections of track staged in rural iconography: tunnels under mountains, trestle bridges and serpentine routes through the green countryside. The main viewing area, glass-enclosed, opens onto a lovingly recreated view of downtown Bridgewater as it existed before the train station, roundhouse and track systems were ripped out and replaced with shopping malls.

"The express train is coming through," Jackson exclaims. "Look, Daddy, it has a baggage car and a flatbed!"

"And a caboose," Theo yells, then goes totally silent, as he often does when visual input overwhelms him.

The boys move at will through a low-ceilinged room at least twenty times the size of their sandbox. On the walls and in glass displays throughout the museum are the exhibits that Wally has constructed on the history of the Halifax and Southwestern Railway that served southern Nova Scotia— but no longer, not for decades. His exhibits celebrate the men—and they were all men—who worked for the railway. Wally has blown up photos and candid snapshots of train engineers, conductors, managers, executives, telegraph operators and machine-shop men on their last day at work after decades of the rail life, some hugging their wives as they stepped down from trains. There are newspaper clippings of retirement parties, a photo collage of the local train crash that killed exactly one person eighty years ago, and many beautifully forlorn images of old train stations and sidings in the middle of the local nowhere. The museum also has many valued collectibles that Wally has purchased or been given: lanterns, tools, train schedules, travel brochures, signage, dining car china and silver, a telegraph, oil cans. Everything is artfully arranged, and explained with Wally's commentaries, his cutlines mounted on foamboard.

As the boys roam, Wally and I lean over a display case to admire the yellow Bonaventure edition of Canadian National's dining car china and silverware. The coffee cups from the late 1950s and early 1960s in particular take me back to my youthful train rides from Montreal to Prince Edward Island. This is ludicrous, because this china predates any journey I made on a train, predates my birth in some instances. But still, the coffee cups take me to a good place—so what do the facts matter?

"I need a set of these things," I say intensely. "I've been outbid four or five times on eBay. Each time, some guy comes in at the last minute and I just give up. I just need four cups and saucers."

"There's a lot of that stuff flying around," Wally says, rubbing his chin, as if mentally replaying his own bidding battles in the virtual world, painful to recall and too disturbing to actually talk about with me, the collecting novice. "You need patience. Or you'll go broke."

He points to an exhibit case behind us: a sugar dish, in muted silver, glowing softly, flipped upside down so that the stamp of the Halifax and Southwestern logo is visible.

"Wow," I say.

"There are only three in existence, and I've been tracking them for ten years. This is the first time one has come up for sale. And I was prepared to go to the wall financially. Because who knows when another might come up again? Maybe never."

"How much?"

He mentions a figure in the relatively high hundreds; then says he'd been prepared to pay double. "As high as a thousand."

"No way."

"Beautiful, isn't it?"

Usually, I love this kind of conversation. But something else is happening to me today, and I'm trying to figure it out. I stare at the sugar bowl, admire its gentle contours, the logo stamp.

"Wally, why the hell did you start this place?" I finally ask.

He gives me, briefly, a suspicious look, which fades to something more contemplative.

"I've always liked controlling my environment," he says at last. "And as far back as I can remember, I always had this dream of escaping. It was a dream of forts in the wilderness. With a lake and trees. And always a train in the scene. Trains were always in the dream."

I keep asking him questions. I find out that he grew up in Ottawa. His mother moved there from Liverpool, Nova Scotia, looking for work, and met her future husband, Wally's father, who moved into town from the Saskatchewan prairie, also looking for work. Wally isn't melodramatic or keen on confessional behaviour, but it's plain that there has been some disappointment in his past. A career as a paramedic burned him out. The railway museum has taken a long time to get off the ground, and he pays the bills doing cabinetry and building model train worlds for private clients. His eyes brighten when he starts talking of what his train world means to him, the passion for it, the energy applied to recreating the past and keeping it safe, in a sense, for all time: under glass, protected. And he positively beams when he mentions Sheila, his wife, his partner in life and business, a cheery woman of Mi'kmaq origin who makes jewellery that she sells at trade shows and in the museum gift shop. The boys love Sheila and Wally.

"It's what makes me happy," he says, shrugging. "Being here, with the museum, and with Sheila. It's like a honeymoon."

Wally has made a world from nothing; he's found sanctuary in controlling the variables, or as many as he can gather in one place and nail down with carpenter's glue and bits of foam. His museum is the safest place in the world for him. And this safety has kept something alive in him that has jumped from him to the trains, and from there into me and my boys.

A man can make a world from nothing and it can be a good thing. I don't presume to understand the darker side of Wally's passion, his obsession with the hunks of silver, pottery and rust from a dead railway. But it seems the creation of his museum has offered him a soulful respite from the things that bring you down in life.

As Wally and I talk, I realize I, too, have made a world from my fantasies of sanctuary and remove. I, too, seek to control the variables, to fashion a safe haven: a family under glass. What's the difference between us? Wally is an adult who can make his own choices and live with them. But what choice did I give my wife and our two boys when I brought them out here? Do I expect to hold danger at bay and to prevent time's forward motion? Have I fetishized the idea of home—of family—and isolated us from an opportunity to build genuine community? What have I done?

—

That evening Alison and I have to go out around six; the kids will stay behind at their grandparents', watching train footage DVDs as a prelude to their sleepover.

Because the rain is intermittent, the sky not fully congested, we're under the hopeful impression—misguided, as it turns out—that driving thirty minutes inland will produce a radioactive sunset, a sweltering dusk. It's humid and buggy when we step out of the car on the dirt road near Jackson's school. Misting rain. One hundred per cent humidity. Deep puddles everywhere.

"Did you bring the bug spray?" I ask, swatting the air.

"Ours has scent in it."

"Scent?"

"Remember the last time?"

"It's friggin' non-toxic *citronella,* not Chanel."

"Still. You know what these people are like."

"Perfume Nazis who think it's better to be eaten alive."

As we run through the buggy mist toward the school, a shingled building that belonged to a local church, it occurs to me that part of Alison's resistance to moving to Nova Scotia permanently is purely aesthetic. Not that she marinates her lingerie in perfume, but she loves exotic aromas designed for the body. What civilized person doesn't?

A few months ago at a meeting for parents of the children in Jackson's class at the Waldorf school, a woman startled us with a sneezing fit, announcing in a strangled voice that she was experiencing an allergic reaction to perfume. We spent a half-hour discussing the evil effects of perfume on the immune system. After the meeting broke up, she stared intently at each person heading for the door, probably expecting someone to confess. I filed past her, bracing for the possibility of being sniffed.

Tonight we're attending a fundraiser organized by a movie producer who moved to the area from Toronto and whose children attend the school. The fundraiser has a sweet concept: every several weeks, a film from a different country is screened, preceded by a buffet meal featuring food from that region of the world. In typical Waldorf fashion, all parents are invited to contribute a dish and to work at staging the event and cleaning up. The fundraiser has proven to be a big hit, particularly among retirees, who love culture on a budget.

Inside the kindergarten, where the food and drink is being served, the humidity is intense: a sweat farm. We're coastal people now; mugginess and heat are largely unknown in our microclimate. But it's a gentle place, full of little chairs, scarves, dolls. I like being here. Not a violent action figure in sight. Or a soft drink machine. The Waldorf approach is perfectly out of step with the rancid hyper-competitiveness and homework-driven approach of the other schools we investigated for the boys. Still, there's kook-iness in the ideology.

"Tell me this," I say to Alison over dinner. "Why this fear of right-angles business? What are they afraid of—*corners?*"

In his writings, the founder of Waldorf, a German mystic named Rudolf Steiner, had evidently suggested that right angles were, on the whole, a bad thing.

"Something to do with the arrogance of rationality," Alison says.

"Corners are evil. Up there with serial killers."

"Waldorf celebrates more organic forms. Natural forms. You don't find right angles in nature, apparently."

"Do you want to work or live in a house made by a Waldorf carpenter, cross a bridge made by a Waldorf engineer? Fly an airplane—"

"Larry, you're shouting."

I make nice after that. I eat all my curried dishes: chicken, chickpeas, mushrooms, with rice, naan. I thank the cooks. I talk to people in the crowd. A pleasant bunch: the naturopath, the garlic farmer, the movie producer, the midwife, the bookstore owner, the waitress, the waiter, the retirees. There is the usual absence of people I would call local, the folks who have lived in the county all their lives. In general, the locals are turned off by the vibe at the Waldorf school—but also by the fees. Why pay money to send your kids to school when you could send them for free? The local folks who favour Waldorf tend to have children with learning disabilities or other problems adapting to the public system. Anyway, the lack of local support and government funding means that the Waldorf school is always a donation or two away from having to lay off its teachers; fundraisers such as the film-and-food nights are essential to keeping the experiment in alternative education going.

The movie screening is held in a classroom upstairs even more unbearably muggy than the kindergarten. The movie is a musical comedy, *Bollywood Hollywood*, a love story about a young Indian man from suburban Toronto trying to satisfy his family by lining up a bride. Two hours of laughs. Wonderful fluff. The only problem is the seating: unforgiving wooden classroom chairs. When I get up after the credits roll, a major back spasm hits.

Alison has to help me to the car.

"Honey," she says gently. "What am I going to do with you?"

I insist on driving. I'm fine once seated in the car; the spasmed back muscles are compressed, unable to send pain signals.

We drive for a while in silence, both of us apparently ruminating on a pleasant evening as the Mazda negotiates the coastal route to Foggy Cove. I'm feeling relaxed except for the occasional insane microsecond when I imagine hitting a deer, killing us both, leaving the boys orphaned.

"Doesn't it make you want to go back to Toronto?" Alison says into the marital tranquility.

"What makes me want to do that?"

"The movie. Something romantic about the city."

"Alison," I say. "The Indian community in the Greater Toronto Area live mainly in the armpit of"—I name two large suburbs west of the downtown core. "Suburbs stolen from the farmland and dotted with shopping malls and super-sized McMansions. A cookie-cuttered mess. I do not see the romance. What I see is the illusion on the screen."

"You're so *hard* sometimes." She pronounces this too coolly, no plaintive edge in her voice containing a request for me to refute her. No, she's offering up only a conclusion.

I say, "I loved the movie—"

"Do you ever see through the illusion out here?"

She's looking straight ahead.

"Alison, that's not fair."

"How happy are you out here, really?"

"It's been raining for a month."

Silence for minutes—but I can't give in just yet. "I'm tired of working my tail off for a life I don't want in Toronto."

"Why can't we just eat out at restaurants less often when we're there? Why don't you do yoga to work off your stress?"

"We need tons of money to live the way we currently do."

"I should start my business again. Put the kids in daycare!"

"You don't mean that," I say, my voice rising. "Neither of us is keen on daycare."

We keep arguing, a bitter exchange. Then I pull out the big weapon: the threat to sell the Nova Scotia property. The magic bullet. The cash would clear our Toronto mortgage, reduce our expense level considerably, allow us to restart Alison's fashion business and enable me to be a stay-at-home dad for a few years. This suggestion upsets Alison, as she senses it is motivated by spite. If I can't have my way and move us all to Nova Scotia, my argument goes, then let's get out of here entirely, and completely reverse our roles—after all the work we've done to create the current and largely workable balance.

What a whiner I've become!

We retreat into silence as we enter Foggy Cove.

When we arrive home, she leaves me in the car and goes over to her parents' house to check on the kids. I step outside and fall to my knees.

My back kills.

My conversation with Alison leads to questions that nag me for days: How real is Foggy Cove? Rather: Do I want to live in Foggy Cove as it exists now or as it will exist in future? What exactly is the movie in my head? The illusions I refuse to see through?

Indisputably, Foggy Cove works on the sanctuary porn front.

You need to be creative with the camera now and then, staying clear of two or three trailer homes amid a platoon of stately capes, and resort to editing software in post-production to erase the satellite tower and the monster home that sits just a bit too proudly above the treeline. But even a blind cinematographer could summon a Hollywood moment here.

Life in Foggy Cove is what I'd call an authentic simulation of rural—not precisely the real thing, and that has its attractions. No one is driving four-by-fours on the beach or hunting deer within shrapnel range of the house, and while it would surely be fun now and then to help a neighbour raise a barn or haul firewood on a sub-zero winter morning, if this were a community where people still worked together on that basis, you'd probably also have to help them slaughter the pig or pull the calf out from inside the mother cow or butcher the steer. That would not be so much fun, although very instructive in the facts of life. Most nights, Foggy Cove still feels like a wonderfully lonely, marginal place, far from excitement, culture, crime, where signs of human habitation, even the utility poles, seem demurely respectful of the forceful natural elements.

It was once a truly isolated community, almost cut off, no roads into the big towns aside from cow paths, requiring a sail by open boat to trade or sell goods, speak to the law, see a doctor, go to the summer fair. The life then wasn't about luscious sunsets and matching each gourmet course to the right wines. There were grim realities. It was an era when some folks probably drowned a sick old cat in the creek behind the barn instead of opting for a lengthy regime of steroid treatments, as we did with our first cat, before her fatal heart attack. (She was then cremated and returned two weeks later in a lovely pine box, attached to a sympathy card from the veterinarian expressing sorrow at our loss.) Forty or fifty years ago, Foggy Cove was a place where—if you were looking for *slow,* as so many people say they are now, but aren't, as far as I can tell—things were exceptionally slow, maybe a few telephone party lines, a dirt road into Lunenburg, a horse cart to get you there. *Live near the beach—are you foolish in the head? Freeze your arse off. The next big storm will drive the waves into the sandbanks, and where will your basement be then? Sunk, that's where she'll be, guaranteed.*

Those moments, those voices, were long gone by the time we arrived. Should we mourn their passing? Some here definitely do. But it's not my past, so mourning it would be a lie. Now that we're regulars on the scene, it wouldn't be totally ludicrous to start mourning, in advance, for the Foggy Cove I already know; the place is changing faster than its property assessments are rising. We have a road association with dues-paying criteria, a three-member board and meeting minutes sent out by email. Our conservancy group agitates for protection of the coastal ecosystem by networking with other such groups on the Internet and spending many long hours discussing government policy on these matters. At town hall meetings, people complain about property taxes, economic development for businesses and youth, the accessibility of the health care system for seniors. And there's always the waft of actuarial speculations in the air, the logic of white-collar concern on everything from the guidelines for waste recycling to the availability of the newest Hollywood DVDs at the general store.

Foggy Cove is another chapter in the history of coastal property development. An old story, in North America, Europe, everywhere, where rural meets the money, and the money moves in, and decides that things need to be improved, secured, formalized, debated, lawyered, assigned, subdivided, graded, connected and, eventually, gated.

We bought our land cheap, before the big boom. Mostly luck, but I worked hard at the research, to the annoyance of practically everyone around me. It wasn't sweat equity that paid for the construction of the house, but hard cash from the black arts of corporate writing—speeches, advertising campaigns, marketing reports, business plans—for mostly large, international companies. The stuff I still do part-time for cash.

We're privileged to be here, but the deeper sense of wealth comes from being out of synch with our peers. In winter when no tourists are around, we are the youngest family in the village. And being younger by comparison to everyone else, it seems we're playing hooky from the narrative of middle-class responsibility, which requires that escape come much later, after the final corporate outsourcing moment, after the pensions activate and the kids are long gone. I feel a bit like a drug dealer or one-hit pop star: I've got so much just for taking a small step outside the mainstream.

The serious employment here is mostly related to tourism and the retirement money that has arrived from out of town. There are long-time Foggy Cove residents, born and raised here, who will deploy their tractors to cut your hayfield or plough your road after storms, mostly to keep themselves amused. Some commute into Lunenburg for office jobs such as managing the website at the real-estate firm. And there are always cheerful locals around—possibly quite wealthy, on paper at least, because of the land boom— who pay the bills with caretaking work on the vacation properties: cleaning house, washing windows, stacking firewood, resetting the fire alarm after it accidentally goes off the tenth time this month because of a software glitch that nobody can figure out.

There are also building contractors from all around the county who are working the Foggy Cove opportunity very hard. And so they should, given the money on the table. This place is colonized, in the summer, by a growing cadre of executives, bankers, investment fund managers, property developers, media and advertising types (like me), high-tech entrepreneurs, management consultants, doctors, lawyers, teachers and accountants who have come here from across North America and Europe to buy and, increasingly, build their dream vacation home.

Foggy Cove as rural community—dead.

Long live Foggy Cove!

Jackson's birthday party, May 22.

The rains have subsided, but not the flooding.

All of us are at the grandparents' place. A constant thundering in the main room, the boys in hard motion. In the kitchen, shouts over water taps being repeatedly turned off and on, the clatter of pots and pans, the usual miscommunications and long-established inefficiencies between my mother-in-law, Vivian, and her daughter Alison as they prepare a feast. Vivian is a wonderful grandmother, great with out kids, generous and hard-working, a fabulous cook who does not remotely understand the fuss about moderating the butter and sugar in her chocolate brownies or raspberry crumble. She has the kindest eyes, which convey a mix of sensitivity and skepticism, and a gentle voice gone raspier in recent years—a timbre the boys call rascally. As gentle as she is, she's territorial concerning the kitchen. It's best to stay clear of her in moments like this, although the boys are not in full command of that logic.

On Alison's signal I sit down at the end of the long table, opposite Stan, who has Jackson and Theo on either side of him. He, too, has learned to avoid Vivian's kitchen, at some expense to his facility as a cook. He's allowed in only to boil water for tea and to uncork wine bottles. And so there we sit, four males, the adults inert, the boys chomping raw carrots smeared in hummus, while two females control the flow of food to the table. I don't take patriarchal pride in my uselessness, but it's not unpleasant. Stan contentedly sips a cognac.

In his vigorous seventies, lanky, seemingly stoic and taciturn, Stan prefers the shortest and most oblique of explanations on most subjects, which on occasion can cause confusion. A playful guy, and crafty, he has a profoundly sensitive way of handling the boys in their recreational destructiveness. He knows that grass can be reseeded, decks repainted and walls repaired easier than building a precious relationship with his grandsons. Mostly retired, he works as a part-time venture financier from his basement office, raising money for oil wells in Kazakhstan and gold mines in Bali. I've learned a lot already from Stan about raising kids.

When Alison and Vivian join us, we all hold hands for the prayer, a Waldorf ditty.

> Blessings on the blossoms
> Blessings on the fruit
> Blessings on the leaves and stems
> Blessings on the root

This we get through on memory alone. Done.

But Jackson insists we do the longer prayer, and the grown-ups look at one another evasively. It starts out okay.

> For the golden corn
> For the apples on the tree
> For the golden butter
> And the honey for my tea

And then any choirlike unity breaks down, totally. I mangle verses to clear signs of disapproval from Jackson. Stan and Vivian utter gibberish, below audio threshold. Alison stumbles on a few lines but harmonizes with Theo and Jackson at

> For fruits and nuts and berries
> That grow along the way
> For birds and bees and flowers
> We thank you
> Every day

The boys tuck into their plates. Tonight they don't need much parental cajoling to eat their vegetables or refrain from excessive fidgeting. We made it clear at the outset that little boys who are good are likely to get large slices of the chocolate cake that Vivian has baked into the form of a steam engine. The cake lacks historically accurate or technological detail, missing the coal car linked to the engine, a fact noted by Theo without malice toward his grandmother, but the icing sample offered to the boys clearly aced the yummy test.

Dinner quickly segues into dessert. The only conflict of substance between the boys concerns the eating rights to the excess of icing hanging from the cowcatcher. After the division and consumption of the icing, with each boy claiming to have the larger of the precisely equal shares, Jackson leads his grandfather over to the TV, wielding the DVD remote. I tune out. A classic parental episode of attention deficit when grandparental care is in the room.

I stand with Alison by the big windows.

Our arguments of late have fluttered from resentments into unstated compromises: we're leaving in two days to go to Toronto for a week, as a family. The intent is to check out the Waldorf school there in the likely event we return to live in the city in the fall; also, I have clients who want to schedule meetings with me. It will be good for all of us, we think, to get away from the rain and fog, give Alison a chance to see some friends, go out to dinner, do some shopping.

"I'm keen," I say. "But I can't do dinner with——" I name a couple with whom we occasionally socialize. "I drive them nuts. They drive me nuts. When I'm talking to her, her eyes dart like a snake."

"Well."

"She just chatters on and on. Anyway, the last time was a disaster."

"You were going on a bit too much about Nova Scotia."

I have a knack for causing bad reactions in others on this topic.

"Then let's call——" Alison names another couple.

I shrug no.

She names another twosome.

"You get depressed by the size of their house," I say.

She squints back, hurt flickering at me.

"I'm sorry." I stroke her cheek.

"Up," she says. "Up, not down." Sometimes I cup her face in my hands, caressing her cheeks; the operative word is always *up,* as in mummy like everyone else doesn't want her skin sagging. She wants it taut, forever. So stroke up, Daddy. Up. So up I stroke, until she smiles.

"You have to be in a better mood," she says. "And nicer to me."

"How about——" I name a fourth couple.

She makes a face: "You get competitive with him."

"I just try to hold my own."

"You nearly pulled another Lobster Boy performance the last time."

The blaring of the TV, some industrial noises, a symphonic soundtrack. Alison looks, then whispers, "What's that?"

"The *Battle of Britain.* Why?"

Alison shouts, "Dad!"

Stan shuffles over, looking to me for support.

"It's a DVD—they skip over the violence," I say. "No murderous parts. Right, Stan?"

"I thought the boys might like to see the airplanes," he says innocently. "But it is proving a little hard to avoid the shooting."

"Dad, this isn't such a good idea." Alison moves past him toward Jackson, who is doing some amazingly fluid scene-shifting, despite the fact that no one has taught him how to use the remote.

Mother and son tussle for control of the technology.

I can't look at Stan directly. Not for a minute did I believe that he could edit out the murderous parts—but what's a man to do? Deny the grandfather a small pleasure?

Alison secures the technology and prevents Jackson from spiralling into a meltdown.

Theo throws cake on the floor, and starts to dance.

A typical evening.

After the party, we trundle home across the wet field. The boys have stayed up much too late and eaten too much sugar. But they soon lose the struggle against sleep. When I do a final check on them, it appears that they have each appended a yellow happy-face sticker to their pyjama tops. Across the brow of the sunny globe-face is the word *Wal-Mart* in black.

What can you do?

Not long afterwards, their tired parents are in bed, eyes dancing across the pages of books.

"It's not like I become Lobster Boy all the time," I say.

"Honey, even once more is too much."

"I just find people's responses weird. You'd think we were running a slave plantation out here. Or had moved to Afghanistan."

When I mention Foggy Cove to people, there are often curiously polite responses: curious about the deficiency of sensibility that motivates a person to brag about building a cottage in Nova Scotia that is next to nowhere, not Muskoka or the Hamptons or Lake Como, and polite not to mention this deficiency. Some people are genuinely interested, positive, full of softball questions. When I'm in top form, I'll quiz them on their sanctuary dream and listen for long periods without bringing the conversation back to Foggy Cove. When I'm less effective, I'll talk too much about my good fortune, then, feeling guilty, I'll tell a near-perfect stranger, Listen, come out, bring the kids, it'll be great.

"Promise me," she says. "No more Lobster Boy."

"I promise."

"If you feel him coming on, say you're sick, give me a signal."

"Okay."

"Good."

"Not even a single claw? As a protective gesture."

"Divorce court, honey."

"Okay, goodnight."

"Goodnight."

Lobster Boy night. Where the term was coined.

Lobster Boy: me.

The victim: a big-time high-tech entrepreneur, a business-man, late fifties, the founder of a public company that pro-duced networking widgets for networking-widget-buying corporations. As an executive experienced in dropping spoor on the status trails of upward mobility, he was also a vocal presence on government task forces on weighty issues like The Global Challenge of Corporate Competitiveness in the Twenty-First Century. He could be counted on to be visi-ble, his face occasionally in the business media, or sternly reproduced in annual reports among the board of directors.

We met for the first time at a business cocktail party at his home, to which spouses were included, as they say, as if spouses were a uniform or ID badge. It was a trophy house in a power neighbourhood of the city, each room recently over-themed. Lots of art on the walls, mainly featuring proud stags in coiffured European landscapes, very adult, bourgeois chi-chi.

Later in the evening, a few drinks in me.

Okay, I was trying to schmooze him, even though I'd promised myself to be careful; this man had influence with a firm that was a client of mine. A portion of my income indirectly depended on his patronage.

He had opinions, and they would be heard, and I would listen, admiringly, silently. Then I would leave, enlightened, grateful for the instruction, and enrol in an Executive MBA program to acquire the mental hygiene and corporate deportment to do my part in transforming Canada into a Nordic Singapore: a disciplined, hyper-competitive, low-cost, benefit-free manufacturing zone where expressing minor reservations about any aspect of global capitalism would be akin to breaking wind in public, and thus deserving of a caning or the confiscation of my medicare card.

Chief among my mistakes, aside from engaging him in conversation in the first place, was raising the subject of Nova Scotia, and my plans to take a sabbatical there, maybe live there half the year, commute by Internet sort of thing. This was an inelegant way of conveying that I was a man of financial means and geographic range, capable of configuring my laptop to receive email in a business-class lounge.

He couldn't resist giving a tutorial on how the new realities of globalization, and the flow of money and influence from the developed to the developing world, made my decision to retreat to Nova Scotia not only idiotic for me career-wise, but also ethically bankrupt. Canada needs to get globally competitive, he said. We need lower taxes so that we can invest in productivity and turn out many more engineers and scientists and MBA graduates per capita, or else China and India will eat our lunch. And Nova Scotia? Why would you live there, a welfare province, sucking away our hard-earned money—for what?

So you can all sit on your asses.

We didn't come to blows, but there was shouting, finger-pointing, obscenities, doors slamming; in short, it was a *memorable* party. Lots of fun—but only in retrospect.

And as I hit back at him, I became Lobster Boy.

Early on I tried to get a word in edgewise on the apparent lesson of nineteenth- and twentieth-century capitalism as it had manifested in the West: that economic wealth and civic vitality flow best *from* investment in strong institutions and by sharing the wealth for the greater public good. This was a thought I wanted to pursue, not claim as theological truth. I wanted a conversation, a dialogue.

He said, That's crap—have you ever been in business?

For like twenty fucking years, man. Every day I wake up in business. I can't believe the arguments coming out of your mouth. So crude, really.

You're quite a piece of work, he said.

It is a well-documented fact that some of Canada's top high-tech companies have always had their noses in the public trough, rooting around for tax credits and low-cost loans to finance research, product development, overseas contracts and manufacturing plants (sometimes in despot regimes). I knew about that; I'd been involved in some very large draws on the national purse for the purpose of helping a company go global. This was money that originated as taxes taken, presumably, from the pockets of everyone in the country, including Nova Scotians.

My opponent had, of course, done it all himself, an entrepreneurial Zeus, his business springing fully formed and profitable from his own head without any public assistance, or so he pretended.

A few days after our argument, I checked into the finances of the company that he founded; there were references in its annual reports to research-and-development tax credits in the financial statements. No surprise. And a petty satisfaction.

Lobster Boy wasn't the favourite dimension of my character, but it was authentic, appealing to those who like forcefulness in a man and a righteous willingness to mix it up without worrying about social etiquette or the advice of a spin doctor. I pissed a lot of people off too, with an ugliness in spirit, nourished by the ugliness in others. But where was my self-control? In my social and business life in the metropolis, I failed too often to keep Lobster Boy caged. Could I be blamed for wanting to run as far away from him as possible?

Why do we assume that being authentic involves exiting from the circumstances and momentum of one's actual life and striving for an elevated plane of existence somewhere else? The prevailing wisdom is that the clutter and stress of daily life brings out what is most artificial in us. Why do we believe we've above it all, destined for so much better, if only there was time to think, meditate, and get really tactile with the land, the elements? Why must we stand on cliffs or stagger up the monastery steps or kick our toes through the sand in order to feel in the moment? Why can't we be authentic in the authentic moment itself?

A busy airport, summer season chaos. Alison leads us through the check-in for the Toronto flight, her bodily attachments including her purse, a magazine, the snack cooler and a backpack containing the boys' crayons, colouring books, trains, tape dispensers. The boys also cling to her body and pepper her with questions, testing her knowledge of jetplane physics and of conveyor belts within the airport luggage system. I'm bringing up the rear, a typical airport dad, goofily dressed in beige shorts, sandals, a blue polo shirt, commanding a luggage cart piled so high I can't see in front of me, doing an incompetent job of keeping the car seats balanced on top of the four large suitcases. For someone who has travelled so much on business, gliding through airports and security sectors disdainful of mere civilians and seasonal travellers scared of every last drug-sniffing dog and machine gun, I'm now the poster boy for disorganization in motion. We arrived two hours early; I'm a mess.

My wife is calm, a figure of elegant aloofness, her posture erect but not rigid, her face quite still, except for a slight clenching around a tiny smile that I can never read, or read well enough, even after all these years together. It signals her brief escape into a state of absence—a solitariness—that doesn't diminish her control of the family situation in the slightest; her ability to zone out into a private world is surely a survival strategy among a brood of males who all demand everything from her at any hour of the day. Her inwardness seems neither an aggressive statement of desire to be left alone nor a coy gesture to draw attention. No, she's simply *gone,* yet still a part of us moving toward the check-in counter.

It has taken me many years to understand some of the causes of the turbulence below the demure surface of my wife's presence. They aren't weird pathologies, in my rude assessment, just the usual tensions of a well-adjusted adult trying to reconcile her place in the world.

"Daddy?" Theo doing his monkey act, climbing me.

Alison waving, Come on, honey, over here.

Jackson complaining that no way is he allowing the big blue suitcase to be checked into the belly of the plane, because this means he won't have access to his bedtime books during the flight.

I asked her to marry me in the Montreal airport, maybe five minutes after we had checked in, very early Monday morning, June 6, 1988, after a cheeky weekend in that city. For reasons unclear today, we were on different flights heading back to Toronto; I told her to think about the question on the flight and give me an answer when she landed. The most outlandish thing I've ever done. The most romantic.

Toronto. Breakfast at Whole Foods, mid-town, in the café upstairs that fronts on Avenue Road, where the city's top cosmetic surgeons hang their shingles. It's a neighbourhood anchored by money, implants, facelifts, the Four Seasons, upmarket everything. We are staying in a modest hotel a five-minute walk away.

The boys and I are eating cups of muesli yogourt, honeyed up. Layers of organic fruit. A holistic parfait. The bill for three of us—ugh.

Alison is doing retail therapy. Not picking up her phone.

Bami and Baloan—still the principal characters in Jackson and Theo's imaginary world—are being invoked at the table.

"Theo, are you a vegan?" Jackson asks.

After a pause, Theo says he isn't.

"But are you a vegan in Bami-and-Baloan-Land?" Jackson counters.

"Yes," Theo says. "Because I'm Bami!"

"Yeah, that's right."

"And you are Baloan," Theo says, pointing a yogourt-encrusted spoon at his brother.

"I am Baloan," Jackson says with pride. "Baloan is a vegan."

I seek clarification. "Jackson, why are Bami and Baloan vegans?"

"Because they're allergic to all things made from animals."

"Do you want to be a vegan for real?"

"No, Dad."

"Why?"

"Because then we couldn't eat steak and burgers and stuff."

"Only in Bami-and-Baloan-Land?"

"Yeah, Dad."

"Only in Bami-and-Baloan-Land, Dad," Theo says.

He, too, is starting to say Dad now instead of Daddy.

Our condo isn't far from here, leased out to a banker from Puerto Rico who is in Toronto with his wife and two young boys for a year of professional development at head office. Our situation in reverse.

Feels like summer outside: plenty of exposed midriff, toned bodies on display, cars. Pollution count high enough to present health hazards to children, seniors and the infirm. I'm easily startled by the urban noise and the semi-nudity of buff women of all ages. I'm from the boonies now.

"Do you want to move back to Toronto?" I ask the guys.

"Never," Theo says solemnly. "I want to live in Nova Scotia forever."

"Good, Theo. And you, Jackson?"

"We don't have a pool in Nova Scotia, Dad."

"But we do have the lagoon and the beach."

"But we can't go for Greek food after skating on Thursdays."

"No, but we can go to the train museum when it rains. And we can go to Granddad and Grandmummy's for dinner and chocolate cake."

"Yeah," Theo says. He is with me, each step.

I'm prepared to counter-argue with Jackson, childishly, until he concedes—but he zigs not zags on me.

"Dad, do you want to move back to Toronto?"

How can I be playing this game with them?

I say, "We'll go where you monkeys are happiest, okay?"

—

The Toronto week came and went as some weeks will: too fast.

Back home in Foggy Cove, I'm in my office, watching the boys playing in the sandbox. Alison hovers over them, arms folded, lost inside herself, clearly unhappy.

We had three days of sunshine and beach weather when we got back, but it's now relentlessly blustery again. Misting rain. Damp, damp, chilly damp. The boys are, as usual, oblivious in their simulated train world, trussed up in fleece and rain gear.

Alison wears a baseball cap pulled low, a yellow rain slicker.

In Toronto, she transformed for herself and for everyone around her: blond hair, red lipstick, summer dresses, strapless shoulders, gorgeous laughter. Now she looks like an exhausted skipper on a scallop boat, bored, dreading the next wave coming over the gunwales, but stuck there, waiting for the giant traps to reach the surface.

Honey, I think, I'm so sorry.

I reach into a desk drawer and pull out the journal I kept on our honeymoon to Italy and Greece.

Two months of daily entries—the first time I did such a thing.

In 1989, we quit our jobs and spent most of our savings on a two-month trip that included extensive interludes of archaeological tourism at ancient sacred sites throughout Greece, in Athens, Mycenae, Delphi, and on the islands of Crete and Santorini.

When I start reading I'm not sure what I'm looking for. I keep trying to find something profound in the notations I made about my first experiences at the great temples, but that doesn't work out too well; the passion for expression is evident—and has proven resistant to every effort to

kill it so far—but the craft isn't there. On the trip, predictably, we tried to be different than the other North
American tourists we saw, many preoccupied with guide
books, camera settings, vocally uncertain in their grasp of
the local currency. I thought we looked reasonably local,
except for one tic that gave me away, the habit of compul-
sively checking the precise location of our passports, hidden in a pouch uncomfortably Velcroed around my waist
between underwear and khaki shorts. But our hearts were
in the right place: we hadn't wanted our internal clocks
telling us we had only twenty-eight minutes to genuflect
solemnly at the temple before returning the headsets and
getting on the tour bus.

Embarrassingly clear from the journal entries was my
objective to invest every moment of the trip with *meaning*,
to connect my experiences in life with something grander
lurking behind it, a truth that explained action, motivations, silences, the mysterious gaps between people as well
as the glue. In some respects this ambition for inventing
personal myth is intuitive and healthy, a natural process by
which we all learn about the world and acquire the maturity
and grace to function in it and toward others. But in our
media- and narrative-obsessed culture, I wonder if it isn't
also a pathological response, indicative of a frenzied
dependence and perverse insularity that I see in so many
people who analyze themselves to a fault at the expense of
moving their lives forward productively, contriving existence as a cinematic script in which their psychological realities and deeper emotional conflicts are framed in terms best
understood by screenwriters and sitcom-makers. I know far
too many people for whom life is, I guess, a story in search
of events to explain it, not the reverse. As a writer, I'm prone
to self-analysis as an occupational hazard. But when you
live too much in your head, when you focus too much on

fictionalizing yourself as the hero in your life drama, and I've done that myself, that can't always be a good thing.

In Greece I was a tourist with things to do and places to see. I was newly married, and consciously preoccupied with all that. It was time to get serious. There were practical as well as philosophical matters to attend to, namely: how would Alison and I embrace the future together?

The question hasn't gone away.

Alison, outside, alone, with our children.

Me, inside, alone, reading the journal.

This space between us—what else does it contain but distance?

Are there stories we need now, lurking in the rotting paper of those honeymoon impressions that I jotted down so long ago?

Are there myths worth creating about how we arrived here?

Do I dare remix the cues to memories I laboured to preserve and romanticize, viewing them no longer as finished product but as raw material that, in a new form, might tell me something about myself and Alison that we didn't already know? Something useful to help us through a rough patch? We're stalemated, just a little; we've been over the same territory so many times. Like vinyl to the stylus: the same needle, in the same groove, at the same speed—this eventually produces cackle and hiss. It's not the end of the world, our situation, by no means. But I'm willing to go into the past and take what I can from it. I want to talk to that honeymoon couple in Greece, share in their discovery of each other, map their expectations where they converge but also diverge. And then take it from there.

This desire to meet in the flesh the twenty-nine-year-old

version of myself and my bride presents logistical difficulties. But on the page, far stranger things have happened.

A miser can have ghosts appear in his bedroom all night long to replay his life and project his future, scaring the dickens out of him, before improbably turning him into a generous man.

A time machine can fly a man backwards and forwards.

Why can't I send myself into my own past—if only on the page?

Who wouldn't do this if they could—if not to change destiny, but simply to say hello to who we once were.

All journeys change us; we're never the same individual at the finish line as we were in the starting blocks.

Enthralling and terrifying—

PART II

SYMPTOMS

2.1

HONEYMOON IN GREECE (Mythogyny)

Athens, September 1989

AT DAWN THEY LEAVE the shabby pension in the Plaka, the air still breathable, the metallic odour of yesterday's car fumes infused with a lemony accent. He starts to chatter away as they walk, already manic, telling her that with each step they are more or less re-enacting the sacred pan-Athenaic procession. She still has the smell of the communal toilet lingering in her nose. The most disgusting thing.

A group of vendors along the high street are already in action in their kiosks, cursing theatrically at one another, mostly in good humour as they fuss with tabloid magazines, cigarette cartons, sweets. In an alley, a toothless man stands behind a grill, roasting nuts while muttering prayers. Flicking his amber worry beads. It's a motion that reminds her of the wrist action involved in tricky yo-yo stunts.

She knows all too well that her husband is waiting to be encouraged to reveal more about the historic relevance of the procession route, but it's too early for this marital ego stroke. This morning he doesn't wait for her encouragement. He relates the ceremonial purpose of the route taken by the ancient Athenians, once a year, up the slope of the Acropolis and toward the temples to celebrate the goddess Athena on her name day.

"All citizens and even some slaves were invited," he says, as if addressing a student. "The priests made sacrifices, said prayers, and the rest had a good meal on the sanctuary premises in honour of wise Athena, as the protector of the city, as the warrior virgin goddess."

She asks him to slow down, she can't keep up. She would love a strong coffee, gritty espresso, a ton of brown sugar. "The temple will be there in five minutes, Larry. It'll wait for us. It's waited a thousand years."

"The point is dawn, Alison. As I've told you."

"I know, honey."

Honey. This gets on his nerves. An endearment she uses when she's really conveying annoyance, but perhaps too tired to express it openly, too diplomatic in these early days of the honeymoon. He realizes that she's trying to go along with his game, but she's more sullen than she needs to be. Defeats the point of cooperation and compromise, he thinks. He slows down, doesn't want to get into an argument over small stuff. No need for that. And, besides, he's giddy: soon he'll be approaching the Parthenon, not through an image in a book or on a screen, but by walking up to it himself. He hopes the power of the temple's presence will overwhelm him, as it has so many of its acolytes throughout history. But will it? Not that he really expects a total pilgrim moment of soul-destroying illumination. The journey was long getting here, true, but it wasn't that arduous. His feet aren't blistered, nor are his knees scabbed or bleeding. He doesn't feel broken up inside or vulnerable to the presence of a goddess. He isn't weeping or speaking in tongues. He has cameras, credit cards, the address of American Express, where they can get more money if they run out. He has her. She has him. He takes her hand as they walk, and they share a look that's supposed to mean they're in agreement that this is an adventure, that this is what they wanted.

They arrived the night before by overnight ferry from Italy, along with beer-chugging Scandinavians from whom they kept their distance. On arrival at Piraeus harbour, they walked into a crowd of pension owners (and their hawkers) and quickly settled on a middle-aged woman in the crowd, dressed elegantly, with pearls, a cigarette holder. She drove a Mercedes sedan. She took them to a small, street-side room, not so clean, but pristine compared to the communal toilet in the hall. Before turning in they ate a cheap meal in the Plaka. It took great discipline on his part not to take a cab up to the temple. It had to be dawn for the first visit.

They're ascending now, a winding paved road. He wishes this were a hundred years ago, and that the path was dirt, not pavement, goats at each switchback, not someone selling tourist maps.

She gives him a look. How many times has he gone on about this?

Up they go, at his pace mostly, the tension of her resistance finally giving way to curiosity and wonder, and up they keep going, wakeful and both happy to be here together, up through the gates of the Propylea, past the caryatid sculptures, the robed priestess figures chiselled from pentelic marble, Athena's handmaidens, her posse holding up the Erectheium.

"Is this beautiful or what?" he says.

Again he tells her why they need to be standing in front of the east pediment of the Parthenon as the sun rises over the mountains, not after, or the morning is *ruined*, because we need to watch those first rays penetrating the columns into the recess of the sanctuary where, way back when, when this place was more than a ruin, the morning sun would have struck the shield of the monumental statue of Athena inside the cella and set everything around it aglow.

She lets him go on, erasing the fact of having heard all this too many times. She knows that if this had been the first time he'd given her the lecture, it would be entertaining. It *is* entertaining in this moment, on the spot—but not the twenty rehearsals. She doesn't know how she can convey this thought without hurting him. Decides that there's no way, actually.

He thinks that he'll drive her crazy if he insists on blathering, because she has eyes of her own, a brain, an art history degree.

As they walk around the Acropolis, he enjoys the experience on the most basic terms: it's a conquest, a notch in the bedpost of his education. He achieves that objective in about fifteen minutes, leaving time to wonder whether it's possible that his attraction to the temples resonates on a deeper level. What level would that be? Is it possible that the temple offers an invitation to commune with forces larger than his own hungry intellect? He doesn't see himself in need of anyone's benediction or protection, let alone that of a goddess on a hill who never lived except as myth carved into marble. But as he debates all this with himself, a sensation weasels into his mind. He will later describe it as a fleeting awareness of what it must be like to crawl on bended knees through the incense, to lay the animal upon the altar, to wail at the wall from sunrise to sundown, to circumambulate a mosque for days in a chanting trance before the greatness of God, not as mere symbol, or as myth made timeless and universal by the power of art, but as a force living in the sanctuary, available for conversation.

"Cat got your tongue?" she says playfully. "Hello, hello."

She's standing in the path of the rising sun, the light so strong he can barely see her. He steps to the side, shifts the angles between them. Golden light, golden arms, golden legs. Honking cars below. The thrum of traffic roaring away from a stoplight. He suddenly feels hot all over, and weakened; the mass of the temple looms at him, and he's afraid that the columns will topple forward, crushing him. He starts to gibber. In a monotone he recites long sections of a university paper he'd written, oh, ten years ago, when he took on the assignment of the Parthenon, dissected its harmonious proportions and sculptural program six ways from Sunday. The words tumble out of him, about how the temple is a masterpiece of visual illusion, its geometry manipulating the eye in so many cunning ways, creating the sensation of a structure majestically anchored, growing out of the limestone hill below it, while also nurturing the counter-deception that you're observing a sky-ship floating free of everything, sailing in the heavens and through the vistas of mountain and sea all around. A riff spools out on how the Greeks built temples not as objects apart from landscape, but as elements within and oriented to it, an organic presence, but also as a medium to glimpse the supernatural, a divine zipper in the sky that every now and then unzips for respectful observers, enabling them to see the immortals, the gods and goddesses. He descends into total incoherence but thinks to himself that he's lucidly explaining to her—to the world at large, in fact—what the Parthenon represented to the classical Greek mind, the fusing of intellectual power and spiritual depth into the quality we might call wisdom, bringing them close to the fire of divinity without being so arrogant as to believe they were gods themselves.

And then he collapses into her arms.

She screams—

Seconds later a man reaches in, wraps his arms around Larry's chest and guides him to the ground.

All quiet except for the pages of the man's journal, also on the ground, flapping in a wisp of wind scuttling past at foot level.

"That was weird," Larry says, elbows on his knees, head hanging. He wipes his brow of imaginary sweat.

The man lifts Larry's chin, looks him directly in the eye.

Alison keeps saying, "What's wrong, what's wrong?" until the man puts his hand on her arm, calming her too.

Larry says, "Do I know you?"

"I don't believe I have had the pleasure of your company before." An accent from the American South: ornate, courteous in its flavour.

"You look familiar."

"Do you know where you are?"

"What?"

"Count backwards from ten."

"I'm fine," Larry says, brushing off the request like a drunk refusing to hand over the car keys. Then he counts backwards—successfully.

"Tell me your name, if you all will humour me for a second longer."

"Larry. Larry Gaudet."

"Larry Gaudet," the man repeats. He doesn't pronounce the last name as *Guh-det,* as it was given to him, but as *Gode-ay.*

Larry tries to stand, and with assistance from Alison and the man, he manages it. "I'm fine, really."

"What's your last recollection before things went AWOL?" the man asks, bending over to pick up the journal.

"How'd you pronounce my last name?"

"Mister Gaudet, if you please, the last thing you remember."

"Oh."

Alison nudges him—

"The temple was attacking me," Larry says, casting a reproachful look at the Parthenon over his shoulder, as if it were a pet or child that had inexplicably misbehaved in public. "The columns were marching at me. How weird is that?"

"Mister Gaudet," the man says. "Are you on strong medications for an illness? Or dehydrated? But I see there's a water bottle on your belt. Well. Is it possible you celebrated too enthusiastically last night, perhaps too many glasses of Metaxa?"

"No, nothing like that. I'm healthy as a horse."

"And the heat—does it bother you, usually?"

"No."

"And the temple was—attacking?"

"Maybe smothering me."

"I reckon, then, you had yourself a little case of Stendhal syndrome. It's not all that unusual."

"Stendhal what?"

"Stendhal syndrome. A psychosomatic disturbance. Rapid heartbeat. Dizziness. Confusion. Hallucinations. It happens to some people when they're exposed to art. Named for the French novelist—"

"I know who Stendhal is," Larry snaps.

The man looks off into the great city for a moment.

"I'm sorry," Larry says. "I mean, what kind of loser am I?"

"It's more common than you think," he says, his gaze wandering over to Alison. "In Florence, especially among the younger American ladies, frankly, seeing all that Renaissance nudity for the first time . . . there are dozens of cases every year, apparently, of disoriented exchange students, wandering the streets. It's all rather charming, romantic, this response to art. Wouldn't you agree?"

"And your name?" Larry says.

"Tony Savoie." *Sav-wah.* Two long syllables.

"You must be from the South," Larry says.

"Antoine Baptiste Savoie," the man says, affecting pride. "From the bayou, near Lafayette, Louisiana. Cajun country.

And you might know that part of the world, given your surname, there, Mister Gaudet."

"I'm Canadian—my parents are from the Maritimes, the East Coast. But I grew up in Quebec. In Montreal."

"A sweet little jewel of cosmopolitanism, Montreal. I've spent time there. The Paris of North America. Lovely, lovely place. Although my favourite is Quebec City in the early fall, walking through the old quarter. That's a sexy town, if you breathe deeply enough . . ."

"That's what they say," Larry says uneasily. "Why did you pronounce my name like you did? It's not how I say it."

"Gaudet is an Acadian name, very old, a proper lineage," Tony says energetically. "Hell, my people come from your people. The great exile from Nova Scotia, late 1700s. There's a bunch of Gaudet clans down our way, and we all and they all say *Gode-ay*. Names like Arsenault, Babin, Daigle, Aucoin, Boudreau, Thibodeaux, Foret. I bet you've heard those."

"There's Arsenault in our family, on both sides."

"You heard of Cajun country—everybody has."

"Like around New Orleans?" Larry offers tentatively.

Tony shakes his head, playfully derisive. "Do you know what Cajun is? It's a bastardized form of Acadian. From the French-speaking refugees—Catholics all of them—thrown out of Nova Scotia by the English, the consequence of some geopolitical kiss-and-make-up between England and France. A failure of my ancestors—and yours—to swear allegiance to the British sovereign. Some of our folks went to New Orleans—forced to, and many died getting there. I imagine you all studied that in school. But New Orleans wasn't, well, the most welcoming of places for poor, sick French Catholics, and so many went over to Lafayette, and farther, all the way to the Gulf Coast, the deeper swamp. Farmed and fished for centuries—did mighty fine—before they found us again, made us Americans."

Larry looks over at Alison, the message being, Time to lose this guy.

But Tony intervenes. "What are the odds of two Acadians meeting up here on the Acropolis? You'd think Athena herself had set us up!"

"Athena—"

"Come on! Let me buy you folks a fine lunch. I know a little taverna on the grubby side of town, owned by an old friend of mine. He'll make you a horiatiki with feta so salty smooth and tasty that you'd think it came from a block hardy enough for sculpting out one of these caryatids here."

Larry looks at Alison. He's bewildered, still, and she's not much better, giving him a searching look. Her eyes are bloodshot. It occurs to him that he's given her a real fright.

"How about dinner?" Larry says, realizing that he's being rude. After all, the man had rushed to his aid.

"Well, that sounds just fine to me," Tony says. "Anyway, I have some work to do. I promised myself to be disciplined here."

"What kind of work do you do?" Alison says.

"It's not exactly work in the nine-to-five sense of the term," Tony says, a sandalled foot tracing figure eights in the dust. "I suppose it's more of an obligation left unfulfilled."

"How so?"

"I've been trained as a historian, always thought I had some kind of book in me, but I could never figure it out," he says in a voice that both Larry and Alison would later agree sounded melodramatic, consciously self-pitying. "I'm what you call . . . between assignments at the moment. This isn't quite a euphemism for being unemployed—but anyway. So I have this journal I keep chiselling in. Nothing in the way of grossly profound insights are pouring out of me, but it keeps me out of trouble."

Alison has another question, but he's moving away. "I'll tell you what," he says, uncapping a fountain pen. "Let's meet in front of the American Express office. Everyone knows where that is. Is nine too late?"

"Cool," Larry says.

"I'll give you the whole sordid history—and find out what you all are doing in this part of the world. Imagine, two Acadians at the temple!"

When he disappears around the Parthenon, Larry sits down again, fatigued. "Very weird."

"Are you really okay, honey?"

"Yeah. I'm talking about Mister Cajun."

"He was very nice, Larry."

"You don't think he looks like me?"

She tilts her head at him. "Maybe a little. Around the eyes and brow. Perhaps the body type."

"You think?"

"But way older."

"How old?"

"I don't know. Forty. Forty-five. Fifty."

"Forty-five. At least."

———

THE JOURNALS OF ANTOINE BAPTISTE SAVOIE

To paraphrase Camus, a person's life is often nothing more than the rediscovery, through the detours of art, of those one or two images that first opened the heart. So Greece it is, specifically, that tugs at my heart. It's a bias that no doubt leaves me open to being charged with crimes against scholarly comprehensiveness. But there's more than one way to excavate a universal message from the ruins of history.

The Greek temple, particularly as roofless and scavenged ruin, does something magical for me, harnessing the energy of rectilinear form shot through with natural light, funnel sky and sun through columns and over gables that shape views of mountain peaks, deep gorges and cities on the plain. There is allure in these artifacts of mythic simplicity, in the ever-crumbling temples of the Acropolis (as surely as Venice is ever-sinking), pockmarked by acid rain, scarred by the vandalizing of treasure-hunters. It seems I prefer the ruined and skeletal over the polished and the plumply restored: the simulated reconstructions I've seen of the Acropolis feel less sacred to me, more administrative, *civic*, a bit like the ancient world's Washington, D.C.

Washington. Did I really spend eight years strolling the Shining City? Will it take eight more years to repossess myself, to scrub away the stardust clogging up the lymph nodes that monitor moral hygiene?

My two little boys, growing up as proper Virginians.

(Mom would not be amused, bless her departed soul.)

My boys, feet in the black loam of their stepfather's hobby farm, so excited at being able to name their new ponies, one each.

My boys, their tanned bodies, so supple and strong, ballooned out in life jackets on the deck of the sailboat motoring out of the Chesapeake on a breezy day, their mother coiled beside them, all golden arms and golden legs, a straw hat, big Gucci sunglasses, her new husband suggesting they putter around, then anchor within a dinghy ride from the yacht club.

At which temple can a man pray for an alternative reality?

To which god must these entreaties be made?

So here I am, dear Athena, the protector. What can you do for me?

Or have you done enough already?

In my late twenties—when I finally got serious about my education—I fell in love with the seductive location of Greek temples, the orientation in the landscape to forces grander and more intimidating than the tavern next door or the prison by the river. Which also accounts for the allure of Stonehenge, Machu Picchu, Teotihuacán, the pyramids. In these places (and others), the product of human genius leads easily to awed contemplation of the inhuman cosmos. You feel your mind drifting to questions you can't answer but which have always been with you and which you believe were summoned by your own curiosity and private yearnings. The Greeks awakened something in me that the Gothic vaults and gargoyled accents of Christian iconography hadn't, not even the famous cathedrals I visited on my first trips to Europe, which I found dank and dark, mainly depressing, despite the architectural splendour inside and out, the vertical massing of grimy stone bordered by slippery cobblestone.

Given my Catholic background, I can't enter a Christian church, even as an apostate, without feeling undermined by guilt, *enclosed* by the weighty history of a living cult still chugging forward, cheerlessly promoting an ancient message. I've had similar responses in mosques and synagogues. You're always cautious, because these are cautious places; you enter mentally crouching as if expecting a blow, resisting the urge to kneel. The assignment for any pilgrim is to submit, not question too much or too loudly. You suspect that all your questions have been thought of in advance, along with the answers; there's a script, and you aren't its writer.

This ruined palace of Athena—does it let me fill in the gaps, and pose my own questions, shape my own answers?

The Greeks, aside from providing us with the iconic presence of the Parthenon, have a legacy as temple-builders, as sanctuary-creators, that spans a good thousand years, from the Minoan palaces on Crete and the Mycenaean citadels on the Peloponnesian peninsula, which date to the early Bronze Age, to the sacred sites of the classical period and later, not only the regal Acropolis, but the alpine splendour of Delphi and Olympia, and many others erected on countless mountain ranges and scrubby plains all over the country that provide awe-inspiring views of sky or sea . . . at Perachora, Eleusis, Salamis, Calydon.

Greece is one degree of geographic separation from so many places that count in the narrative of religious sanctuary. It's only a short flight from Athens to the so-called Holy Land, or the Middle East. Looking south from the Cycladic islands, the southern-most being Crete, we're a ferry away from the sanctuary wonders of Turkey and Egypt. From there one closes in on the lost civilizations of Mesopotamia and Persia, whose influences infused ancient Greek art. If we went in the *other* direction, heading north from Greece, we could look to the countries of lingering influence in Western Europe, all heavily influenced by revivals of Greek thought and aesthetics in a collection of movements we now call neoclassicism, which affected so much of the sanctuary art and architecture we still see on the streets and in the museums of London, Paris, Madrid.

In a fruitful but arbitrary sense, perhaps, classical Greece stands out as one of the great bridging cultures that enabled a number of sanctuary concepts to flow from their primitive origins into more modern manifestations through the temple form, a source of amplification and transmission even today for universal ideas always in search of new homes. Take a look at preclassical Greek pottery or free-standing sculpture from the seventh and eighth century BC, the early *kouros* figures too, and it's easy to trace the geometric patterns, abstract tendencies and narrative approaches to the Near East. The Greeks were resourceful, pragmatic, open to the best influences and always innovative, always evolving. They took inventive hold of Egyptian two-dimensional representation, a way of seeing that had purposely remained static for thousands of years, and, within a few centuries of experimentation, they'd resolutely brought it into three dimensions on the pediment sculpture of the great classical temples, foreshadowing the birth of perspective in the Italian Renaissance.

I know, I know, it is unacceptable in these times—or least in my country it is—to say that any one region functions exceptionally well as the classical centre. It is very convenient to suggest that Greece—or Mexico, Russia, Turkey and so on—was a conduit for the influences and developments migrating from tribal/preclassical cultures populated by preliterate primitives toward the urbanizing/classical and neoclassical centres where we, the civilized, live. This conceit highlights a bias about what the center is, what classical means, an error of perception that these postmodernists tell us indicates an objectifying, dehumanizing, immoral *program* undertaken by the powerful to control the powerless. So be it.

Greek temple architecture first opened my own heart to the beauty that springs to life when patronage, political vision, artistic genius and communal resolve come together in common cause, not to build a nuclear missile or napalm delivery system, but to do something comparatively *useless*, to erect a building that no one can live in, that merely inspires the spirit and provides sanctuary to ideas, principles and myths that still live two millennia later. The Greeks helped me appreciate that a structure on its own could locate and focus human curiosity about where we fit in the cosmos, and provide a means for us to contemplate and uninhibitedly worship—that is, to be reverent and humble in contemplating our ultimate fate in the unknowable larger scheme of things. From the Greeks I understood that we humans started creating and patronizing sacred places as a formal strategy for appeasing the invisible forces of the spirit world, to improve the crop yield, distract the enemies across the mountain, make the animals or the concubines fertile. The Greek sanctuary was an arena within (and around) which the community told stories to itself to fill the mystical void. I was fairly dumb not to have realized the role of the sanctuary in my own culture. Although, it's always like this: the ideas fed to you at home for your own good never taste as good as those grasped in the first steps beyond adolescence when you're out in the world, discovering it for yourself, on your own terms.

The preceding comments presume much; the ancient Greeks didn't think like me. Their gods were real to them, the picture of their moral universe, not cartoon characters or action figures. But whatever they were to their creators, you can be relatively certain it was the conception of the god that shaped the sanctuary, not the other way around.

What does a godless man do for protection?

———

Sweltering afternoon in the pension, the blinds shut, the drone of cars outside the window. He fails to snooze for long. She tries to read, then puts the paperback down.

"Let's not go tonight," she says.

He raises himself on his elbows, scrutinizes her.

"What?"

"What if he's some weirdo?"

"We're just going to dinner."

"But where?"

"Will you relax?"

"Larry, you're the one who needs to relax. You nearly fainted."

"I'm a swooner. Jesus."

"I had a similar response in Florence, actually. Just like Tony said. Right in front of *David.* I didn't faint. But I felt odd for days."

He turns toward her. "I bet you did. Those long limbs. That rock in his hand. Although, did you notice, his, well, his equipment, wasn't exactly . . . impressive."

"He was in a state of *repose,* goofhead."

———

THE JOURNALS OF ANTOINE BAPTISTE SAVOIE

In many sanctuaries of my acquaintance, I've often walked the labyrinth, veering toward the heart of the sacred story, then veering away, only to return again through a different avenue to the moment of revelation. The moment of truth. As you experience the patterns, you tell yourself the variations are worth the repetition, and that there is dignity in meandering through the competing truths of who you are. Sometimes to keep moving is all you can do to stay sane.

Who have I shown the world?

The interrogator in Saigon, after Tet.

The man dropping leaflets from the sky over Santiago.

A fart-catching spook for Kissinger, hanging Makarios out to dry.

Afghanistan? Never mind.

With Larry Speakes, in the Oval Office, two southerners doing good old boy BS on the old man: sir, this evil empire line, in the speech. The quiet anger in Reagan's eyes, a lay preacher if there ever was one. The man kept the line in. Should have known; he'd been in advertising.

A twelve-year-old boy catfishing, in hip waders. Gators, ya'all don't mess with me. Whistling past the graveyard. Shotgun or no shotgun.

Telling her, it's not working . . .

Our two little boys looking at me. Every second Saturday. Eyes like lollipops. Come home, Daddy.

The ugliness of the labyrinth—the monsters of our own making, circulating, feeding on sacrificial tribute.

Monsters in the basement.

———

They arrive an hour early at Syntagma Square to make phone calls home from the Greek national PT&T office nearby. Through the dusk-shadowed streets, there are views of the Parthenon. Aloof in sunset.

"It's like a boat in the sky up there," Larry says. "Really, it is."

"Watch where you're going, honey. It's a red light."

Transatlantic echoes in the booth.

"Yeah, Dad. Even more Greeks here than the old neighbourhood—what?" Listens, then: "They speak English, but I've picked up a few words of Greek, not just the swear words, Dad."

Alison spots Tony Savoie in a café across the street, near the back of a crowded patio, seated with other men, leather-jacketed characters in sunglasses. One wears a bandana around his head, a kaffiyeh, like Arafat, the other a Nike baseball cap. Both are cracking pistachio nuts, eating them voraciously. Untouched glasses of ouzo in front of all three. Tony is listening gravely as the bandana guy talks. His journal is closed on the metallic tabletop, the silver nib of the uncapped fountain pen gleaming brightly. He does look like Larry, she thinks. Maybe a Larry who's seen things her Larry hasn't. And hopefully never will.

When Larry emerges from the phone booth, she points Tony out.

"Oh, good. At least he showed up."

"We shouldn't interrupt—"

"Come on, let's see what's going on."

He leads the way. As they wind a meandering path across the patio, the two leather-jacketed associates stiffen up. One gulps his ouzo and flashes Tony a grimace. Tony turns, a surprised look.

"My Acadian friends," he says. "Bon soir!"

Larry says, "We didn't mean to interrupt."

"I was just finishing up here."

One of Tony's companions has vanished. The second is standing now, fumbling with a cigarette pack. Tony does nothing to make introductions. The second man leaves.

"What language were you speaking?" Larry says.

"Arabic. The bill is settled—shall we go?"

"Where?"

"Costa's place. It's a little walk down this way."

Alison says, "Your friends . . . we didn't mean to—"

"Ah, my friends. At best, they're associates of old friends. To make a very long story short, there's someone in my orbit who is having trouble—well, he's having difficulty emigrating from Beirut. A question of visas and so forth. And I was invited to look into the matter while I was here."

"Sounds mysterious," Larry says as they start walking.

"I've worked in this part of the world before. In a diplomatic capacity for the U.S. government. Early 1970s."

———

The Journals of Antoine Baptiste Savoie

I left Catholicism behind at ten. I was too literal-minded to absorb its metaphysical premise. My early tutors in the family, my father's sisters mainly, but also the school system, failed to set up conditions in which the myth would take, so to speak. I was befuddled by the idea that God always existed and could be everywhere all the time while living within everyone as Himself the Father, the Son and the Holy Ghost. There was no awe; it just seemed implausible, even for a barefoot bayou boy.

I will admit that when my parents were blown up in the swamp, and when the swamp then caught fire, I had a moment when I thought they'd been struck down by God, or a god. But they were just in the wrong place at the wrong time, off for a Sunday by themselves, a small raft on the water, corn muffins, picnic basket, a jam jar of bourbon juleps, so strong and sweet, swimming in mint and peppermint leaves. How were they to know the oil company was drilling for natural gas nearby? That natural gas could burp its way up and explode in your face?

The swamp burned for a month. Hades on Earth. But I could not blame a Catholic God for that, only a very large corporation.

When I started to read heavily in my later teens, including the more accessible, shorter works of European existentialists and the summary analyses of the great philosophers provided to me as a college freshman, there was no turning back to official religion.

Vietnam sealed it. I could see the visions of transcendence that motivated the enemy. They would have taken on any belief that got them out of underground sleeping arrangements and eating rats.

I was no hippie back in '67 or '68, and didn't walk into Saigon (or crawl out) talking about free love and peace. In the bayou, you didn't see hippies. You didn't burn draft cards. You joined the army because your Uncle Claude in Baton Rouge knew the recruiter personally and said you could get a college education for free if you put in a little hard time in the rice paddies, killing gooks. You didn't think. You didn't disrupt conventions. You didn't yell into megaphones about the pigs and the proletariat. And you didn't—well, you didn't do much. I came home from Vietnam (metaphorically, if not geographically) susceptible to conspiracy theory and utopian solutions to social inequality. So, predictably, I came to view Christianity as an enslaving cult of long-standing malevolence toward its brethren, a propaganda machine, a political entity, a reactionary in the social realm. Opium of the masses sort of thing.

At Yale as an undergrad (my admission courtesy of a commanding officer, a rich boy, Tommy Buchanan, who owed his life to a fluke of crazed intervention that came from my gun out of fear), I tuned into the history of art and architecture on the basis that the house of God was a house of cards. It was best to view God's vast aesthetic assets on Earth—paintings, music, sculpture, poetry—as an appropriation of the talents of artists and artisans who required church patronage to put food on the table or to avoid being broken on the wheel. It was best to reclaim these works for the history of art, the history of truth, divorced from context and purpose, which, let it be said, was to manipulate the faithful, to have people fall on their knees before tithing grain and a virgin daughter to the feudal baron or the convent.

It was best not to see the temple as a holy place, but instead as an inventory of creativity in the myth-making arts that could be scavenged as artifacts for intense study, not ritual veneration.

My parents would have been—confused by my education. My biases.

But the bayou experienced in isolation? It nurtures an appetite for mystery. You don't become an engineer or lawyer or doctor when you raise yourself. Not with my Cajun resentments. You want to talk to God, or make yourself into one. You want to live in myth. As priest or pimp. And you want weapons. Could be words. Could be guns. But you aren't walking through any neighbourhood of the soul unarmed.

I never bought into that storefront voodoo bullshit in the Big Easy, that Creole magic sold to tourists. Hell, no. That wasn't real.

I've visited temples and churches and sacred sites the world over under the guise of being the neutral observer who interprets his insights through the specialized language of art history. I've never gone anywhere as a religious believer or disciple of any sect but that which reveres the individual pursuit of self-knowledge.

Conscious intent doesn't speak to everything, does it?

———

The taverna is rustic in the way Larry has long dreamed of, no wider than a bowling lane, bright blue walls, tiled white floors, wooden tables and chairs, all charmingly warped. On the walls, tapestries feature quilted approximations of the Parthenon, and family photos too, seemingly from the 1950s. Not a tourist spot.

Their entrance is a movie moment: Tony is embraced as a brother, with effusive hugs and kisses by the proprietor, Costa, a bald-headed linebacker of a man. Larry and Alison are welcomed as if members of Tony's family, requiring a parade review—for their benefit—of the children in Costa's family, and his wife, tiny, pretty, unwarily shy, restrained by her complete lack of English.

A table at the back, near the kitchen. Costa pulls up a chair, pouring a round of retsina for everyone. "The Tony. I receive your telephone call, and we talk all night, and it is three weeks later. Only tonight you come?"

"I've been busy, my friend. As you might know. Busy, busy."

Costa nods. "Yes, we will have our talk. But now we drink to our health, no? And we will be nice to your friends!"

"And, Costa, seeing your family, finally. Too much time has passed."

"And my wife's parents are living with us too." Rolls his eyes.

"I miss my little boys."

"And the mother?"

"The mother. She is there. With them. In America."

Tony raises a toast. "Opa!"

The first bottle of wine is emptied before the olives and peppers arrive. The second bottle comes with a large horiatiki salad, toasted pita bread, a plate of grilled seafood— sardines, octopus, squid—and bowls of tzatziki, hummus, taramasalata. Alison is content to eat and watch the two older men compete for laughs. Their brotherly displays are effective, if strained now and then. When a silence extends too long, another toast is raised. Some pleasantries make an encore appearance.

"So, the Tony, my friend, we are both in the family life now."

"Two little boys, Costa."

"And—" Costa stops before mentioning the mother again.

"And you too," Tony says, picking up slack. "A big family."

"Three little girls. They love their father."

"Yes," Tony says gravely. "Girls love their fathers forever."

"And your boys?" Costa says.

"Designed to break their fathers, of course. Drink my whisky, crash my car. But I understand they're less complicated than girls."

He says this raising a toast to Alison; she blushes.

Larry tries several times to enter the conversation, but the other men mainly treat him as a witness—an audience—for their reunion act. Alison observes that Larry refuses to pick up the cues of the supporting role he's expected to play; now and then he does steal the floor through doggedness alone. The men respect that, retreat for an instant, gulp wine, before brutally relegating him to the front row again. As the second bottle empties in repeated toasts, Costa withdraws with a waiterly bow and soon returns with a third bottle, but his manner has changed; he's the proprietor again. He pours himself another glass but leaves it untouched. He doesn't sit down but stands behind the chair, his hands gripping its back, as if massaging a tension-filled neck. Then he backs away, on duty now, greeting new customers, some effusively, although it seems to both Larry and Alison, as they later discuss, that Tony's arrival was a special event.

"So you and Costa go way back?" Larry asks.

"You might say that."

Larry lets the silence ask the question.

Tony continues: "Think it was Cyprus, the first time. '73."

"You guys, what, worked together?"

"Something like that."

Alison sees Larry winding himself up: he wants to probe and be probed. He thinks his forays into Tony's past come across as cautious expressions of gee-whiz interest between budding friends, one older and therefore deserving of more verbal airtime out of respect for seniority. He thinks he's being as deferential as he can be. Alison detects in Larry's questions a desire for responses that will allow him a lengthy counter-response. Eventually Tony reveals an association with the Reagan White House: a special adviser to the speech writers pool for eight years, pretty much the whole reign, offering the historian's point of view. He says this in the weary spirit of someone who knows the questions will keep coming.

"Wasn't he just a stooge?" Larry says, garrulous, thrilled to be around a man who'd been so close to real power and celebrity in the flesh.

"Oh, I wouldn't say that," Tony replies. "You look at any of the great speeches, Bitburg, the *Challenger* tribute, evil empire, the letter he published when he was diagnosed with Alzheimer's. I could go on. Reagan had some of the best speech writers in America working for him. But if you see the final drafts of his speeches, nine times out of ten, he's rewritten large sections, often on the fly. He said what he wanted to say. Made some kind of poetry out of clichés . . . but there is something to the argument that while he was a man of strong beliefs, he could be manipulated. Yes."

"And you made sure the history was right?" Alison said.

He gave that some thought. "Errors of fact were corrected, yes."

"Wasn't it propaganda, plain and simple?"

Alison hears the effects of wine in Larry's voice: not antagonism but a loss of carefulness.

"Reagan believed what he was saying," Tony says. "So I don't know what that makes it. Propaganda is a big word.

Implies a deceptive surface, a manipulation. But in Reagan, there was no such separation between surface and depths."

Larry jumps into the ensuing silence and then goes on too long about a theory of propaganda he'd read about in a book but is now having trouble explaining. Alison likes that Tony is tolerant of her husband, not condescending. His periodic looks in her direction don't contain, she thinks, a coarse evaluation of her sexual potential, although he does appear to deeply drink in what he sees of her. This causes her to lower her eyes once, no, twice, if she's honest. He likes women, certainly, but there are no coy or crass hints, or subtle undermining of her husband. His persona doesn't shift into pickup overdrive when Larry goes to the bathroom; it's as if her husband is still sitting there. He seems harmless, but she's dated an older man before, so she knows what harmless is, and how it becomes something else fast. She likes his effort at restraint, finds it courtly, and appreciates his ability to engage and study her. He's gentlemanly in a way her husband isn't, not yet. There's something sad about him, an aura of regret. She doesn't trust that so much: he wears his sadness like a crown, as a sign that he's a man of deep thoughts.

She gives her husband a long look. She loves his reckless spirit, his bandwagon energy to throw himself at the world. He's the first person who hasn't confronted her aimlessness, her confusion at life, and made it seem like a bad thing: only as a fog they will walk through together in creating their life as an unstoppable adventure.

"I've written speeches too," Larry says. "For executives, nobody famous, of course. I write stuff for corporations and magazines. Brochures, speeches, journalism, white papers . . ."

"One day you will want to write books," Tony says.

Larry thinks this is a question; it isn't. He has much more to say about his career plans—but Tony turns to Alison, learns about her interest in fashion, the design school she'll be attending when they return to Canada. Tony doesn't give the impression of utter fascination with either of them—both Larry and Alison will agree on this. He can't entirely disguise the rote even-handedness with which he's alternating his questions between them.

"And family?" Tony asks.

"Like kids?" Larry responds, as if procreating were something Amazon tribes did between bouts of cannibalism. "In the future—but there's a life to live."

"And you, Alison?"

"I don't know."

"How old are you?"

"Twenty-five."

"Too young to start with babies, huh?"

"We have a cat back in Canada."

"And where is this life you want to live?" A question for both.

"I'd love to live in Europe for a while," Alison says. "The food, the culture. Maybe work for a fashion company, like in Italy."

"So you want to be the next George Armani."

"Giorgio," Alison says, a full-bodied Italian pronunciation.

"And you, Larry?"

"I'll go anywhere. Do anything."

The couple is unsure where Tony's leading.

Alison: "And your family, Tony?"

"I am kinda going through a divorce. Not quite true. I am divorced, legally. I do see our boys when I want, generally."

"Oh," Alison says, panicked by the thought of asking him more.

Tony seems to be reaching for the words to make everything sound as smooth and inevitable as the wine they're all gulping too fast, but Larry interjects. "So, Tony, come on, this book, you're writing . . ."

"You mean, this journal I'm keeping."

"Whatever you're writing."

"Would you excuse me for a minute or two?"

"Sure."

"I'll be right back."

Tony steps away from the table toward the kitchen behind them.

"It's getting late," Alison says.

"We just got here."

"And you interrupted him, Larry. He was—"

"Going to talk about family? The last thing he wants is that."

"I'm getting a little tipsy. Can we leave soon?"

Ten minutes later, Tony returns. "Sorry, I had to make a call. I'm planning a trip to Crete and needed to confirm the arrangements."

"We're going to Crete too," Larry says. "We're just going to fly there after a week in Thera. Santorini, you know."

"Is that right?"

Costa arrives with desserts, baklava, a bottle of ouzo.

"Crete," Tony says to Costa. "My friends here are visiting . . ."

"Your first time?" Costa asks, his tone expressing intense interest.

"Costa is a Cretan," Tony adds.

"We can't wait to go," Larry says.

Costa looks at Tony—something passes between them.

"Me, I am thinking," Costa says. "Spring is better. This time of year, the weather becomes not properly predicted. Rain. Big wind."

"I thought the weather didn't get bad until late October," Larry says. "Anyway, we have to go, with the excursion tickets we bought."

"Then I know where you must go!" Costa announces brightly. "To the south coast, near where the Matala is. The

Cat Stevens used to live in the caves there on the beach. The hippie guitar player. You know?"

Larry says, "But isn't Matala a bit—touristy?"

Costa, hands on his hips, pretends to be cross. "Am I looking like the dummy to you? Of course not. Matala is nice for renting motorcycles and seeing the Australian and American girls who wear nothing but the tiny strips across the"—he cups his breasts—"No, you stay in Pitsidia. There is great beach there. Nude beach. It is loved by the German lesbians but nice people. Nice little family restaurants. Quiet. This is the perfect traditional Cretan village." Then he vanishes in a sequence of waiterly nods.

"Pitsidia," Larry says. "Cool."

"So you're flying there, then?" Tony asks.

"We go out, let's see, the Thursday after next, but we have places to go first, Mycenae, Delphi, Thera," Larry says. "Alison's father kicked in for the plane fares. And my dad. It's a honeymoon."

"And so you should enjoy it—"

Larry interrupts: "So the book you're working on?"

"Oh that," Tony says, shrugging. "It's just some impressions I have. Some ideas about where I came from. What I've seen."

"I'd love to hear more."

"It's about the history—the history of protection." Tony isn't reluctant to talk, but he makes it clear there's something ludicrous in what he's up to. "The idea of sanctuary—the religious, political, contemplative dimensions. The history of protection in its broadest meaning."

"The history of protection." Larry feels out of his depth.

"We seek protection from many things, Larry. From our own ignorance, the gods whoever they may be, from other humans. We even seek protection from ourselves, and who we've become."

"A historical approach."

"It started out that way—but I've kind of gotten off track."

Alison says, "So you're going to Crete for research?"

"I've been in Greece for six months now. And the Middle East in general. Going over old ground, the sacred sites, trying to reconcile some things I thought I believed a long time ago and perhaps believe no longer."

A group of about a dozen people walk in and take the long table across from them. An extended family. Costa emerges to play stand-up comedian, three bottles of wine in hand. A bouzouki player behind him, riffing away. The restaurant has suddenly become crowded and noisy because of this family, absorbing the table of three into its field of celebratory gravity, pushing them toward laughter.

Tony exploits the shift in dynamics to move the conversation back to the Reagan years, into yarn-telling, into straight narrative, and Larry takes the bait. Tony seems more settled now, as entertainer, bringing Larry into his world, nourishing him on insider information: how Reagan used the teleprompter; how he wrote out his speeches onto cue cards, the words and phrases compressed into phonetic shorthand; how you'd never understand the man in a private moment, but only on a stage or podium.

"That would have been cool to see all that," Larry says.

Larry and Alison decide they like Tony. They succumb to what they intuit as fatherly gentleness. No one is drunk, not fully. But Alison is yawning now, her leg pressing into Larry's: it's really time to go home.

When they leave, no bill is presented by Costa, or demanded by Tony. This confuses the newlyweds.

"It's on the house—on me, I mean," Tony says. "It's taken care of."

"Are you sure?" Alison asks.

"Yes."

As they stand to leave, Larry says, "Let's get a drink somewhere."

"We can do that," Tony says neutrally. "But perhaps Alison is tired."

"Honey?" Larry asks, turning to his wife.

"A quick one, sure." She's too weary to argue.

The air on the street revives Alison a little as they saunter to the bar where earlier in the evening she spotted Tony and his two associates.

"I'm ready to quit any time," Tony says after they arrive. He seems totally sober after ordering Greek brandy.

"We've had a great day," Larry says.

"A man with Stendhal syndrome, that's a man I can talk to."

"You're making fun of me, man."

"No, I'm serious. I've had reactions like that."

"To art?"

Tony sips his brandy. "To a lot of things, Mister Gaudet."

"There you go with your Cajun pronunciation again."

Tony eyes him. "I'm a little surprised that a man who faints at the Parthenon—who professes to be a man in love with the culture of the world—I'm surprised he's not aware of the lost country of Acadia, which is the country that brought him forth."

"Where I come from, you just never talk about this, that's all," Larry says, an apology in his voice. A desire to please, a keen desire. "If you're French in Canada, you're assumed to be a Quebecer."

"Acadia is a diaspora tale to break your heart. Taught me what little I know about myself. I mean that." Tony gulps down the brandy.

More pressure of Alison's leg on Larry's.

Tony says, "One more round?"

"I think we gotta crash," Larry says.

Alison makes a move to stand up. The blatant yawn, nearly angry.

"Hey," Larry says. "What about Crete?"

"What about it?" Tony is laying out crumpled money.

"Are we going to see you down in Pitsidia?"

"I confine myself to Heraklion. The ancient palace."

"Knossos. That's a big draw, man."

"In the history of sanctuary, the labyrinth is key. So, Knossos."

"That's where they kept that friggin' bull."

"The minotaur. Man-bull."

"Hey, maybe we could visit it together."

"My schedule. I'm not sure."

"We're gonna be in Heraklion—not next Friday, the Friday after. We get in Thursday evening."

"Tell you what. Jump on a bus to get you to the site around nine. We'll spend an hour or so. Then you can go on to Pitsidia and enjoy your holiday, the rest of your honeymoon."

———

The Journals of Antoine Baptiste Savoie

Larry: lives in a bubble that appears as fragile as soap suds until you poke the membrane. Not so easy to get in. Or out. But there he is, right in front of you, transparent, readable. Flaws of insight that'll destroy or create him, or both. Self-constructed ego, the building project undertaken without the proper permits or engineering oversight. Blueprints he himself hasn't yet seen. He will topple a thousand times but rise each time—oblivious to what tripped him up. He thinks he's indestructible, and I wouldn't bet against it.

Alison: also a bubble creature, trying to paddle out of the suburban womb. Opaque out of fear, and reticence. She's the woman at the window, closing shutters for siesta, stealing glances at you bullshitting with your buddies in the alley. You'll look up and catch only a turning head, a swatch of blond retreating into afternoon gloom, languor. Hers would be the seductive laugh—low-pitched, thrilling—you hear down the hallway at the top of the third floor, the private floor, the door under which an inch of light escapes. Ego not fully formed. She has talked to many architects but can't make up her mind. Tries on different modes of representation, uncertain. Something very uncontemporary about her. Reminds me of Alessandra, graceful yet awkward, but still she's attracted to adventure. Familiar with—and accepting of—the vanities of men.

Conclusion: each completes the other's labyrinth.

———

Mycenae

They walk into the king's throne room, the megaron, on what would have been the top floor of the ancient citadel. This presents horizon views across the green, sunlit plain, a breeze in their faces. It's late in the autumn afternoon. The setting sun makes the ruins look more photogenic than when they arrived in the flat light of noon. It wasn't much of a megaron any more, the walls and roof long gone, a slight depression in the stone floor where the hearth had been. The citadel walls remind him of a mouth full of dying teeth, the crowns all gone, only slivers of exposed enamel above the gum line. He says as much to her, and she replies, "The roots are alive. It feels eerie here."

A lot of the site is like that, a floor plan defined by rubble and ramps, but he agrees with her—the citadel has a more forceful presence than any other structure as far as the eye can see. They get an intimidating sense of its lost grandeur by walking around the exterior of massive cyclopean walls, some several metres thick. They wander into rooms on the lower levels that were once enclosed, like the spooky hallway near the cistern. They also visit the famous entrance with its lintel stone supporting a pediment sculpture of two lions facing each other.

They come to a corner that overlooks a ravine. He isn't sure whether the story unfolding in his mind is all tourist propaganda, or something proven by archaeology, or the trace elements of the Homeric poems lingering in a memory cell. It's thrilling to fantasize that he might be standing on the spot where King Agamemnon made the fateful decision to sacrifice his daughter Iphigenia to appease the goddess Artemis in return for getting fair sailing winds to carry the war fleet to Troy.

"I wonder what our friend Tony makes of this place," he says. "What kind of occult Cajun bullshit would he be throwing at me?"

She isn't there when he turns around but several paces away, in conversation with an older Greek gentleman, a dark-skinned, white-haired man with jaunty blue eyes and a dandy air about him. He's talking excitedly to her, jabbing on the tourist map in her hands. He has an oboe strapped across his chest, and is accompanied by a large, friendly dog. Neither Alison nor Larry can understand a single thing he says. They finally figure he's a shepherd, as now and then he shouts across the ravine to a dozen animals or so, grazing on the slope of the mountain. The shouts stir the animals into descending from their perch, creating a racket because some have bells around their necks. At some point the shepherd stops talking, shakes their hands and drifts away.

She says, "What a sweet old man."

"He may not be that old, he might just look old, the sun damage."

And so they walk on from the megaron and join the crowds, which, she says, remind her of an army of ants swarming. He says that sounds about right, because this place feels like it had a military purpose, not as gentle as the Minoans. "The people who built this place, it was all war, tribute, protection." She thinks about that, then points out the grave sites outside the citadel proper. "Is that where the common folk lived?"

"The royal support system. In times of war they were invited inside, behind walls. I think. Probably. You don't want them dying on you."

She laughs. "The queen still needs her nails done."

The sound of an oboe reaches them as they meander toward the main entrance. They both look toward the mountain, and in the distance they see the shepherd leading the flock up the slope.

Jazzily tuneful.

He says, "What do you think it means?"

"I don't know what it means. Enjoy it."

———

THE JOURNALS OF ANTOINE BAPTISTE SAVOIE

The classic definition of sanctuary refers to the most sacred part of the temple, where consecrated objects are kept, often called the inner sanctum, the most legendary one being deep within the precincts of King Solomon's temple. The Ark of the Covenant was supposedly housed there before it was appropriated as a movie prop by Steven Spielberg.

What constitutes a sacred site is a broad subject. The first thing that comes to mind is an edifice of substance and dignified presence, usually with an auspicious history or highly mythologized past; cathedrals, churches, mosques, synagogues, temples and monasteries all fall into this category. But a sanctuary in my definition is any place or site that provides people with the experience of communing with or being sheltered by their deity (or deities). It can also be a community, a city, a geographic region. The Holy Land, for example, which encompasses the current (as of writing) boundaries of Israel, Palestine, Jordan and Syria.

In Athens, the Greeks worshipped the Acropolis, a rocky hill in the middle of town where temples had been built for hundreds of years prior to the construction of the classical buildings around 500–600 BC. In India, Hindus have long revered Benares, a densely populated city on the Ganges plain, considered the home of Shiva, the destroyer god; many worshippers still go there to die, or their corpses are brought there for burial. Muslims, Christians and Jews all hold Jerusalem sacred for different reasons. Jews believe that King David built the temples of the first Holy City of Israel there; it's also an article of the faith that Jerusalem—after the Babylonians conquered it—was where the Jewish diaspora was launched. Christians are obsessed with Jerusalem because this is where they believe Christ was crucified. Muslims hold that their Prophet Muhammad built the al-Aqsa mosque above the ancient Jewish temple, referred to as Temple Mount, located on a rocky outcropping, known as Dome of the Rock.

A sanctuary can also be a landscape devoid of structures or human inhabitants—mountains, streams, rivers, fields, deserts, caves, the ocean. Just about every type of natural landscape has acquired religious significance or reverential attributes for somebody somewhere. For Hindus, the Ganges River, or Mother Ganges, or Ganga Ma, is sacred, the myth being that its waters poured down from heaven; to bathe in the river is to cleanse yourself of sin and negative karma. In Shinto, the oldest religion of Japan, Mount Fuji is venerated as the home of the spirits, or kami, of the cult. The ancient Greeks oriented temples precisely within the cleft or valleys between mountain ranges, believing that it was the landscape itself that was sacred, a belief shared by many primitive or pagan cults. A religious sanctuary can also be a hybrid of structure and nature, a shrine: a pile of stones sculpturally arrayed on the plain, a sacrificial altar on the hill, a tea hut beside a garden stream.

A site can be deemed sacred for many reasons, often because a god or mythological character appeared or performed a miracle there. In Lourdes, the Virgin Mary apparently materialized before a young girl and led her to a spring of healing waters, now a grotto where millions of pilgrims visit every year, seeking cures for the incurable. At Mount Sinai, God's voice thundered from the heavens at Moses and burned the Ten Commandments into stone tablets. The basilica at the Vatican is reputed to have been built over the site where Saint Peter was crucified by the Romans. In Makkah, the most sacred site in Islam, the Muslim prophet Muhammad was born; each year millions of Muslims make a pilgrimage to this Saudi Arabian city. Everyone changes into white garments—symbolizing purity, humility and equality—before circumambulating the Kaaba, or house of God, a boxlike building maybe fifty feet high, believed to have been built by Abraham and his son, Ishmael.

Acquiring a contemporary perspective on sacred sites can be an intriguing exercise when we step outside conventional definitions of religion into the domain of celebrity power and popular entertainment. Graceland. Movies stars. Rock stars. News anchors. Athletes. What constitutes a god is always in flux, and, therefore, so is the religious sanctuary, because what is held sacred is also a moving target, a reflection of a society's obsessions and fears, its dreams and fantasies. I can't imagine theologians familiar with the works of great prophets and biblical scholars being thrilled with this line of thinking. But as exaggerated as these comparisons are, they counterbalance the idea that those of us in the modern West have progressed beyond religion, superstition and mythology. We're just as obsessed today with mythological gods as the ancient Greeks and Romans were, and for many of the same reasons, including a need to believe that there's a parallel world on the fringes of ours where we'll be better off. The old-style pantheon was home to such powerful characters as Athena and Hera. The closer I look at the global myths we perpetuate around celebrities—especially entertainers— the less I'm sure that there is any difference. In the hearts and minds of millions of people, these figures are idealized constructions nurtured on fictional premises and, in fact, experienced by their fan base almost entirely as beings beyond reach.

The idea that religious sanctuaries don't always have a physical presence in touchable human terms—this isn't a new idea. Christians have always had the Kingdom of Heaven as the ultimate sanctuary, offering redemption from the world of Original Sin. Tibetan Buddhists have long oriented their spiritual yearnings to a paradise called Shambhala (the inspiration for Shangri-la), although for many of these believers, it's not just a mythical heaven, but a place that exists and will eventually be found, somewhere in a hidden valley in Bhutan. For devout people and religiously inclined tribes throughout civilization, a sanctuary is just as likely to be a vision or path of transcendence to the afterlife, or a moral code or value system that provides spiritual solace in corrupt times or evil environments. This is sanctuary within our interior world, often informed (or perverted) by outside proselytizers. The notion that people have *souls*, their own inner sanctum, is a creative application of the sanctuary principle, an act of metaphysical ingenuity shared by many religions.

Let's also consider the faith we invest in the symbolic languages and art that convey the mythic meanings of a sanctuary to its cult membership, including holy texts— the power of words and stories. The Bible, the Koran, the books of the Veda scriptures, Confucian wit, the novels of Ron Hubbard, the red book sayings of Mao are famous as prophetic documents containing scriptural revelations that inspire the faithful. In the beginning, there was the word. To put it ever so glibly, words will set you free. There's shelter in the protection of words, but also in other aesthetic qualities deployed in the sanctuary, the fables in stained glass, Hellenic sculpture, paintings in Renaissance perspective or Egyptian relief, or any artifact in the service of the cult: pottery, candles, jewellery, the chalice, the cross, the menorah, the black stone at Makkah on which the sins of Islamic pilgrims are wiped away.

The history of religious sanctuary tracks along with the history of innovation in art and architecture, or at least it used to until godlessness became a rallying virtue of twentieth-century modernism. This tracking owes much to the reality that religious cults were a mechanism by which political ideas and community order could be established or exerted over a population. Spiritual leaders often received profligate patronage from kings and emperors to help communicate the appropriate message to the target audience. In many cultures, the king and the spiritual leader were one and the same. Regardless of the separation of powers (or lack thereof) between church and state in the ancient world, religious sanctuaries by their design often mythologized virtues that reflected civic as well as spiritual concerns. The Parthenon in Athens celebrated rationality, wisdom, reverence and poise—the principal traits idealized in classical Greece, the birthplace of democracy.

At the soaring Gothic cathedral in Chartres, France, which reached twice the height of the tallest cathedral previously built, there's a very strong message about the Catholic God being all-seeing, all-powerful, Someone to Whom the faithful will listen, reverentially, fearfully, scared shitless, actually. Rising vertically through massive columns, arches and flying buttresses, the Chartres cathedral is a myth-presenting system that was state of the art for its time, arguably the greatest example of stained glass-making in history, with 176 windows depicting parables and characters from the Bible. On the outside walls there are more than two thousand stone figures. The investment in such artistry served as much more than just entertainment; this cathedral (and others like it) forcefully illustrated the idea that religious dogma defined the boundaries of daily life. If there's a modern equivalent to Chartres—to the pyramids, Greek temples, the Duomo in Florence and other notably grand religious sanctuaries—it would have to be the television, the means by which the prevailing cultural values are transmitted today, using the power of artifice, first-rate storytelling and mass distribution to remind us who we are and what we stand for and where our disposable income goes.

In short, the sanctuary principle in religion or spirituality manifests in a multitude of forms, in structures, landscape features, metaphysical concepts, aesthetics— and within the body itself, in our souls or consciousness. I would also surmise something else: myth, or the myth-making capability in humans, shapes the religious sanctuary, and the religious sanctuary, exists to protect and nurture the myth.

Some sanctuaries take protection seriously, insanely, come to think of it. Think of the crypts we've constructed for our nuclear arsenal, the heavily guarded sanctuaries on the far edge of prairie fields and within nuclear subs under polar ice, the buried tubes and silos of killer instinct. With myths imposed on us by religious cults and often symbolized or brought to life in sanctuaries, we can do many things, from building societies and bombs to dismantling them. Whether these sanctuaries manifest in a temple high on the hill, a bias hidden within the brain, or a slogan or thigh displayed upon a billboard, they exist as structure and ritual form, the veneer of meaning, representing all we'll never fully understand about how we came to be.

———

Santorini

The wedding ring slips off her finger, a simple band of gold sinking into the sea, a family heirloom lost forever. She's blissfully unaware of this, floating in a sunny honeymoon moment, in the placid, bath-warm buoyancy, and she's still unaware a few minutes later as she walks toward him, tiptoeing on hot, black volcanic sand. It's the nudist part of the beach, far from the crowd, and they're both naked, and it

feels innocent, totally unsexy, as if they were frolicking tod-
dlers, because there are no gawkers here, only two cavorting
towel-preeners, the Danish couple, whose every predictable
move comes off as a puppet gesture from an invisible art
director staging a fashion shoot.

She discovers the loss on the crowded bus back to town;
they return to the beach by taxi at sunset. He snorkels into
high tide, diving toward flickers in the depths, finding only
fragments of shell and stones catching the light while it
lasts. Each time he rises to the surface for air and to check
his bearings, he thinks ahead to the claustrophobic hours
they will spend in jewellery shops in the tourist quarter in
each village and city along the way, the quest for a replacement, the rationale they will improvise to explain the loss.
It's only a ring, the ring was cursed, it had a tragic past, so
much sadness, the death of your mother, it wasn't meant to
be, let's start fresh, let's start our lives together properly.

A few days later they will find a ring they both like, but it
has an inscription, a date, from the 1970s. They decide to
think about the purchase overnight. At dinner, Alison
abruptly says no.

No, not that one—what if the woman who owned it
died young, like your mother, or got divorced?

She's quicker and more instinctual than he is, and art-
ful at creating an elaborate backstory to justify her snap
judgments. She's already visualizing a dramatic arc emerging
from the symbols and their settings—the lost ring, the sea,
nudity, a baptismal moment, the marriage, the honeymoon,
the new ring, the new bond, the life ahead.

When they leave Santorini by ferry for Crete, he con-
cludes that it's best that the ring be found in Florence, the
last stop on the trip, where a few years earlier she had a summer of culture, an Italian boyfriend, a room with a view, a
siesta under the Tuscan sun. The ring would be found there

several weeks later, their honeymoon acquiring scenes from a place where life flows from the education of the senses, and even a conversation about the freshness of the olive oil provides an excuse for a seduction.

———

THE JOURNALS OF ANTOINE BAPTISTE SAVOIE

Imagine being born in the early moments of the evolutionary drama, at least several million years before the Old Stone Age, long before the Paleolithic cave dwellers incised images of bulls on the walls of their sanctuaries in celebration of the natural world as Universal Mother but also to signify their love-hate relationship with the animals they killed for food and clothing. Let's go very far back: imagine you're among the first gill-breathing creatures to raise a snout while paddling webbed claws through the nutrient-rich soup of the planetary womb, casting an amphibian glance landward, blindly intent on conquest and other strategies of pre-bipedal survival.

How frightening was your life?

How alone were you?

How lacking were you in explanations?

Your existence would have been a nightmare.

Researchers tell us that unborn babies dream in the womb. And the first land creatures—what were they but the babies of evolution, orphaned on the beaches of an incomprehensible experiment? It's not so hard to imagine post-cephalopodic sentience marked by a capacity to dream, to nurture fantasies of escape from such a hellish goopy estate.

What if you'd survived those initial moments in the transition from water to land? You would have taken cover, and over time, much time, your descendants, and their descendants down through so many thousands of generations, would have developed much better survival strategies. They would have learned to find, kill, grow, cook and preserve food with increasingly better tools; take shelter from their enemies and the elements; and indulge in elaborate mating, fertility and funerary rituals. In the dark nights around the fire, in the huts and caves, they would have told stories about gods and demons, and drawn pictures to impress, frighten or hold power over someone in the tribe, but also because the world was too frightening to be understood solely through the prism of human action.

The first hominid brains may have been unsullied by advanced cognitive activity. But even back then, I suspect, there was a genetic disposition toward stories, parable, sermons—anything to help early humans reckon with the predicament of existence. They would have decided to believe in something besides themselves, the forces behind the scenes, pulling the strings, investing the lion or the eagle with energy or malice. They would have made up stories to explain the inexplicable weather, the inscrutable night sky, and to silence the mewling of the children and the braying of the hungry and the complaints of the aged. And their stories would soon have taken on new meanings and uses.

The best storytellers would have carved out a niche as priests, shamans, prophets on retainer, adorning themselves in colourful garments, garish pigments, confusing dialects. They would have supported their patrons in the construction and consecration of special buildings and shrines to honour the ghosts they evoked and to institutionalize their power; they would have helped create sanctuaries as emblems of manipulation for all those humbled or frightened by their vulnerability to the cosmic vastness. Which was everyone.

———

Nearing midnight the ferry glides past the Venetian fortress at the entrance of the Heraklion harbour, cutting through black water and past the impromptu flotilla of moored sailboats and other pleasure craft. Revelry on a big yacht, disco music, flashing lights, bikinied women, pot-bellied men, cigars, champagne glasses, laughter.

Larry stands on deck, tethered to luggage and to Alison, enjoying the breeze. He's drawn to life along the quay, a grouping of small fishing boats, visible at the edges of light created by the yachts. On one boat, two men are stacking nets, father and son, the latter pausing to wolf down a sandwich taken from a black metal lunch box; on another, a half-dozen men gather around an open engine hood, greasy arms reaching into the guts of the problem, shouting instructions and happily trading insults. Larry's Greek is improving, but he doesn't need it to understand what men say to one another on boats that wouldn't survive a single storm on the North Atlantic. He feels a kinship to these men, mired in their wharf life, one he's known his whole life: the tourist in the family, come home for summer, thinking he knows what's what and who's who. Even the feeling of being the outside observer, he thinks, can feel like home, if you keep looking long enough.

And then he sees the man in the Nike baseball cap. And Costa. Tony's associates from Athens. Both smoking on the deck of a yacht.

Larry says nothing to Alison, thinking he'll tell her later. She's had a bad day, seasick on the choppy, grey-flecked seas, unhappy that her husband had evidently misinterpreted their travel itinerary, only realizing this yesterday, causing a little panic, a needless argument. They were scheduled to fly to Crete on Friday, tomorrow night, not today as Larry had told Tony Savoie in Athens. It was impossible to change the tickets without incurring costs he didn't think they could afford. She's unhappier, still, that he insisted they take the ferry instead so they wouldn't miss the Knossos tour with Tony tomorrow.

Larry is expecting a grimy, air-polluted world in Heraklion, the largest city in Crete. But as they step off the ferry and join the crowds in the maze of streets, he's not thinking about air quality. Or Tony's friends. The travel guide said Heraklion could be dodgy after dark. So Larry is moving them along as fast as he plausibly can, a little annoyed that Alison is dawdling, complaining. He relieves her of another bag, and on they go; there's not much around to quell a tourist's disorientation—a few toughs, a panhandler, youths on street corners, delinquency in the air. But then he sees the sign for the pension, overhanging the street.

The room is a sanitary comfort. Two single beds. A bathroom.

She doesn't feel much like talking. And gets into bed. After a minute, she says, "The light is bothering me."

"I'm just reading for a bit."

"I won't be able to sleep. It's late. Come to bed."

He's tired too, otherwise he would go out to a taverna, as he did in Santorini, a book in hand, a glass of Amstel, a plate of olives and bread, the illusion of being the intellectual on a journey of exploration, making mental notes for the travel memoirs he'd write one day.

He gets up to check the double lock on the door, turning it this way and that, noisily, and Alison grumbles, and then isn't much impressed by the kiss to her forehead. He climbs into bed again, turning off the table lamp. Decides the moment has passed that he can say anything to her about Costa and Baseball Cap on the yacht.

She's asleep before long. It's hours before he is.

———

The Journals of Antoine Baptiste Savoie

The ancient sanctuary designers were fond of creating sophisticated entry protocols. A favoured tool: labyrinths, or labyrinthine processional routes, through which pilgrims were often led toward a more intimate setting, the private shrine where homage is made to the god or goddess. Labyrinths are found all over the world, dating back thousands of years, with many based on spiral or circular patterns found in nature. Circles and wheels are shapes that are universally held to be sacred for their wholeness, symbolizing union with the divine forces. In the Hindu tradition, some temples are encircled by a path called a *parikrama* that allows worshippers to circle the home of the deity while saying prayers. In early Native American cults, the labyrinth was called the medicine wheel. The Celts referred to it as the never-ending circle, and in mystical Judaism, it's the Kabalah. In medieval times, French Christian pilgrims who could not make a pilgrimage to the Holy Land walked the labyrinth in the Chartres cathedral instead, and for this reason it's sometimes called the Road to Jerusalem. For penance, the faithful would traverse the labyrinth on their knees.

At Knossos, the ancient Minoan palace on Crete, once inside the building you soon end up walking in circles, moving deeper and lower into the site through hallways and down long ramps that seem to double back and branch off, here and there. This downward spiral of the labyrinth eventually brings you to a lower courtyard, away from the residential apartments and administrative offices, along the route of an ancient procession that traditionally concluded with an event called the bull dance. Young men and women would attempt to seize the horns of a charging bull, in honour of the animal considered sacred to the Mother Goddess who ruled the Minoan cosmos.

The labyrinth represents the meandering path of the soul. A nice idea, but practically it works as a technique for disorienting people, taking them out of their daily habits of mind. Navigating a labyrinth reminds people that spiritual exploration requires a journey beyond superficial externalities into internal profundities. Labyrinths are not the same as mazes. There are no dead ends and you can't get lost. The idea is to take a circuitous path to your spiritual destination, quieting the mind in the process.

———

A hot, dusty morning, searing sunlight. Larry had expected the site of the palace restoration at Knossos to loom as poetically into his field of vision as Mycenae and Delphi had. But the bus disgorges them in the midst of a drab suburb. Bulldozer sounds from a nearby construction site. Concrete apartment blocks. The palace looks like a bland office building nearly collapsed to its foundations after a big earthquake, before the wrecking ball finishes the job. But as he looks past the blighted streetscape, he sees a vista of rugged brown fields, dotted in cypress and pine trees, extending toward a panorama of gorges, high ridges and even higher peaks of a mountain range that goes on forever. He can imagine that fifty years ago the air around here was often stilled to a glued poise by molecules of pine resin, fragrant with the aroma of sage and rosemary, not throat-irritating as it is today with diesel fuel emissions and the coconut sunblock someone is wearing in the lineup at the ticket booth.

"Mister Gaudet and Miss Smith," says Tony Savoie.

"Hey, Tony." Larry hasn't yet mentioned anything to Alison about the previous night's sighting of Tony's associates.

"It's hard to really see what this place was," Tony says as they wander inside onto a ramp that flows down to a colonnade below grade. "The Evans reconstruction leaves much to be desired—but if the German fellow, Herr Schliemann, had got his hands on it, we'd have a chalet."

"Schliemann was a thief," Alison says, "wasn't he?"

"Which archaeologist of the eighteenth or nineteenth century isn't by today's standards? Schliemann was a genius at smuggling artifacts."

"Lord Elgin," Larry says.

"Oh, of course, of course," Tony says dismissively. "Schliemann was at least an entertaining thief. He was sort of a junk bond trader type of his era, a self-made man. Travelled the world making money and stealing it. Cornering the market in California gold dust, the Russian one in indigo. When he finally moved to Greece full-time to excavate and plunder, he used friends to find him a bride who was beautiful and well-educated but very poor. Why? Perhaps he needed love in the way he needed Greece—a beauty powerless to resist him. He lived like a god, even going so far as to rename his servants after characters in Greek mythology, and he insisted that messages be written to him in ancient Greek."

"Anyway," Larry says, interrupting, "this place has the feel, a little, of a Holiday Inn, maybe an amusement park— trying to do Greek revival—that got hit by a paint bomb."

Tony is nonplussed by Larry's humour, and continues with the lecture. "On the other hand, Arthur Evans was a Victorian man, quite proper. So you can imagine the biases. But he did sink a lot of his fortune into excavating here and

restoring the palace. It looks gaudy—the plastering, repaint-
ing. But when you think of the pottery, the frescoes, oh, so
many beautiful artifacts in the Heraklion museum. It's
priceless. This place has been a sacred site for eight thousand years, the excavation layers showing clear evidence of
Neolithic settlement. But most of the site we see today—
that's from the Minoans. Different theories about how the
civilization was destroyed. The earthquake, but also by the
Dorians, Achaeans, Mycenaeans."

Near the excavated storage magazine, where the Minoans
kept their large ceramic jars of oil and water, Alison begins
to feel better, out of the hot sun and dust. Tony and Larry
are a few steps ahead, embroiled in some pointlessly competitive exchange. Then Tony suddenly stops, turns to
Alison. Larry walks a few more steps before realizing this,
then reverses course to join them.

"Can I read something?" Tony asks, flipping to a marked
section in a travel guide. His manner suggests that he
intends to read to them whether they like it or not.

> After the Athenians killed Androgeus—jealous of
> his victories at the pan-Athenaic games—his
> father, King Minos, waged war on Athens to
> avenge this death. The Minoan king prevailed,
> and as tribute, demanded that seven Athenian
> men and seven women be sent to Crete every
> ninth year to be devoured by the Minotaur.
> When the third sacrifice came round, Theseus,
> the son of the Athenian king, decided to join the
> sacrificial ranks, intending to kill the monster in
> the labyrinth at Knossos. He told his father that
> if he succeeded, he would return with white sails
> hoisted, instead of black sails. When he got there,
> with the help of Minos's daughter, Ariadne, who

had fallen in love with him, Theseus killed the minotaur. Ariadne had given Theseus a ball of thread, which he unravelled as he walked into the labyrinth. Getting out then became a simple matter of following the thread backwards. However, when Theseus returned to Athens by sea, he forgot to change his sails from black to white. The King of Athens saw the black sails, and, thinking that his son's mission had failed and that Theseus was dead, flung himself into the sea and died.

Alison thinks he isn't the Tony from the evening in Athens. He's manic, sly—where's the gentleman? She's also exhausted from the travel, the stress of losing her ring.

Larry's a little afraid of Tony now, but still drawn to him; he wants to know what Tony's up to with the Arabic guy and Costa. Is Tony a spy, maybe?

After what Larry thinks is a contemplative pause, he says, "The idea of the monster, you know, living beneath the surface of the palace, in the labyrinth, it tells you what the Greeks thought about the challenge of civilization. Below the luxury and society, there's always some kind of pain, or cost, right? You feed the monster what it demands, the blood and flesh, and you become a monster as a result. No matter how well hidden the monster is, if you keep feeding it . . . you are, like, the monster."

"Or kill the monster, and you pay another price," Tony says. "The Minotaur is a metaphor for what lives in all of us. Or most of us. The Greeks certainly understood the subterranean realities of power and aggression, the dark forces, the murderous aspect of humanity that, of course, they invoked as the situation demanded. But they demanded that it be kept on a leash. Chained in the lower layers of what we might call ego, or consciousness. Still, better to know the enemy within. Is a monster in a basement always a bad thing?"

Larry shrugs, wants to fight back, but can't find the words. Tony isn't waiting for eloquence from Larry and resumes talking. "In the big poem, Dante confronts the 'infamy of Crete' at the seventh circle of hell. I trust Dante, always. But I prefer Picasso's perspective. Some of his work from the 1930s shows the bull raping and killing. The usual statements. But in other paintings, the monster is presented as a lover, in a consensual relationship with a woman. What the hell does that say? That he pretends to understand what woman are looking for? No wonder the feminists hate Picasso."

"Or maybe—"

"But these conjectures, Larry, they're literary, romantic. Where do they get us, ultimately. Speculations divorced."

"Divorced?"

"Divorced from the origins of the myth. The Minotaur was probably a Greek adaptation of the Baal-Moloch myth of the Phoenicians. Related to human sacrifice. During times of war, in the very distant ancient world, young men and women were given to the victors as tribute, and there was likely human sacrifice, possibly to gain favour with the gods but perhaps, as well, to diminish the enemy in a very countable way—by killing them. So killing the Minotaur, this signals the respect the later Greeks had—if not for human life, then for stopping the practice of blatant human sacrifice. Maybe. It also fits a theory many have of the Minotaur as a Cretan sun god, their version of Zeus. Remember, his birth was the outcome of a coupling between earthly queen and sacred bull. A coupling inflicted as an indignity on the queen's husband, King Minos, by Poseidon, to punish Minos for his greed and arrogance— but never mind. Quite a nasty trick by Poseidon, making a man's wife get the hots for a sacred bull. But if you're going to get cuckolded, it may as well be by someone with bull sperm, I suppose. A man-bull, the sexual extreme."

"I guess there are many ways to look at this." Larry is crestfallen. He can't begin to match Tony's effortless improvisations.

Tony turns to Alison. "How do you see the Minotaur myth?"

"I don't know much about it."

"But what about the summary I just read?"

"I like the part about the ball of thread."

"You do," Tony says neutrally.

She shrugs. "She showed him the way through the labyrinth, and how to get back to her."

"You liked the love story?" Tony says, as if catching her in a preposterous lie. "But then he left her."

"She liked bad boys," Alison replies. "Boys her father wouldn't approve of. She took her chances."

"So everybody got what they deserved?"

"I guess so."

"Now, Alison, you can do better than that."

Larry finally realizes that Tony is badgering his wife. "Hey, Cajun man." His voice is a confident balance of jovial and harsh. "Enough already with the tutorial."

———

THE JOURNALS OF ANTOINE BAPTISTE SAVOIE

This desire to hurt them—where did it come from?

Was it the naked ambition of the boy, the careless expense of energy? The unfocused appetite of the girl, how she walks toward locked doors expecting them to open as easily as blowing out a candle?

I am a disgrace—

But how to atone?

The verb atone means to reconcile or become at one with something. Atonement is an esteemed reflex in the history of the sanctuary. It's among the classic rituals of penitential self-reflection across many spiritual disciplines, including the Hindu practice of sannyasi, involving the renouncing of worldly possessions, which is often accompanied by a desire to wander in poverty until death, bereft of material comforts or human family.

In Christianity, the doctrine of atonement is a complex bit of theological business that boils down to the claim that Christ died for our sins and, for this reason, we must never forget His sacrifice or the fact that we were born into sin. Sinners we shall always remain, until Judgment Day. So there is much to atone for in becoming at one with the Almighty Father, which not only involves prayer and good deeds, but searching out pain in equal measure to the guilt one is supposed to feel for being an eternal sinner. The logic is tortured, but you get the point; it's about humbling yourself to grovelling insignificance before the Maker.

Atonement is a concept that more powerfully comes into play as we get older, acquire the scars of living, our memories fraying but still reminding us that we've spent too much of ourselves chasing material things and wild adventures, often hurting others in the process. Some of us turn to spirituality when there's nowhere else to go.

When we destroy the things we love, such as our families, marriages.

When we strip away the veils of acquired persona and discover—nothing's there, nothing worth protecting, anyway.

Am I permitted to pray for forgiveness?

Should I seek soulful vindication in the undertaking of menial, even humiliating activities?

Should I kiss the feet of the monk? Tramp barefoot in the snow to fetch his water or firewood?

Clean toilets and bedpans at the hospice?

What should I do?

Some people seek spiritual connection through self-inflicted pain, the mortification of the flesh that has long been a tradition in some monasteries, sleeping on straw beds in cold cells, no blankets or warm pyjamas, no talking, only praying through the night on your knees in darkness. And there are those in the monastic milieu who favour violent self-punishments, like submitting to the whip.

From whom does a mythless man seek atonement, if not from the god that he has made from himself? It seems bizarre and grandiose; but who can grant me forgiveness but myself?

How far from home can you get before there's no way back?

What is dying in you? Or already dead?

———

On the bus back to the pension, Alison says. "I don't understand you. He was insulting."

"He apologized. Profusely."

"I'm not up for another night of you two. I'm going to bed. We have a long bus ride to Pitsidia, very early."

"I know, I know."

"Why are you going drinking with him? You'll be out all night."

"It's just a drink."

"Whatever."

—

Larry and Tony.

A café patio near the harbour.

A table at the water's edge.

Black night. Fog over the water.

A bottle of Metaxa between them.

"I'm sorry Alison couldn't make it," Tony says.

"She's tired. We have a long day tomorrow."

"Yes, so do I."

"Can I ask you something?"

"Fire away."

"I saw something the other night. Your friend Costa. And one of the men you were talking to in Athens. With the Nike cap. On a yacht."

Tony looks at him.

"When we came in by ferry last night."

"I thought you were flying in."

"A mix-up. So we took the ferry instead."

"Oh."

Tony leans forward, arms on the table, eyes closed. "It's really not all that secret," he says, opening his eyes. "But it's nothing we should be talking about. We're involved in a transaction."

"A transaction."

"It's nothing illegal. *Extra-legal* might be the right word. A miscommunication between governments—well, one set of governments and a group that wants to be a government and never will be, I suspect. Not in my lifetime. There's a hostage in this miscommunication. A hostage we're trying to free. In Beirut. Not as complicated as it could be. But there's tribute to pay, and we're part of the payment system."

"So you're still working for—"

"I work for myself."

"It sounds cool," Larry says, uneasily.

"There's a certain excitement—but cool? No, not that."

"I don't know," Larry replies with sudden bravado. "It's like I wish I could be more like you. Doing all this historical writing, travelling the world. And being involved in this heavy, heavy stuff. Where the action is. Do you think . . . how would I . . ."

Tony isn't listening, but scanning the pages of his journal, lingering here and there, turning a page or two, lingering again.

"Tony?"

Tony looks up. A smile Larry can't figure.

He closes the journal slowly, fingertips softly raking the cover. He drains his brandy.

"Larry, let's talk, one displaced Acadian to another."

"Sure, man."

"There's a ball of thread in your hands, son."

"A what?"

"I suggest you walk backwards, following that thread."

"Cute."

"You're as capable as anyone, Mister Gaudet."

"But what?"

Tony hurls the journal into the harbour. Splat.

It floats, unopened, into fog. Gone.

"You threw away your journal, Tony!"

"My heart's not in it."

"You're weirding me out."

"The heart I speak of here—it's not an appetite to *develop*. I'm in love with something else, the work you find so cool. And once you're addicted, it's tough to give up. The messiness, complications, the beautiful inefficiency of it, the universe of lies that hold it all together and give it—I guess—a truth unique to me. I can't give it up. I try. I have tried. There have been long stretches—as even my ex-wife would admit—where I've denied the appetite, taken out the garbage on Tuesdays, talked seriously with my neighbour about which lawn mower to buy, which football pool to join with the other men on the street. I have tried. Yet here I am."

"But why throw away your journal?"

"The paper of it is gone, drowning. Drowned. But the process of transferring the journal from my head to paper . . . something got lost. And it's too late for me to get passionate about finding the lost parts."

"You speak in riddles, man."

"As one displaced Acadian to another?"

"Go ahead."

"My friend, you are at the mercy of at least three kinds of histories. The history you were given as a youngster by those who wanted to control you. A history you think you've rejected. A toxic dump of biases that never degrade. There's a second history, which you are consciously inventing as you go along, a kind of manipulation you do in your own head, out of hopefulness and plain ignorance. And there's a third, the scariest history—everything you don't want to learn about yourself. Think of how vast that history is already, Larry. How unreachable. Think of all that you've left behind. Hell, I'm sure there are more ways of looking at history, but it is my proposition here tonight"—he pauses to pour them each a hefty brandy—"that we reconcile ourselves, you and I, as kindred spirits, explorers who create our lives in more dimensions than is good for us."

Larry feels a too-tight grin on his face, a liquor flush and exhaustion too, but he finds it in himself to raise a toast, wordlessly. They clink glasses, drain their brandies.

Tony stands up, stiffly, offers his hand.

Larry doesn't want the evening to end. There's so much more he wants to know. He says, "It's not that late—where you going?"

"Back into my alternative history, Mister Gaudet."

"Your what?"

"Do you know what a sannyasi is?"

"No."

And then he disappears, this time leaving Larry with the bill.

They walk through the lemon grove, away from the quaint little village nestled under the hills.

"Look, no houses, nothing, no utility poles, nothing," Larry says. "It's like it all was, maybe thousands of years ago."

She loves the midday heat, the grit in her sandals, everything. The ocean is a blue sliver in the distance. "You're walking too fast," she says.

"If there are nude German lesbians, don't you think we should get there as fast as possible?"

"You're warped from reading *Playboy*," Alison says after a pause.

"*Penthouse*. Like when I was thirteen."

"Try eighteen or nineteen."

"Sixteen, tops."

It's an hour since they checked into the pension behind the main square. They love the old woman who speaks no English but somehow conveys to them they're welcome to use the courtyard in the afternoons to make meals, or read, or sleep.

They're tired of temples and trying to visualize the processional route and ramps of labyrinths; there's no more reading aloud the synopses of the cult rituals that took place in this or that sanctuary.

In two weeks from now, they'll be on a plane home.

They're entering the sweet spot of the honeymoon, an interlude where they'll be each other's sanctuary. This will endure most tellingly in memory: beaches, food, wine, laughter, intimacy. Days of thoughtless pleasures, the buoyancy of swimming together in a warm sea, floating face down, snorkels sucking in air, minute after minute staring into the clear depths to the sandy bottom, no fish life except minnows.

As they approach the end of the grove—a twenty-minute excursion from the village—they see the excavation site.

He says, "The guidebook says Kommos is a Minoan site. From the later period. An important harbour. Possibly a major palace complex. A Canadian couple from the University of Toronto is doing it. Important work."

They walk past it toward the beach.

———

The Journals of Antoine Baptiste Savoie

There's a grandeur in the history of sanctuary that, to me, suggests that humanity can't be all bad.

Our species has gone to considerable effort and expense to ritualize its cosmic ignorance. The origin and purpose of the sanctuary as a pathway to a state of religious rapture or mystical awareness, as I see it, is usually linked to a communal achievement: helping people, a tribe, acknowledge what they don't understand. While this function of the sanctuary is still relevant and indeed everywhere in forms we recognize and some we don't, there's also been an important *inversion*. I'd argue that many people who seek out or invent new forms of sanctuary today evidently do so to celebrate the mysterious characteristics not of any god, but of themselves. They are the gods.

We are the gods.

The powerful have always erected monuments to themselves, much like Tamerlane did in the fifteenth century when he wasn't marauding, building his mausoleum in Samarkand and other mosques in Turkistan. Egyptian pharaohs, Catholic popes, a succession of Roman emperors and British monarchs—they all saw (and still *see*, in some cases) themselves as gods or god surrogates and surrounded themselves with material glories to advertise this fact. Think also of American robber barons, the East Coast industrial oligarchs, the West Coast media men such as William Randolph Hearst, who built his retreat at San Simeon.

Many had historians on retainer, let it be said.

You expect grandiosity and paranoia from the powerful—a willingness to devote resources taken from the very many to manifest the dreams of the very few. You expect that they will want their stories to endure. You expect that they will be propaganda machines. But I'm interested in the mutation of that myth-making prerogative beyond the royal hearth and presidential office into the population at large. This seems to me a radical shift from the ancient world. I'm not talking here of modern celebrities, the people transformed into gods in the minds of those enthralled by and addicted to popular culture; I'm more intrigued by the motivations of the millions of sanctuary creators in my culture who emerge from a much broader trend, the rise of the individual as the most sovereign unit of organization. Not church, state or corporation—but the person. You. Me. I. I'm interested in our appetite to create and tell stories about ourselves, our desire to live as myths in the making.

Is this a secular or a religious activity?

The next time you're in the presence of someone with a story to tell about who they are, how they came to be, and where they're going, listen as an anthropologist or theologian would. Evoke the spirits of enlightened observation. Will you hear a modest voice, tempered by contemplation on the eternal questions, or the echoes of endless self-absorption, a person blinded by the reflection in the full-length mirror?

Amen.

2.2

ACADIAN IN EXILE, PART I

I'M OFTEN ASKED how to pronounce my surname.

In the Montreal neighbourhood where I grew up, English, not French, was the language on the streets. There I said *Guh-det,* which was how my parents said it. As a teenager confronting the French fact of Montreal—of Quebec—I stretched it out to *Gaah-dette.* When I moved to Toronto, people told me my name was *Go-day.*

And there's the version from my parents' Acadian fishing village in Prince Edward Island, which had been anglicized by the time I started to visit there as a young boy. There, Gaudet is pronounced *Goody,* which was perhaps not the intention of Jean Gaudet, the farm labourer who brought his name to North America from Martaize, France, in the 1640s, a man known in some genealogy circles as the "Abraham of Acadia," having apparently fathered his first child at forty-seven and his fourth (and last) at seventy-eight. His children in turn produced twenty-two grandchildren, giving the clan its start here as one of the enduring names of Acadian descent.

Larry Goody.

Around the time Alison and I got together in the late 1980s, I had just published a magazine article, commissioned as a "going home" exercise, the desired outcome a portrait of my awakening to personal heritage. I opened the story with an image of my mother's casket, "a glinting, metallic container" ascending a conveyor belt into the belly of a 737 on the tarmac of the airport in Montreal, the plane destined for the Island. My father and I were going with it, readying ourselves for three days of visitations before the funeral. I intended to summon melodramatic effects with that airport scene, but as I'd sat there in that waiting room watching the casket being loaded, I hadn't felt anything at all: I'd been in a state of shock.

In the arrival scene along the main highway, I took the reader through a cultural wasteland before revealing the splendour of the coastal village, its postcard attributes. I exaggerated the white-trashy aspects of the scenery farther inland for contrast: " . . . the bleakness heightened by the occasional house—shacks, really—with yards adorned by abandoned cars, doorless refrigerators, clotheslines running from porch to telephone pole and, against the shed, cases of empty beer bottles stacked to the verge of toppling." Some of this was true.

Next came a passage that has a callous edge that unnerves me as I read it now: "Fresh out of the salt water, the lobsters can crush fingers and open gashes with their claws, but tossed into a pot of boiling water on board and eaten 10 minutes later, a lobster is the closest thing I know to culinary nirvana." Although I've cooked truckloads of lobsters in houses and barns, only once have I eaten them on a boat. No matter, it's clear I wanted to convey that the village was one big beach party. The mythical boat-boiled lobsters in question, surely, felt differently. Also, it takes about fourteen minutes to properly cook a lobster.

There were many attempts at bringing local characters alive and revealing the very dull but journalistically required facts of village life: the tons of fish caught annually, the age of the vintage organ in the church, the criminality of the economic conditions in the old days, the trope that vandalism is on the rise among Today's Ignorant Youth.

I commented on the sensitivity of the village males, plainly suggesting they were all strong family men who fished hard, told good stories, shed a tear now and then, brewed a little moonshine on the side and were generous and hospitable to all outsiders. Some of them were like that—but how many? I also referred to the wellspring of spirituality underlying the harsh realities of rural life by manipulating some words uttered by my maternal grandmother as we walked together through the cemetery. She told me that she often saw the ghost of my mother outside her window, wearing a white dress.

I made the claim that, despite the hardships of the fishing life and the inbred qualities in the culture that can make village life claustrophobic and isolating, the place was a paradise.

> . . . where you can wander down to the beach to boil pots of lobster and snow crabs, steam clams, drink beer and strum the guitar with friends who will sing until their voices crack. Someone will give you meat pies, bags of frozen codfish fillets and bottles of homemade strawberry jam with your name on the label. On the road, drivers in oncoming cars will acknowledge you with a casual nod or a wave, even if you are 'from away.'

Sanctuary porn; and not of the highest quality.

The story I didn't tell was that I blame my mother's premature death by stroke partially on high blood pressure caused by the melodramas in the village, the death of her sister from breast cancer, the drunken antics and domestic problems of her siblings and their families, the illnesses of her parents.

The theme I could have pursued but didn't, except in passing, related to the fatalism of Acadians disenfranchised from their rural roots, lost in the city, lacking the strength or wherewithal to exploit the new environment, unable to create or sustain homes for themselves and their families, ultimately living through the prism of a refugee sensibility marked by sentimental attachments to lives they never really lived, in the village, on the farm. When we lack a home, the pretence must do. But if I had been looking for sanctuary-as-home, I lost time by singling out—and promoting—the emotional address as the Island. But it was too painful to contemplate the situation at the real address: Montreal, Quebec.

Among the earliest European settlers to Canada from France in the mid-1600s, my distant ancestors, the French-speaking Acadians, were expelled from Nova Scotia in the 1750s—turned into refugees—and brutally dispatched by the British colonial authorities to other British and French colonies across North America, or sent back to England and France. The Acadians were exiled mainly because they weren't English Protestants; they were French Catholics, homegrown North Americans, who mostly tried to stay neutral in the ongoing wars between the imperial European powers, which often played out as proxy conflicts in their territory. However, they were, in fact, willing to swear allegiance to the British Crown, and had done so since the early 1700s, the caveat being that they weren't required to take up arms against the French, or the Mi'kmaq with whom they'd developed cooperative alliances after generations of mutual and relatively peaceful coexistence. But in the 1750s, the British colonialists expected much more from the French, an unconditional oath of allegiance, suspecting them of secretly supporting the Mi'kmaq and also the French Catholic clergy in undermining British rule. Not incidentally, the Acadians possessed some of the best farmland in Nova Scotia, which was likely of no small interest to the colonial authorities and to commercial interests in nearby British colonies such as Massachusetts, New York and Maine. To make a long story short, the Acadians were deemed ready for an ethnic cleansing and the confiscation or destruction of their property, farms, chattels, dignity. Deportation. Those who stayed behind had no part in the power structure. They hid out in the woods, eating berries and rabbit shit. Instead of moving to Louisiana, or dying along the way in sinking ships or being murdered by highwaymen in the Carolinas, they remained under economically marginal, culturally depressing conditions. Two hundred years later or so, some descendants of those Acadians who stayed behind finally moved away from Eastern Canada on their own accord—like my parents did—because at last they got the message to get out: their home provinces didn't provide reasonable opportunities for their economic, social or political advancement. Maybe they were tired of being dirt poor and the savage conditions that resulted, for example, in nine of the fourteen children in my father's family dying of one preventable disease or another. No matter: upward mobility was at hand. There were highways, cars, radio, TV and awareness of different places in Canada with enough food, toilets *inside* the house, running water, winter clothing. But as my parents tried to get established in Quebec, they should have taken note that it was a Canadian province with aspirations to become its own country.

Here's the situation:

The Acadians of Eastern Canada, as a group, had been pretty much turned into English-speakers by the time my parents left the Island, except in pockets of resistance in cities such as Moncton and villages here and there across coastal New Brunswick; otherwise they had been forced—more or less—to speak English to do business, attend schools or socialize and marry beyond their dwindling numbers. In leaving their largely anglicized Acadia, perhaps my parents would have been wiser to continue west to Ontario, where they could speak the language most natural to them. But no, they stopped in Quebec: Gerry and Vera Gaudet, principally English-speakers, decided to move into a world where a French majority was on the verge of giving vengeful voice to its gripes at the British. The only reason I can intuit for them staying in Montreal is that the city did have a French element, a French fact and spirit, which was more or less on life support in Prince Edward Island. Maybe they were drawn to what they'd lost. That's an interesting thought. Also, Montreal was closer to the Island than Toronto or Calgary; the decision might have been that simple. Get off the train at the first big city. Whatever their reasons for staying in Quebec, they arrived where an ethnic nationalistic rebellion was percolating. The Québécois French—there were six million of them—had constitutional safeguards and political mechanisms to ensure they weren't, en masse, anglicized. And they did have grudges against the residual British-descended ruling class, anyone who spoke and lived culturally in English, *les maudits anglais.* Some Quebec intellectuals were creative with the terms of victimization, referring to themselves as the white niggers of North America. Yo, white niggers? Of North America? Were my parents the white niggers of Quebec?

Exaggeration speaks many languages.

—

In the past two generations or so, Quebec has effectively evolved into a nation within Canada—if not in name then certainly in deed.

One of the first acts of the separatist Parti Québécois government when it came to power in 1976 was to make French dominant in every aspect of provincial government and commerce. If English could not be eliminated altogether, it was to be contained by edict and patrolled by "language police." Individual privileges, such as freedom of expression, had to defer to the collective rights of the Quebec majority.

Individuals in a minority position have only privileges?

The collectivities of the majority have inalienable rights?

Coming from a family of anglicized Acadians denied their rights for so long, you'd think I'd be more sympathetic to the French cause in Quebec. For much of my life I've defended the nationalistic aspirations of Quebec outside the province and, in fact, outside Canada, to those who describe the language laws as fascist, or complain that Quebecers are potentially treasonous destroyers of a great country. Why would I do this? Especially when the province has trampled my rights as I interpreted them.

Perhaps it's something similar to what they say about those who grow up in unhappy homes; apparently some get very good at putting on the smiling face to the outside world out of shame about the real situation. It's not as if my embrace of dime-store psychology doesn't have a weird precedent. The architect of the Quebec language laws, a psychiatrist-turned-politician, Camille Laurin, once famously described the goal of independence from Canada as "collective psychotherapy" to help French Quebecers with their "inferiority complex."

The Québécois French take offence when it is suggested that they oppress their minorities; they argue persuasively that they're the minority in Canada, in North America, so why can't we leave them alone and appreciate the progressive social democratic society they've created? As an anglicized Acadian, I see myself sometimes as Exhibit A in support of their argument. But still, I was required to see myself as one of *their* minority. Who did we belong to? To them?

My parents kept their heads down. Their priority was putting food on the table. My dad played in an industrial hockey league and bowled for fun, and spoke a lousy *joual* at the machine shops where he worked. My mother fretted about everything, emotionally tied to the Island. Now and then she would complain, in an occasional bout of gin-soaked bitterness, about the attitude of customers in the department store where she worked who demanded (demanded!) to be served in French. Imagine that! We missed an important fact of life in Quebec: We Acadians weren't French enough in language, culture and political loyalty.

We were Canadians first, not Quebecers. This didn't seem so absurd as a working principle; but as I grew into my later teens and confronted life outside the neighbourhood, it became apparent to me that I'd been incubated in a cultural minority, the English. I was the most absurd genre of cultural bastard: an English-Acadian in Quebec. And no one was writing language laws or holding royal commissions or constitutional conferences or creating distinct society clauses to protect my destiny and my individual privileges from the hegemony of collective rights.

I left Montreal for Toronto in 1985 to get away from the politicized climate, even though by then I spoke enough French to be functionally if not always grammatically bilingual, the result of countless night courses and other linguistic immersions. As a teenager I'd played basketball in a community league in a tough French neighbourhood. I'd drunk beer in taverns with the French-speaking machinists and secretaries who worked at my dad's shop. As a result, I picked up a working-class version of the Montrealer patois, jumping between French or English as situations demanded and as best I could. But I was restless. There were other reasons to leave Montreal. I followed a girlfriend who had found a job in Toronto, believing that I, too, would have better career prospects there. I was right. By then the Montreal economy had weakened considerably, relative to Toronto, which had been recently energized by the hustle (and spending power) of hundreds of thousands of ex-Quebecers, like myself, seeking an economically brighter future, a less politically turbulent social milieu.

Prior to the Toronto move, the plan had been New York. I had a friend living there, a Montrealer, attending film school; he was learning to write scripts and eventually he became successful at it. We spent weeks together in New York, hanging out in bars, going to museums and plays, talking to women who attracted, ignored and scared us. I didn't have the brains to stay, intimidated by my lack of money and U.S. immigration laws. My friend, an English-speaking Jew, has long since moved on to Hollywood. He's said that he'd move back to Montreal if it wouldn't be economic suicide, and if he and his wife and children spoke French, which they don't; so he continues to live in the suburban blandness of Los Angeles. I knew many Jews who left Montreal after the separatists came to power; Quebec, with its well-documented history of low-grade anti-Semitism, had nothing to offer Jews but trouble, given that they were mainly living as English-speakers. I also knew Jews who stayed, damned if they were going to be pushed around, not with what happened in Europe: they were tough, and had real anger, and I admired their clarity of purpose.

I couldn't be clear about anything, and I tried to see both

sides of the Quebec situation. I was earnestly in training to
be a writer, and falling in love with contradiction and para-
dox. Practically speaking, I didn't realize that, in the end, I
would have to fight in some way to make my life in
Montreal work. I didn't fight at all. I just left.

Alison and I moved back to Montreal after we got married
in 1989. She is an ex-Montrealer too. We were determined
to engage the new spirit of French Quebec by going native.
We moved into a large flat on the upper floor of a duplex in
the French-speaking bohemian area, the Plateau. Our landlord was perfect in our central-casting minds: a gay actor,
indépendantiste, middle-aged, unilingual French. He rented
to us likely out of shock. An English-speaking couple? *Les
autres? Ici? C'est fou. Complètement.* Maybe so, but Montreal
was suffering from a hard recession, worsened by the fallout
of the language wars, the resulting tentativeness of foreign
capital to invest there, the loss of hundreds of thousands of
English-speakers who'd moved away like I had. The retail
sectors of the city were boarded up in places on many high
streets, bankruptcies galore, rents dirt cheap. My landlord,
who lived below us, was probably grateful for any tenant
who looked reasonably solvent. We were almost a stereotyp-
ical gay couple, come to think of it: We had a cat, an
adopted tabby, no kids, loved art, owned a second-hand
Honda. We took French lessons and dusted off our imper-
fect bilingualism, ate *steak frites* at bistros on Rue Saint-
Denis and stomached the suspicions of our English friends
who wondered why we'd gone overboard with all this
French immersion. Alison went back to school to supplement her art history degree with a fashion design certificate.

We seemed like characters out of a coming-of-age novel,
but looking back at that time now, it feels like a novel steeped

in alienation and disillusionment, not a paean to a home-coming or an end to exile.

I was not a model of fluid integration into the business scene, as I was still writing speeches for clients in Toronto, although I did take a three-month contract with the PR department at Bell Canada, the phone company, at its corporate offices in Montreal. The experience wasn't an exceptionally happy one: I was retained to write corporate materials in English, which were translated into French, and this made me, within the mostly French-speaking office, something of a social pariah. The lurking question always was: why couldn't these documents be written in French first, then, if necessary, translated into English?

Bell Canada was an officially schizophrenic company, operating in both Quebec and Ontario; it took the bilingual approach, though English was more equal than French. The language police were not happy.

The biggest problem of adaptation to our new life in Quebec was that Alison and I spent more time interpreting life through the media than building authentic bridges into the culture. In both languages we watched TV, read the papers and absorbed a frenzy of professional opinions on the political situation that, it seemed, was always poised on the brink of catastrophe. Regrettably, we forgot to lead our lives on the street where the world felt different in the daily exchanges with real people. The media realities and the politics preyed on us: we wanted Canada to stay together, and we wanted to stay in Quebec—in Montreal. We didn't know where we fit or whether we could fit; we had the sensation of being on the front lines of a struggle, the English-speakers behind enemy lines, fraternizing with French-speakers who saw us as double agents. We were uncertain and in the end discouraged. So in 1992 we left again.

2.3

THE CHURCHILL TRAIN (Velocity)

Manitoba, January 1997

THE TRAIN CHUGS into polar wilderness. We're beyond all
roads now, into trackless snow, the skyline ragged with ever-
green trees. At the speed we're travelling, the darkness is a blur
of night, a fog of jittery sameness across the window, tiring
on the eyes, like wearing glasses with the prescription slightly
off. Gazing out into the vast sub-zero weirdness of northern
Manitoba, I settle into my bunk in the sleeping car, under
heavy blankets, sedated by the wine at dinner. My memories
of the overnight train rides of my youth didn't have a clanging
audio component, the din of steel wheels on frozen rail. Back
then, sleep won out over the train racket and the excitement
of starting my summer vacation on a journey from Montreal
to Prince Edward Island. This is different: I'm thirty-six years
old going far north on business, in deep winter, and I'm about
to be denied restful sleep for the second night running.

We left Winnipeg the previous evening, near midnight,
for the fifteen-hundred-kilometre journey on the milk
run—the only train—to our destination on the shores of
Hudson Bay, the town of Churchill, a port for the big ships
travelling to the isolated outposts in the High Arctic.

I hear swearing and look out into the aisle: my creative
director is on his knees in pyjamas gripping the boxy, black

vintage Hasselblad camera, twin lens reflex, all manual; it looks like a very expensive scale model of an old-fashioned boiler furnace. He's searching for something on the floor, peering under seats as he crawls up and down the aisle.

"The winding mechanism," he says. "A screw's missing."

My buddy and collaborator, Johnny Pylypczak.

We each have our own four-section: two rows of two seats facing each other, which fold down into bunks and can be closed off for privacy by sliding-door partitions, and locked if need be. Otherwise the car is empty.

I join the search but find nothing except a beer bottle cap. The Hasselblad was purchased for this project. Pre-loved, and it still cost three thousand bucks. I don't know why we aren't using a modern camera, although I'm under the vague impression that batteries die in the brutal cold and then the electronics won't work. Johnny thinks we'll get cool effects, futuristic-nostalgic, romantic. The Hasselblad will produce the look and feel that Glenn Gould, the patron saint of this journey, would have liked: it's a Nordic machine, cold German metal, perfectly designed, like a Bach score, precise and balanced and poetic in its restraint (years later Johnny corrects me: Hasselblad is, it turns out, a Swedish company).

"You brought pyjamas?" I ask mockingly as he fiddles with the camera to see whether it will still function despite the missing screw. He ignores me. His pyjamas are a muted black wool.

I stand there, unashamed, in my high-tech underwear, a full-body suit of bright orange that more properly belongs on the speed skating oval. It's designed to let moisture wick away from the body, but since I have no plans to exercise into a sweat—or wet the bed—the technology is wasted on me.

"The thing about all this solitude business, it gets pretty isolating after a while, after like a minute," Johnny says quietly.

"In the name of creativity, we're here."

"A distance from everything creative. Give me the city any day."

"As a writer, I understand this need for distance."

"As a writer, you understand words."

Contemplative, soft-spoken, poised in creative and business matters, Johnny has long cultivated the appearance—the subtle but expensive haircuts, goatee, quietly fashionable clothing—of someone confidently in the role of the blasé guitar player from a too-famous rock band, not the frontman who swallows live bats or drunkenly exposes his genitals to the crowd. He exudes the quiet-intense vibe of George Harrison, and is much given to dark humour, complicated silences. Still, he's like me in fundamental respects, a blue-collar kid who played too much street hockey instead of studying or going to church; utterly clueless that his future would, improbably, involve advising large corporations on how they present their message to conquer the world.

He squints at the camera for a long, silent moment, as if the thing is sending messages only he can hear. Without looking up, he says, "What you were saying at dinner about refugees, the killing."

"What was I saying?"

"My people." He says that mock-proudly. "What about their stories?"

"I would think we know a lot about that. Everyone ran over the Ukrainians, right? The Nazis on the way in and out. The Soviets."

"But it's not like Spielberg doing the telling on the big screen."

"The Jews, they're great at that stuff, totally. They get behind the myth-making. Invest big-time. A real cultural core competency."

"These winding mechanisms."

"Compared to the Chinese, the Jews really have it together. When is the Chinese diaspora going to tell its story? That's the big one."

"We'll just go to the Hasselblad dealer in Churchill," Johnny says, deadpan. "Assuming we ever get there."

"Mao killed seventy million Chinese. When are they going to get a Spielberg to tell that story? Ten Spielbergs is what they need for that."

"They need to get to Hollywood. Then kick ass. From the inside."

"Johnny?"

"The camera will work. Flaws can be put to good use."

I crawl back into the bunk to confront sleeplessness.

Another drink won't do the job. I'm tired but also wired, fretful about the assignment. Another half-hour passes. As a last resort, I try an old trick, pretending I'll get work done. I have a transcript of *Idea of North,* the radio documentary that Canadian pianist Glenn Gould produced in 1967, which was inspired by a train journey he'd taken along this very route. I pull it out, hoping for an insight or two. This kind of wishful thinking, put into action after two glasses of wine, has had soporific effects before. As soon as I start to read, my mind wanders. All I can think about is how ludicrous this assignment actually is, how unnecessary.

Johnny and I are making this trip because I persuaded our client, MTS, the telephone company in Manitoba, that its annual report for that year should be a thematic remaking, in print form, of *Idea of North.* That program was a landmark event in Canadian radio, and Gould was widely admired for turning the documentary form inside out, creating what he called an "oral tone poem." The program was based on interviews he recorded with five people with experience in the North, spliced together as if everyone were taking part in a conversation on the Churchill train.

The technical guy on the project, Lorne Tulk, said it was "the real and imagined effects of geographical isolation . . . the jumping off point for Glenn's exploration of solitude."

I loved something Gould himself had said about those who desire to get away from it all. "Something really does happen to most people who go into the North—they become at least aware of the creative opportunity which the physical fact of the country represents, and, quite often I think, come to measure their own work and life . . ." Whatever this "creative opportunity" was in Gould's mind— the ability to commune with one's inner essence, write a book or score a concerto, or be at peace with the world—I exploited his comments in the brief I provided to MTS executives, explaining my Churchill proposition for the annual report.

> Gould used the "physical fact" of the Manitoba landscape as inspiration for exploring ideas about Canadian identity and, as well, to engage his own creativity. For MTS, there is much to say about the physical fact of our presence in Manitoba and the creative opportunities we have to serve Manitobans, as we have for the past 90 years. We have our own idea of North: by connecting Manitobans to the world beyond, we have a pivotal role in Manitoba by using communications to strengthen the human community.

The logic is shaky, but we were in the realm of corporate propaganda, where you make do with the feeling of logic, an eloquent and sometimes contradictory arrangement of thought patterns and word associations, the sensation of logic, maybe, without the boring rectitude of actual coherence. My brief wisely omitted any reference to solitude, which is the last thing that MTS or any profit-seeking enterprise ever needs. For a business to be profitably creative, it needs to engage people. I know that and had demonstrated it myself, as an entrepreneur. Over the previous six months or so, as it turned out, I had proven useful to MTS, assisting its executives in drafting a strategic plan that was approved by the board of directors. Then, as part of a team that included many investment bankers and lawyers, I transformed that plan into a prospectus and executive speeches, the basis of a marketing roadshow used to justify the privatization of the company and to sell nearly $1 billion in shares to potential investors. MTS was the largest initial public offering in Canada that year. So I understood very well the need for sending a strong message to the financial markets. MTS didn't in the least require an annual report that emphasized that its revenue-generating market was situated in a vast, frozen, people-less tundra. Pragmatically, MTS needed to attract new investors to buy its shares and corporate bonds; many of these investors worked for large financial concerns on Bay Street and Wall Street and they did not, as a general rule, romanticize the business potential of the frozen tundra, unless seeking an investment in mining or oil exploration. To impress these sorts of people, MTS needs to emphasize that it is a telecommunications leader in the vibrant metropolis of Winnipeg, a city of 600,000, where the company has invested hundreds of millions in networking systems that would make it obscenely profitable over many years. In its first year as a public company, MTS has a fiduciary responsibility, a legal obligation, to portray itself as a competent, ambitious and competitively energized company deserving of shareholder confidence and the support of its employees, customers and regulators.

For the annual report, my job is to ghostwrite the CEO's letter to shareholders and the theme article. Johnny is a partner in the design firm I retained to produce the report. When I brought him into this project, he jumped at the chance to go north, and instead of doing what he'd normally do—hire a photographer—he decided to do the shoot himself. For the amusement, he said.

It's amusing, for sure, but is it the right thing to do? Why am I relying for inspiration on Glenn Gould, who was famous not only for his musical genius but also for extreme flakiness?

During the privatization I earned credibility with management for my dedication; I lived in Winnipeg, mostly in hotels, during the entire job. MTS had no reason to suspect, as I am now beginning to, that maybe all the deadline pressures and late nights and stress, not to mention the months of being at a significant distance from my life back in Toronto, is finally taking its toll. By the end of the MTS job, I'm in a familiar trough, depressed that I'm squandering myself, sleepwalking through life, churning out propaganda for a living. Punishing hours, seven days a week. Alison and I are still debating whether to have children, though we've been married eight years. It would be more sensible for me to head back to my life with Alison in the slender Victorian home in a gentrifying Toronto neighbourhood where I could write the annual report in my sleep, without leaving my desk. But it's hard mustering excitement for going home to twenty more years of mortgage payments. Going north is a delaying tactic, an escapist moment, a petty rebellion, a way of avoiding the question that can still haunt from time to time: when are you going to grow up?

The *Idea of North* transcript has things to say about that.

> 5:23: Well, the only way I see this happening is in an extended ride north . . . I mean a long, terrible, trying trip, perhaps to Churchill by

way of Thompson . . . going and coming . . . and for those that face it for perhaps the first, second or third time, there's an almost traumatic experience . . .

I'm going under, finally. But I keep reading the transcripts, the purpose now being to *fight* sleep with all my might; the more I resist its inevitability, the quicker I'll get there. A sublimely normal moment. The characters in Gould's story reach me through a narrowing channel, their voices fading, my eyes flailing across the print, the master volume in my brain turning lower while the train clatter gets louder. This kind of moment in the isolation of bed is a vulnerable time, the desire to dream awakening, preparing us for the nocturnal creative life, when we see things differently, with less rancour if no more honesty than in daylight.

Smoky-cold, the heat from the train condensing in frozen air. Windows bordered in frost. Hissing sounds, diesel belches. Fat snowflakes in serene descent. A light snow. Windless. A slate, overcast sky. The sun is a gauzy presence, heavily filtered by clouds, barely there at all.

At this time of year, there are only five or six hours of light useful for photography. The train has been stopped outside Churchill for an hour. Eight in the morning, the arctic daylight only just taking hold.

"The light will be gone before we get there," Johnny complains.

"If we miss the light, we're here another day."

"We'll buy stock images. Another night, no, not possible."

We're both still in our sleeping outfits.

"Polar bears," I say nonchalantly.

"Where?" He perks up.

"Not here. But in Churchill. It's what the place is known for. In the fall, people come from around the world and go out into the wild in these huge moon vehicles."

"Like those weird buses that take you out to the plane?"

"Sort of. With way more armour. Polar bears have been known to dismantle bulldozers and trucks. They thrive on tire rubber—seriously."

He contemplates this. Or appears to. He may not have been paying attention, although he's looking directly at me.

"Johnny, it's winter," I continue. "The bears are probably gone out on the ice by now. On the other hand, with global warming, there's less ice out there. Or the ice arrives later. Who knows what we'll find. I've arranged for us to be given machine guns, grenades and land mines."

His eyes flicker only as the weapons are mentioned.

"Do you do that often, just space out?" I ask.

"A solitude moment," he says, maybe sarcastically.

Johnny has heard my riffs on solitude before, and he isn't persuaded. As we sit there, ostensibly quiet, my head whirrs away on the theme, replaying the riffs I've been feeding Johnny.

Why crave solitude? Because we can't hear ourselves think, that's why. The clatter and billboards of the metropolis, the gossip and grudges of the small town, the latest news of the civil war or terrorist tragedy, the gleam of impatience or unsatisfied lust in a lover's eye—all these things, and so many others, get in the way of us, make a mockery of us. Too often, we can't figure out what really matters in life because our signal-to-noise ratio is all out of whack.

We retreat in the belief that apartness, or aloneness, is required to clear our heads, get a better perspective, shed a dying skin, separate what's profound from the superficial; and we fool ourselves that making this distinction is possible. We decamp into otherworldly spaces and hide in shacks to get in touch with whatever we desire to be, or want to create, or need to avoid in order to stay sane. We go places to neutralize the unhappy voices and unmentionable dreams in our heads by experiencing the beauty of the howling wind or the sky reflecting light from a rising sun or falling rain. And we have our tricks to go inward: yoga, meditation, a hot bath, long walks, a walk on the wild side, embraced to protect or nurture something in ourselves; a connection to a god or landscape, the hunger to apprehend the shades of meaning in a memory, a relationship, a work of art, an illness; there's even the perverse allure of getting some distance from those we love, if only to remind ourselves, idiots that we are, how much we appreciate them in our lives after all.

Solitude is never going to give you absolute clarity on a pressing matter that requires a resolution this week or next month. On the contrary, a true moment of solitude, when it does occur, usually defeats any practical intent you hope to achieve with it. The inward journey doesn't operate on a train schedule.

We've all learned to keep our noses in books on subways, airplanes and waiting rooms as a means to put distance between ourselves and the violence of necessary motion in everyday life. We do many things guided by the logic of solitude, and expect that we'll be the better for it. Sometimes we *like* that other people know we're hiding and can only reach us through our proxies. So we give them the email address we no longer reply to, not the personal address to which we spend our waking hours joined at the virtual hip like the cyborgs we really are. We forward our calls to a harried assistant who lies badly on our behalf. We record messages in a monotone that suggests we've been lobotomized or graduated to a very strong antidepressant . . . I will not be returning calls until such and such a date, so leave a message after the tone.

The train jerks into motion. . . .

Johnny and I proceed to install ourselves, gleefully, in the expensive winter gear we each purchased for the trip. I have state-of-the-art outerwear, visibly branded with corporate logos, and a goose-down jacket, with a fleece underjacket, zippable by design. Zippers and black mesh pockets all over my body; by now I've more or less lost track of where my wallet is. Although I can feel it on me when I pat myself down, I can't find the right pocket among all the layers and sublayers. I wear a facial fleece mask of the kind favoured by bank robbers, my orange thermal undergarment, fleece sweatpants, shell pants, knee-high snowmobile boots, thermal socks. I have mitts—as big as bear paws—with which I can't grip anything, and wool gloves underneath that are useful for gripping but in which your fingers would freeze unless protected by the mitts. Johnny is also absurdly overlayered. All my fault: I assumed we would need to wear several layers on the train, and was disappointed that this wasn't so. Trains have improved from the drafty, steamheated, rickety machines that Gould travelled on; we have sleek, electrically heated steel cars in which one can lounge around in a T-shirt and shorts while frost makes designs on the window.

Johnny is also weighted down by two large camera bags, in addition to his garment bag. I've brought along a digital video camera, tape recorders, battery packs, my laptop and accessories and a garment bag. We sit there sweltering, like astronauts being taken over to the main launch pad, trying not to feel ridiculous while the TV cameras get the last seconds of real-time footage before liftoff.

I give Johnny a thumbs-up. I feel good. I believe it will all work out, as all my projects with MTS have. Why not? This is an annual report, not rocket science. Something good will come of this, even if it's only a story. I can easily imagine people at dinner parties saying, You did what? How interesting. Please, go on. Tell us more. This is all so very fascinating.

> 25:38: You get lots of people attempting to create a style of their own, to be known as characters. And this is wonderful . . . people should have styles . . . and this becomes part of the front, the stance . . . people get to believe this is the way they are, even if that's not the way they were when they first went in . . . you come to believe in your own role.

The Churchill train station is a long canopy over the main platform attached to a forlorn building, dangerously icicled. We step down from the train, creaking in winter wear, the only passengers except for a few railway workers who camped overnight in economy class. It's colder than I think possible. We're met by the telephone company rep, a repair technician, a hefty guy, late twenties. He's gloveless, no overcoat, only a fleece sweater. Acid-washed jeans, baseball cap and running shoes, not boots. Evidently hungover but glassy-eyed jovial all the same. He walks us over to the company pickup truck requisitioned for us. He says it'll be difficult to get lost in Churchill; there's only one road outside the town proper, following the shoreline, and it's only cleared of snow for about five hundred metres. Before vanishing into the snow, which has started to fall heavily, he cheerfully advises us to be careful; a sick polar bear (or a smart one, I think) has neglected to head out on the sea ice for the winter and is hanging around the dump, rooting for food, not far from where we plan to shoot images of a satellite tower.

Churchill is what I expected: the spread of jerry-built bungalows across the tundra, a community centre, a commercial zone distinguished mainly by the pizza joint and tavern, and the port with its docking facilities for big ships. Here and there, tourist shops sell Native crafts, moccasins, beadwork, amulets, fur and leather. The main mode of conveyance around town, expectedly, is the snowmobile. The roads are hardpacked snow, and lots of fun to navigate in a four-wheel drive, eight-cylinder truck. I spin out a few times, on purpose. Fun.

As we shoot film in the early afternoon, the wind and snow become severe, nearly whiteout conditions. I drive while Johnny trolls for and collects photos on the Hasselblad. When we get out of the truck, I carry the camera bags, handing Johnny a new lens or film when required, keeping an eye out for the polar bear that never appears. The snow and ice start out as atmospheric backdrop, as the draping for objects that are supposed to symbolize the idea of communications. Satellite towers in a snowstorm. Telephone poles against the horizon. The snow drifting poetically across railway tracks that curve away from town, converging at some distant place where civilization and cable television exist. But Johnny soon loses interest in all the obvious symbolism. He spends a long time on his stomach shooting the snow itself, focusing on beautiful wave patterns. When he's through, we head back to town, with several hours to spare before we have to catch the train south. We drop off the truck at the train station and walk over to the tavern, lugging our bags. The sun has fallen out of the sky faster than I've ever seen before.

The tavern is a sawdust-floored honky-tonk, kitted out with local men (and a few women) surrounding the pool table. Country music on the jukebox. We order a Hawaiian pizza and beer in a quiet corner of the room.

"All your digital video on this trip," Johnny says. "Hours of tape."

"Maybe I'll make something with it. A documentary."

"I bet those tapes stay in the drawer forever."

"You create a ghost for yourself. The ghost is there. But it doesn't always have to be visible. It stays dark, *undeveloped*, but it's still there."

"In English, please."

"An archive has power even when you don't use it."

He sips beer, thoughtfully unimpressed, then says, "Like a memory?"

"Something like that."

When it's time to head over to the train station, the night sky has begun to clear but not fully.

"The northern lights, on a good night, we're supposed to be able to see them from here," I say. "Aurora borealis."

"At this time of year?"

"I thought so. I'm not sure."

At the station, we each make a few calls at the payphone. After that we board the train and store our gear in the bunks. We're bagged but still restless. I have a novel to keep me company, but I need diversions from mental activity even peripherally connected to contemplation. Beer and chips is the better strategy, maybe blackjack, or poker. Our plan is to stay on the train until we arrive in Thompson the next morning, then pick up a rental car and drive back to Winnipeg, a nine-hour-trip south (presuming good weather) through the boggy wilderness, skirting Lake Winnipeg. Our travel agent said, Why not drive from Thompson, you'll get back *much faster*, as if it's no more dangerous than walking across the street for a bistro lunch on a summer day. I never questioned whether driving to Winnipeg from Thompson was a good idea in winter, even though you're explicitly advised not to travel that road at all unless you have survival gear. Which we do. But still.

We go to the bar car as soon as the train leaves the station. It's empty but soon fills up, mostly with the members of a men's hockey team heading back to Thompson after a tournament in Churchill, maybe a half-dozen Native men in their twenties and thirties, tough-looking guys, boozing it up, smoking heavily. Bad teeth, nicotine fingers, scars; one guy looks like his face has been run over by a snowmobile. They don't pay attention to us, but I'm tense, and keep looking over at the bartender for reassurance, a muscled white guy, big moustache, who keeps the booze coming, business as usual. The hockey players soon become seriously drunk. Johnny doesn't look bothered, but that's never an indication of what he's thinking. I can't be sure whether I'm overreacting or whether we should hightail it for the sleeping car and lock ourselves in.

Then a young Native man walks into the bar car and asks whether he can join us. Of course. A surprise. I assume he's with the hockey team, but plenty of folks in this part of Manitoba are Native, and they're not all one another's best friends or play on the same sports teams.

Donny is tall, wiry-strong, with tattooed arms and thick glasses held together with duct tape. A sweet kid in the way of someone who has led a hard life but takes things in his stride because there's no other choice, or maybe he simply doesn't know that some people have it a whole lot better. Soon enough we know that his family is a mess, and he's heading south to meet an uncle who is going to help him find work, once he gets out of jail. Donny has been given no advantages. What he has, though, is youth and vitality. He just wants to hang out, talk to someone new for a few hours. He's eighteen. I'm struck by his innocence and the vulnerable way he asks about things he knows nothing about, not pretending otherwise. I like him immensely. As we talk, it occurs to me that if only we could all show so much honesty in inquiring how other people live we might learn something now and then. At his urging, we tell him a bit about our work, our lives back in Toronto; it's all fantastically alien to him, as if we're describing an interplanetary space mission or a new laser technique for brain surgery. As the night wears on, we do more drinking than we should, and Donny begins to get braver with his disclosures, telling us about the fights he's won, how you can't go through life scared. A young man getting loaded.

The guys on the hockey team have got even drunker. One fellow has passed out underneath the table. Another sits with his eyes closed, a cigarette burning down—right into his fingers. The rest have fallen to arguing. The guy with the tire-tracked face staggers over to our table and, with a toothless grin, asks us where we're from. I say Toronto, and he thinks about that for a long minute, then mentions a famous hockey player on the Toronto Maple Leafs. Then he laughs as if he's heard the best joke in the world. A long silence. When he snaps out of it, I hear a threat in the way he asks Donny for a smoke, which sets off an exchange between them that I find impossible to follow. They're speaking English, but there are other dialects in there too. Donny doesn't like being hit up for smokes in a disrespectful way, and although (or so he says) he isn't accusing Snowmobile Face of disrespect, he makes it clear that, in theory, he doesn't like being taken advantage of. But Snowmobile Face has his own message to send. That one I never figure out. After a good ten minutes of negotiations, Donny hands him a cigarette—lighting it himself. When the guy finally leaves to roust his friends from under the nearby table, I suggest to Donny that it might be wise if he left too.

"I can't. It's about respect."

"This isn't about respect."

"If I leave now—no, I can't do that. I don't do that."

"Don't be stupid about this."

"I'll take my chances."

Johnny and I say our goodbyes and head back to our sleeping car, leaving the hockey players rolling around in a big pile on the floor. Some are passed out, some getting there fast.

We climb into our bunks without saying much. I engage the lock on the sliding door partition.

That night every noise jolts me.

The next morning as we approach Thompson, a town built mainly to house employees at the big nickel mine, we again slot our bodies into layers of winter wear. Donny comes into our car as we pack up. Where did he sleep? Is there a coach car? Did he crash among the hockey players?

I ask him how it all went last night after we left, and he looks out the window, picking at a scab on his wrist, as if to say no big deal. His look suggests that he believes he knows things that I never will. I feel cowardly. Not that I could have protected Donny or myself if a fight had broken out; he's bigger, stronger, a better fighter, if you take his word for it. But we left him there. A kid, really. To fend for himself, even if it was at his urging. This morning I don't feel right about that at all.

As we get off the train. I promise Donny I'll send him a postcard, care of his mother, to a reserve in northern Manitoba.

It's overcast again, everything defined by snow; the idea of north has begun to lose its allure, this I have to admit. I want to get back to Winnipeg, a good meal in a good restaurant, a bottle of wine, then crawl into bed with a novel, or a bottle of ibuprofen. By the time we pick up our car, and eat at McDonald's (it was either that or the fare at a local greasy spoon, and we opted for what we know), the morning is well advanced.

"Are you going to call your uncle?" Johnny says.

"Another life. Let's get out of here. Now."

—

One of my mother's brothers lives in Thompson, a man in his early sixties. Maybe twenty-five years ago he left Prince Edward Island on the run from his first wife and eight children. He'd been a lobster fisherman as a young man, renowned in the village and beyond for his ability to poach and evade capture by the fisheries officers. Now he lives in Thompson, pensioned off by the power company, his long-time employer. He made a new life with his second wife, and they have a teenaged daughter. Two of his daughters (now adults) from the first marriage joined him in Thompson. I haven't seen any of them in years.

I'd called him from Churchill, and he invited me to visit him. Told me to call him the second I hit town.

I said, Okay, depending on how things go.

I have a fondness for my uncle. He's a good storyteller, with a wry, sarcastic, country sense of humour. But I have no appetite right now for sitting around with him or anyone else, gulping down shots of homemade moonshine, or snacking on smoked eel that his son sent up from Calgary, or listening to his stories about the good old days back on the Island, the wharf lore, the drinking and driving, the cars smashed into utility poles or rolling over capes, and the years when he was driving back and forth across the country on a whim, mostly unemployed, not knowing what else to do. One time in the early 1970s he showed up at my parents' apartment in Montreal with two young men, his sidekicks, one now dead for twenty years or more, burnt in a house fire after falling asleep drunk, the other in prison on a life sentence for killing a family of three for reasons that were never clear except it was understood by all that he was *perverted.*

Thinking about my uncle makes me realize that Donny

or Snowmobile Face could have easily erupted from within the bosom of my own extended family. There are several Donnys among us, their potential rotting fast. And several Snowmobile Faces, too, already rotted. We aren't a First Peoples, but there is destitution in our Acadian bloodline.

Once I was adept at stepping into my *down-homer* role. Or at least I thought so. But these transformations freaked Alison out, the yarns I told about fishing tuna in my teens, the gaffed fish roped to the stern, its eyes the size of tea kettles, still alive, looking up at you with a most unsettling awareness that an injustice has occurred here that could be righted, Larry, if you just cut the ropes and gently remove this hook from my gills. I had long riffs on the converging themes of alcohol abuse, male bonding stupidities and fast-moving vehicles; a number of my cousins died because of drunken errors in judgment. Alison was unhappily startled by my relish in becoming one of the local gang on our first trip together to PEI, where we stayed with my sister.

I courted my wife in museums, holding hands and exchanging whispers before Dürer portraits in Toronto and Gauguin's erotic landscapes in New York. We applauded the Royal Shakespeare Company after it had performed all three *Henry* plays in one day—nine hours of Shakespeare. We went to art house movies and, afterwards, there were dinners of antipasto and affordable Rioja, shared between candles, across red linen tablecloths, the quiet table in the back. It was a stretch for her to believe that I was once a feral boy who, from the age of ten, had swum in harbours teeming with fish guts and diesel fuel, a hunter of codfish and tuna, a recipient of poached lobsters, a receiver of fists to the face in dance-hall arguments, if not always the best deliverer.

In truth, I was a city kid; I had only spent summers on the Island. But I also never read a proper novel or book of any quality, or walked into a museum or concert hall, or took a trip to New York until I was twenty. I could hardly string a sentence together when I got to university.

Authenticity? What is it?

On the highway to Winnipeg. I'm at the wheel, singing.

> From this train
> I wave farewell to my love
> Blue sea of her eyes I'll dream forever
> Mining in the dark
> Dungeons of black coal
> My life deep under

Johnny jumps in before the next verse. "Why do you sound like a duck? So nasal?"

"Buddy MacIsaac. A master of the railway ballad."

"Yeah."

"You know who Buddy MacIsaac is? Get outta here."

"I'm not saying I love the music. But he was quite a song-writer, and guitar picker." Johnny is a jazz guitar nut. I'd forgotten that.

"I bet you didn't know Buddy MacIsaac was from Nova Scotia."

"That level of detail, no. That wouldn't be healthy."

"But the hair," I say. "The concept of his hair."

"What?"

"The toupée. Some kind of rat-skin pelt. A statement in self-invention if there ever was one."

"And you're really a fan?"

"Exposure takes its toll. My dad wanted to be him. He spent thirty years learning the guitar solo for 'Dungeons of Black Coal.'"

"Wasn't he a midget? Like, medically speaking?"

"My father was a shade under five-nine."

"Come on."

"Buddy MacIsaac was about five-two, as I recollect. In heels. I met him when I was ten. I went backstage at a concert with my dad. And Stompin' Tom opened the show. My dad knew him growing up."

"He knew Buddy MacIsaac or Stompin' Tom?"

"Stompin' Tom. From Skinner's Pond, PEI."

I launch another tune.

> Well, it's Bud the spud
> From the bright red mud
> Rollin' down the highway smilin'
> The spuds are big
> On the back of Bud's rig
> And they're from Prince Edward Island.

The drive back to Winnipeg goes on and on: ten hours on icy roads through frozen bog, fields and lakes, grey skies, horizons viewable at the same time through both the front and rear windshields. Sunset at three o'clock. When we first drove onto the highway, we faced down the big sign, the public service message, the warning, the recommendation that you don't drive without survival gear, flares, food, a small gas stove, flashlights, matches, etc. Fortunately, it doesn't snow. We drive at reckless speeds, and only twice do we pass cars coming the other way. Our speed is mostly determined by the desire to arrive in Winnipeg in time to have the risotto, endive salad and a bottle of Chianti at an Italian restaurant that I favour. But we miss the last call for food there, and this seems like the big tragedy of the trip. We settle for a bad meal at the hotel and Australian wine that tastes like eucalyptus-infused aftershave.

—

A few days later in the MTS offices in Winnipeg, I explain at insecure length to company executives that our trip has produced unbelievably beautiful images, absolutely relevant to the corporate vision statement. Someone says that a man died on the train somewhere between Churchill and Thompson. He apparently fell off the back while taking a leak. It's the first time I've heard this. It was in the papers.

Is he one of the drunk hockey players? Snowmobile Face?

I wonder whether Donny knows anything about this.

How does someone go missing from a train?

Surely if one of his pals had noticed his absence, the train would have halted and reversed direction. A search would have taken place. But the train came into Thompson on schedule, as I recall. Maybe they only discovered he was gone hours after he'd fallen, and they might have continued into Thompson anyway for help. Surely it has to be one of the hockey players. I can imagine that amid a pile of drunken men on the floor, it takes time to figure out that someone is missing.

I get stupid drunk myself on my last night in Winnipeg and too vocally and incoherently philosophical at a party held to celebrate the closing of the deal that had turned MTS into a public company. A little embarrassing, but my Manitoba colleagues forgive me. They know I've been on the road for many months.

The images that Johnny captured with the Hasselblad are strange and beautiful; as a set of framed prints, they would look perfect hung in a Chelsea art gallery, each selling for the price of a small luxury vehicle. They're resonant to those who understand capital-A art but also accessible to those for whom snow is just snow. Johnny captured the "creative opportunity in the landscape" in the sombre whiteness that framed the ash and smudge of human interference: rails, towers, junctions, trains. As still as the images are, you can sense the turbulence of human presence, the determination to huddle against the brutalities of climate and to generate warmth in the darkness. I also see how this world can drive one to self-destruction.

When Glenn Gould created *Idea of North*, he was already world renowned as a classical pianist, notably as an innovative interpreter of Bach. He'd also developed a reputation as a world-class eccentric. A hypochondriac, he wore heavy coats, gloves and scarves, indoors and out, in all weather, even in summer, and sometimes at the piano. He was cold all the time, whether there was a reason to be or not. He hummed loudly while performing, much to the confusion and annoyance of his audiences and critics. He was a young man when he gave up the concert stage for the recording studio in the 1960s. He believed the stage was a gruesome place, where audiences came half desiring to see an artist fail, miss a note or freeze up. He thought the life of a concert pianist undignified, all the travel, memorizing repertoire, pulling out the same old tricks every night to get the standing ovation. Gould wanted to create and experience music in isolation, without the pressures of live performance. And that's just what he did.

While I was intrigued by Gould's music and ideas, it was the idea of Gould that attracted me the most. By the time I was in my late twenties I'd become a Gould fanatic, reading all the biographies, buying many of his recordings, chasing down trivia on his life. There are many things I could say about why Gould interested me; I suppose what stands out most was his well-documented difficulties in sharing easily in the intimacies of human relationships. Gould kept his distance. He managed relationships on his own terms, often cutting people out of his life when they outlived a purpose, or got too close or demanded too much. Solitude, and the sacrifices he made to achieve it, was a precondition for serving his muse and maintaining his sanity. Unkinder critics have suggested that this fetish for isolation, and rejection of human society, warped his creativity. A warping, perhaps, that inhibited him from becoming a prolific composer of original works, as had been his intention, instead of a sporadic one, a failure even he conceded was true.

The better Gould experts dispute the myth of the isolation junkie. Gould, they say, had good relationships with family, especially his mother and his cousin, Jessie; he enjoyed the company of friends throughout his life, even if he did rotate some people to the outer limits when they got uncomfortably close, or committed a transgression that he would or could never explain. He apparently had lovers throughout his life, romantic entanglements. But when he died of a stroke in his early fifties, those who knew him best said he was a shadow of himself, drugged, bloated. He would often work through the night and sleep well into the day. I imagine he looked very much like someone who had spent too much time alone, certain until the very end that this is what he wanted.

MTS rejects the Gouldian pretence in our visual representation of the annual report and tells us to come up with a new approach, which we create in Toronto, relying on studio photography and stock images.

The result is forgettable, boring, insipid.

The images that Johnny created, though, still have a life. One of my buddies at MTS has hung a set of prints from the photo shoot in his home. I'm going to do the same, one day.

The issue for me that lingers, or festers, is this: What were we doing on that train? Would anything have changed in the bar car had we not been there? If we had said this word or that to Donny or beckoned to the bartender for more drinks, or stayed ten minutes longer or ten seconds less? Had we not been there, would that man have fallen off the back of the train? You may think these are absurd concerns, but guilt is the strangest animal in the internal zoo.

Idea of North is a railway ballad as conceived by someone who was performing Bach counterpoint flawlessly at an age when I was likely still marvelling at two plus two equals four. Gould never spent a single moment of his life getting royally messed up in skanky bars in Memphis or Toledo or brawling in the alley over something someone said to his girl while she fed coins into the jukebox. But he did have other attributes of the anti-hero you often find in the stances of the better country-and-western singers, or certainly within the characters in their songs. It's likely that Gould drove the streets impaired, given what his confidantes have said about his accident record and apparent addiction to prescription drugs. He reminded me of Johnny Cash, favouring the draped black look, except he'd been neutered of in-your-face sexuality and hunk toughness. He was the man in the long black coat, spectral, consciously outside. In some ways, he was a stock character out of hurtin' music himself, a hobo on the run from society and himself, his special insight the product of dishevelled movements in isolation and darkness, the furtive midnight entries into the city by the railway yards after days rocketing through wilderness, ingesting pure desolation. Whenever

I listen to *Idea of North*, I tell myself that despite its uppity reliance on audio collage, Gould wasn't just an eccentric, or a snob, but also a man of the people, perfectly pitched to the tune of loneliness.

On the Churchill train, I was a sanctuary tourist amid the reality of solitude. I should have checked the papers myself. I should have given the dead man a name, if not a face or history. Instead I walked through my meetings in Winnipeg and then went home. The experience had a story to tell me about myself, but for a long time I wasn't listening.

> 32:02: I've seen people who are disenchanted with the north, simply withdraw and concentrate on some activity, collecting guns or stamps . . . just going through the motions.

What I didn't appreciate in the immediate aftermath of the Churchill trip was that scenes had been introduced into my mind that, over time, would demand to be invested with more troubling meanings. Of course, I always had colourful things to say at parties and across dinner tables about the savagely beautiful Manitoba winter, the depravities inflicted on Natives by social injustices, the madness of selling MTS on the Gouldian project. I had anecdotes galore and related them well. But while I had memories, strangely, I wasn't in them as a plausible character. There was no portrait in my head of myself as I likely was then: rootless, directionless, disengaged, a voyeur not a participant in life, unintentionally destructive, too. What was I doing, affecting a paternal friendliness toward a Native kid while my wife, three thousand kilometres away, was wondering whether I wanted to be a real father?

Sometimes I wonder where Donny is. I worry about him without having earned that privilege. Worries like mine he can do without.

In the years following my Churchill trip, I became obsessed with solitude and stepped up the means to infuse my life with it. In its aftermath, I would soon enough become an unthinking slave to the idea that there is creative opportunity in the landscape. I would build a barn by the sea and expect it to protect me and my family. I would bring forth a sanctuary to shelter my search for the lost fragments of myself.

18:53: It takes a strong person to live in the north. When you live in the big city in the south, you can always retreat when you fail in your relations to society. And you can go away and no one really knows the difference. You can't go away when you're in a little village a thousand miles from nowhere . . . so you convince yourself that this is really the life . . . that there's a kind of precious intimacy about all this . . . you've excluded the rest of the world . . . and you've made your own world.

2.4

ACADIAN IN EXILE, PART II

WE CAME BACK to Montreal in 1998, a year after the Churchill episode. The city was on the rebound, recovering from the second referendum on independence held in 1995 by the Quebec separatist government—which came only 50,000 votes shy of winning.

I won't recite the causes of Canada's near-disintegration; this only activates the xenophobic spirit.

Why did we go back? We wanted to come home. Or I did. Alison was less prey to sentiment in this regard; her main concern was getting pregnant. We wanted to start a family. And when I found work in Montreal, we rode my exile delusions into town again. We soon discovered a different city, a more distinctly multicultural spirit, where the English-French duality had receded. There were plenty of new faces and voices, from Haiti, Senegal, Cameroon, Vietnam. The impressive diversity was, in the main, French-speaking, which is what the nationalist program had been about all along. I loved the newcomer or bootstrapping spirit on the streets, having grown up in an immigrant neighbourhood myself.

My problem soon after our arrival was a delayed reaction—the emotional processing, let's say—of the fact that from the time of the first separatist election in 1976 somewhere between 300,000 and 400,000 English-speakers had vacated Quebec, mostly because of the language wars.

So many people whom Alison and I had known from our youth, most of our friends, and nearly all family on both sides were simply gone.

A Montreal diaspora had been created, an exile community that perhaps didn't think of itself as such. What else to call it? It dawned on us that we arrived in Montreal with little more than memories of our losses there. The people we still knew in Montreal, those English-speakers who'd stayed behind, mostly seemed *enclaved* (if such a word exists), tucked into their lives, politically neutered. Our future quality of life, just possibly, required more than picking up bagels at the Fairmount Bakery or ordering a souvlaki plate at Arahova after the bars closed, more than unstinting loyalty to the Habs or the crime tabloids, or having access to cottage country within two hours in all directions.

What do you do when you come home and find hardly anyone there you recognize? The depressing truth: the idea of Montreal-as-home felt more engaging when we weren't living there. So we left again.

I still miss Montreal. I love the spirit of Québécois life. Do I hate the place as well? No. How can you hate something you love? It's not hate. So what is it? Envy, resentment, confusion. All those things, I guess. Would we ever move back again? That's an open question I'm compelled to keep open for reasons I'll never fully understand.

What else can make you feel so confused *except* home?

Until elsewhere becomes your home.

How did Foggy Cove become elsewhere?

If you can bear with me for a few pages, I'm going to double-back or rewind the clock, take a different route through the labyrinth of the story that explains our second departure from Montreal.

One summer in the mid-1990s when we were living in Toronto, Alison and I took a car trip to the Island to visit my family, the first time I'd been there in years. This was pointed out to me, tearfully, by my sister. Donna could not understand why it had taken me so long—as she put it—to come home. My aunts felt the same, but they'd never challenge me like Donna did.

She had left Quebec in the 1980s for many of the reasons I did, and moved back to my parents' fishing village, where she rapidly localized herself. She developed a saltier coastal accent than people who had lived there all their lives. She built a house with a boyfriend, found work and kept the house when her relationship broke up a few years later. When she got together with James, a local fisherman, she began to work by his side during lobster and tuna season. My father was the only one of us left in Montreal, my mother dead for more than ten years by then. As a single guy again, and very lonely, Dad would drive to the Island once every month or two to visit Donna and his sisters. Our family had started to emotionally reconstitute and locate itself in PEI soil. This was a good thing, but, in those years, I could only steal time for very short vacations. And unless I fished lobsters, or bagged groceries, there was no life there for me whatsoever. I also resented how the village melodramas from years past had infected our lives growing up in Montreal, keeping my mother always off balance. I had little desire to make the Island the heart of my emotional orbit. I was married now, and had a different life in Toronto, and there were other places I wanted to live, too.

Also, hadn't my own father warned me—in his stronger days, before he was widowed—that there was nothing good happening on the Island.

I could not say any of that to Donna without wrecking the visit. It would have been very selfish of me. But I found her inquisition off-putting. I wasn't perfect; I was leading a workaholic life to get on my feet and out of the financial gutter. I asked her whether she understood that poverty—and our family had had enough of it—was something to run from. She said she did. After a week, a good week mainly, with a few emotional flare-ups between Donna and me, we left to spend a long weekend in Lunenburg, a detour on our drive back to Toronto.

I'd spent three years in Nova Scotia in my early twenties going to university in Halifax, and I still went there for business occasionally. The reason we went to Lunenburg—although I didn't think this at the time—was that I wanted a seaside experience without family tensions. Lunenburg was only five hours by car from my sister's place.

We arrived in town with mountain bikes, breathable spandex, a titanium roof rack, but no kids, as Jackson and Theo weren't born yet. We did the bed-and-breakfast thing, ate overpriced lobster in chintzy restaurants near the main harbour, wandered through quaint shops in Old Town that sold tourist knick-knacks. We were like any other yuppies momentarily free from their fifty-hour work weeks.

On our final afternoon, we were driving along the coastal route, officially, The Lighthouse Route, picaresque, evocative of words such as schooner, lobster, spinnaker, anchor. As we drove along, the road meandering around inland bays, we made a turn, fully coastward, toward Foggy Cove. We'd heard there were dune beaches where you could walk for miles and never see another soul. And when we came over the hill, it was like the curtain going up in a theatre: we drove through walls of tall spruce flanking the road, toward a glimmer of horizon, and then the entire Foggy Cove basin opened up, the ocean views, the fishing village panorama right there, right below us . . .

A day earlier I'd been suckered by Stonehurst, an archipelago-ish coastal area closer to Lunenburg, a treeless landscape, deep fjords, quiet coves, bulging stone formations and shale everywhere, lunar and prehistoric. It had inlets for kayaking, and granite harmonics, not the roar of beach surf and body surfers. Stonehurst was spooky and lonely; you could imagine glaciers grinding the gears over this terrain, leaving behind rocky outcrops on which you might be able to summon a foundation-less shack; no monster homes need apply.

For several years after that first trip I had fantasies about living in both Stonehurst and Foggy Cove in which silence, tea and books surrounded Alison and me. There would be long walks and precious nights, candlelit, moonlit. We sold our house in Toronto and moved to a rented apartment in Montreal, a more bohemian and less expensive life. Meanwhile, we kept looking for Nova Scotia land. At some point, Foggy Cove became the main obsession; it had beaches, hiking possibilities. Alison preferred Foggy Cove, which meant we could be in agreement, at least on the where if not the why or how.

Then Alison got pregnant, only a month or so after our second return to Montreal, before our disillusionment with the city began to set in again. Jackson's arrival changed everything. White-knuckled excitement, the fear of getting through the next moment, a state of agitation and wonder that I now concede is akin to what I once heard a self-help queen describe as the "terror of commitment" in the male, a phrase she uttered as if there's never been a woman in the history of motherhood terrorized by a newborn's demands. As strange and paranoid as it now seems to me, Jackson's birth exacerbated our fears of making Montreal our home. In that period of intense stress and uncertainty, all normal under the circumstances, we worried out of proportion to the risk that Jackson would grow up a cultural or linguistic outsider, just like his parents had, on the fringes of the perpetual project to make Quebec a nation.

Our son was born in a French hospital, surrounded by French nurses and doctors, and while there was something sweet about that, it all seemed like so much work, stepping into the role of bicultural and bilingual types again. We made the effort, in good faith. But it felt like a project, not a life, as if I were inhabiting a role to prove a point. Somehow my quest to fit in again in Montreal felt inauthentic—a symptom of my inability to let my childhoood go, which is a legitimate source of exile yearning. Still, I felt like an actor in someone else's drama, not immersed in mine. But that soon changed. Six months after Jackson was born, my father keeled over at his machine shop, the big heart attack.

At the funeral parlour, when I went in see him, he was naked under a sheet, on a trolley at the back of an empty, high-ceilinged room where they were packaging him for shipment to the Island. There was a tag on his big toe, too much rouge on his cheek and very bad hair, Dad, puffed out, teased, *so not you*, but they couldn't get the shop grime out from under your fingernails, and for that I'm still grateful.

Birth or death, awareness of the cycle between them, the ticking of clocks, the plotting of your life on some arc where time initially passes slowly and then starts to move along very fast, where making sense of the world is no easier than driving a speeding car, trying to remember a single tree from the forest blur in the rear-view. Your foot on the brakes but nothing slowing down.

His funeral was exhausting in all the expected ways, given the grief let loose, the acceleration of intimacies among relatives one sees infrequently, the protocols for accepting the waves of hospitality at the wake, and knowing when to say nothing at all when shy, older men in overalls, friends of family friends you don't know at all, fidget for words they don't have, almost always settling on a version of "sorry for your troubles," which comes out as one long word, a strangled noise from a place high in the throat where emotional disturbances fester.

After that experience, Alison and I went to Foggy Cove for a week on the advice of her parents—the idea being to spend time on our own, with Jackson. One incident sums it up:

A crisp December day when it was easy to believe the coming of winter isn't a bad thing, the wind bone dry and pleasingly intermittent, the colours sharply defined, a chromatic certainty in every vista, except for the grey-brown of the hayfields, matted and dreadlocked, a crisp rustling underfoot. We had gone for a hike along the ridge of the drumlin hill where we now live. Jackson was trussed in the Trekker on my chest, snoring. It suddenly felt like a sweltering summer day, the sun pretending to be a fat disc in the sky, as if it intended to stay up there forever, as opposed to diving behind the hills in an instant, as it would soon do. Alison turned to me and said, this is it, get the land, here. And we did. Right there. We were the parents of a young child, our first, and we were emotionally all over the place because of a death in the family, our son now without even a partial set of grandparents on my side.

It was hard not to look for meaning in the moment: we were seeking protection, not as recreational privilege but as an authentic need, central to who we were and wanted to become.

How will I feel in twenty years, having used the death of yet another parent in a creative undertaking?

2.5

SUMMER IN FOGGY COVE (Subdivision)

July 2005

THREE MEN, unknown to one another, are squeezed into adjoining seats in economy class, all of us heading home, soaring across the ocean toward Canada. On my left, an elderly German, snappily dressed in dark blazer and grey flannels, a red tie, a green felt hat on his lap, a metal cane at his feet. On my right, a strapping Kosovar, early thirties, jeans, turtleneck, windbreaker.

The Acadian. The German. The Kosovar. All Canadians now.

I'm not supposed to be travelling much this sabbatical year, but there's money to be made, financial commitments on the horizon, tuition fees for the boys, maybe a new car, the retirement savings plan. I've been away for a week, checking out opportunities in the propaganda and speech-writing business, violating the spirit of the Nova Scotia arrangement. I've been living in hotels: room service, dining with clients, my clean laundry delivered the same day, the socks and underwear encased in plastic.

In Foggy Cove, Alison is cooking, cleaning, taking care of the boys and probably half nuts by now.

Early in the flight I keep my nose in a book, then my eyes on the movie, and then I attempt to sleep until this bores me too much. When I let my guard down, the German moves in swiftly.

"I must tell you," he says, as if letting me in on the most bizarre secret. "I am very proud to carry a Canadian passport."

"I must tell you," I reply, "me too."

"I was the first—the first!—to sell ice wine and quality brandy in Nova Scotia." He says this with a shaky raised hand, his index finger pointed, triumphant. Quite shaky. Parkinson's?

"The air in Nova Scotia, on the coast, where I live, it reminds me a lot of the peaty Islay Scotches from the highlands."

"Newfoundland," he replies, not to be derailed. "I was first there too."

I listen for a while as he relives the glories of his market distribution history in the Canadian wine and spirits business. I suppose it's his way of talking about Canada; he expresses continuous awe at the absurd scale and wild beauty of the country, and the goodwill of people everywhere. I've come across people like him when travelling: someone in possession of a single strand of personal narrative that needs to be inflicted upon strangers at the expense of actual dialogue. This man is well mannered and thankfully alert to social cues, unlike other wanderers with whom I've been trapped on long flights. We both know that the book remains open in my lap for a reason, and after a while he tactfully leaves me alone and falls asleep.

Toward the end of the flight, we're handed Canadian customs and immigration forms. The Kosovar on my right struggles to fill it in. At first I think, idiotically, that his hands are too big for the pencil, but it soon dawns on me that he doesn't know how to read or write in English or French. He understands from my hand motions and finger-pointing at the form that I'll help him fill in the blanks.

Jakup Bala. Twenty-nine. Canadian resident. Nothing to declare.

Soon we're talking—his verbal English is rudimentary but decent—about how he arrived in Canada, and it doesn't start out as a pretty story: war zones, refugee camps, families broken up. But we're on a jet airplane moving at six hundred kilometres an hour, so we, too, keep moving fast. I learn about his life as a carpenter in British Columbia, the hopes he has for his young children, who were born in Canada, his wife's love of the mountains and the sea, how he's financially helping out the family back in Kosovo. We become comfortable enough to talk politics, but I stay away from asking whether he fought against the Serbs or was a member of the KLA, or whether anyone died in his family during the fighting. He does say he was separated from his wife during the time they spent in different refugee camps; they were only reunited in Canada.

"In Kosovo," he says matter-of-factly. "UN protection is good for business now. Americans have money. NATO bases coming. The George Bush has the money. Big money."

I nod, then say, gently enough, "So the UN and George Bush will take care of Kosovo." Nothing caustic in my tone or expression. Only curiosity. He shrugs his massive shoulders, burly arms unfolding and opening outwards, palms upturned. A tiny smile. As if to say, What choice do we have?

We go back and forth carefully. I have no interest in drawing out his views on the moral rightfulness (or the means) employed by the KLA and its backers in expelling the Serbs from Kosovo. I only know enough to know I know nothing real. Like most conversations I've had with someone affected by the conflicts in the Balkans, this one starts off in one place, but soon I'm lost and don't know what we're talking about or whether I'm contradicting myself or about to be smacked in the face.

I find myself pontificating about Germany's role in driving Yugoslavia into civil war by recognizing Croatia as an independent country. The elderly German stirs at the mention of Germany. How long has he been eavesdropping? Have I upset him?

I head for safer ground, and soon Jakup and I are showing each other pictures of our children. I give him the full slideshow on my laptop. He pulls out little squares of images slotted into his wallet.

As the plane dips into its final approach, I have a sudden urge to tell both men about my parents and how brutal and humbling their origins were *within* Canada itself. My own parents hadn't fled guns and refugee camps, but they'd escaped privation, poverty, disease and other cruelties inflicted on them out of ignorance, circumstance, and the lingering cultural effects of wars and ethnic cleansings that had caused nasty upheavals and gross marginalization for their ancestors.

I used to think the Serbs were grandiosely weird and too self-pitying because they nursed grudges that went back six hundred years to a time when the Turkish invaders succeeded, in 1462, in conquering Bosnia after failing to do so in 1389 in a battle in present-day Kosovo. But I can see how waves of resentment flow through the generations. It doesn't take much to keep hatred alive. And hundreds of years may pass before a tribe gets back on its feet. Or it may never happen. I wasn't an Acadian version of a bitter Serb. But that has much less to do with a moral quality than having many more options for self-invention.

I get home to Foggy Cove around midnight after dozing in the taxi most of the ride from the airport through modest but sustained rain during which I don't carry my share of the conversation with the driver, a local man in his sixties whom I usually incite into telling stories about the old days. His soliloquies tend to variations on a single theme: the troubles since the fish stocks declined, corresponding to increases in teenaged sexual activity and unwed mothers, the price of heating oil, and the tendency of pot smokers and other delinquents to harass the retirees in the coffee shops.

When I step out of the van, the sea air is resonant with the usual blend of briny flavours, always a pleasant shock. Chilly. Refreshing.

I'm home. I live here now. I'm not just a visitor.

I say goodnight to the driver, and for maybe the fiftieth time in two years, I suggest he come over for a glass of dark rum one night, the hope being that he'll bring a giant moose roast from his freezered stockpile, which he annually replenishes on hunting trips to Newfoundland. For the fiftieth time, he assures me he'll be down this or next weekend.

As he speeds away, I negotiate a path around our car, the red Mazda, tired-looking around the fenders, softly dented and scratched up. It faces the house at the top of the slope of our property, perched on a gravel parking pad bordered by retaining walls of armour rock, an ancient-looking structure of shale blue. The wall creates the feeling of a protected front yard below it. I step down into the yard, pulling my suitcase along at a fast clip. A jolt goes through my arm each time I cross between the irregular slabs of slate in the path.

The cat greets me at the door, nuzzling my legs, wanting either food or affection. I pick him up; he jumps down, unimpressed. Food, then. When we found Rudy at the humane society he was maybe six months old. That day, the caged cats in the main presentation room—about thirty or so—were mostly sleeping or disinterested in marketing their unique catness to the incoming adopters. Rudy, nameless at the time, meowed for all his life, a minute-long sonata of tabby vocal effects. Since then he's been mostly silent. A purring machine, not a yowler. He was groomed to be, as someone once said rather indelicately, the replacement for Samantha, the first orphaned tabby we adopted. Prior to her fatal heart attack at twelve, she'd been surviving on steroids and chocolate-chip cookies.

As I open a tin of high-end cat food imported from the cat delicacy section at Whole Foods in Toronto, I hear a sleepy-hoarse voice, Alison in the loft, stumbling briefly out of slumber—"Is that you?"—then reminding me to turn off the lights and check on the boys before coming upstairs.

I know there's new email, and with the wireless router, I can flip open the laptop anywhere in the house and be connected at high speed to what awaits me. Instead I pour a hefty shot of single-malt whisky and step outside onto the deck.

My throat gives me a signal to swallow a non-existent small lump every thirty seconds or so. A week in Europe always frigs up my throat and bronchial passages. If not taking in car fumes or second-hand cigarette smoke, you're negotiating Europe's quirky dysfunctionality, which once passed for and is still advertised as the pinnacle of cosmopolitanism. On this last trip, it just felt crowded, every square metre spoken for, the place rebuilt countless times, fought over so often. As I sip my whisky, I think about Europe, its ability to start over after each generational disaster, the wars they keep having with themselves, their charming delusions of seamless integration into a multi-country union that makes the much smaller Canadian federation look like a model of entrepreneurial efficiency. Yet they largely dismantled the Eastern Bloc without infernos, the Balkans aside. Credit where credit is due.

In the void of night, I can see a single green light on a beachfront home. I'm glad to be here, with family, released from the strain of posing as a corporate consultant capable of bright smiles and keen promises that, yes, absolutely, we'll get the job done, the value added, all of us on the same page, our core competencies in total synch.

I think of all the money I've spent in Foggy Cove building this house and shaping the property, and the speeches I've concocted to make that money, some of them well written and for good people.

Then I have something of a mini-delusion of grandeur that I'm in a similar if much less plutocratically resplendent situation as F. Scott Fitzgerald's fictional character Jay Gatsby as he walks the grounds of his opulent seaside palace on Long Island Sound. For both of us, I think, the journey of self-invention unfolded on the harder fuels of materialism, chasing money and doing shady work to fund our solitary moments in the pastoral scenery of a lost or never-was innocence.

Lord Almighty, I do have my melodramatic moments . . .

I go inside and downstairs to our library and read the last lines of the great book. Gatsby had moved so fast and blindly toward his unreal dreams of love, wealth and status that he overshot any congress with the purity of his original vision, landing in its tawdry reality, the corrupt facts of the Jazz Age orgy that it's my tendency to romanticize. He paid for his hubris, although Fitzgerald leaves us with the suggestion that a part of Gatsby lives in everyone who believes he or she can escape the past without consequence.

So we beat on, boats against the current, borne back ceaselessly into the past.

In Lunenburg County, the past is borne ceaselessly into the future, mainly for economic reasons.

Some two hundred and fifty years ago, German, Swiss and French Protestants bought a dream of wealth and deliverance in the Canadian hinterlands and came here from Europe on the connivance of the British colonial authorities who provided huge land grants in the middle of nowhere. Here they built a beautiful harbour town that is recognized today by tour operators and their many customers as a UN World Heritage Site for its eighteenth-century architectural legacy. The town is awash with bed and breakfasts, restaurants, art galleries and whale-watching charter boats, catering to the mid-to-upmarket tourist. It is a lovely town, although it's getting harder each year to find people who were actually born and raised here.

The first European settlers soon spread out to Foggy Cove and other communities like it by the open sea. How many of them, once here, wanted to go back? There were no flights between Halifax and Europe then, and the mail took months to deliver. How many mornings did men and women awaken to the brutal task of rendering pasture from land thick with spruce and blackflies and wish they were pushing a cart of leather goods or root vegetables down some cobblestone alley in Vienna or Paris? Or did Nova Scotia become their home, not just by default, or as safe haven from war, poverty, religious persecution, but because the open spaces and hostile climate offered freedom from the oppressive weight of formal culture? Would that have been a benefit in moving here? The opportunity to invent something out of nothing?

The next morning I'm awakened by the sunrise, the incendiary swirl of pink and orange rising higher by the second; it's fast becoming a bright summer day. Everyone else is stirring too, their dreams entering the final moments, judging by little arms and legs lashing out in ninja arcs of unpredictability. The boys are in bed with us, along with the cat, each interloper entwined in a tortuous, codependent relationship to the bedding. Alison is in the middle, the preferred snuggling entity. I'm pretzelled on the mattress edge, fidgeting, having lost the battle for a fair share of the blankets. After absorbing yet another elbow to the ribs, I get up. Rudy rolls over into the spot I vacated, exposing his tummy long enough for me to rub it.

Only a few seconds of stealth, on tiptoes, before I reach the bottom of the staircase. From there each step is a pleasure undiminished by daily repetition. As I fuss with teapot and kettle, I get the usual aesthetic high from running my hands back and forth across the light grey granite countertop on the kitchen island—a solidly cool presence on my fingertips, peppered in minuscule, irregular-contoured dark spots. My first cup of Chinese oolong is soothing, a subtle drink taken in silence while admiring a beautiful perspective, which is what I have. Manicured sheep pasture. Off-camber gravel roads weaving between the homes. Green slopes everywhere. Many homes around here are Cape-styled, quaint relics from the fishing-village past. A few others have formally inventive exteriors, complex volumes, a lot of plate glass, metal and concrete. These homes tend to be dramatically situated, crowning a hill, conspicuous from the dune beach. The best of these announce that the future of Foggy Cove won't only be defined by nostalgic restorations or cookie-cutter vacation homes built with plans bought on the Internet. I'm one of those newer influences, and it's of consequence to me to believe my impact is, at worst, benign. But I have no way to know, not yet. I've just got past the basics: buying land and quieting the title, excavating mountains of soil, pouring a foundation, raising a structure, digging a septic field, sending a few bucks to the beach protection group, annoying some long-time residents with my presumption of belonging, reseeding the hayfield to disguise the septic hump, then fencing everything in—to protect what? Nothing like a fence to make you feel like king of the castle.

As I work my way through the first cup of tea, Rudy joins me. Clomp-clomp down the stairs. Little paws, big sounds. I become aware of a correlation known to parents and cat owners the world over: the smaller the person (or cat), the heavier the footstep. He approaches, doing his leg nudge thing, campaigning for affection. So together we sit, he in my lap. A moment of serenity before family chaos. This is the last day of swimming lessons for Jackson and Theo at the Lunenburg pool.

I focus my gaze along one of the foot-wide pine planks that run the length of the room, a varnished alley of amber with just enough tonal imperfection to remind me that wood is alive, and very seductive on the eyes and feet. I try to empty my mind of all thoughts, but there emerges a picture in my head of the guys—the carpenters—laying the floor down, the room a blizzard of sawdust, the stench of carpenter glue, the mewling of high-pitched saws scoring the underside of each board with two deep grooves, an old trick for allowing moisture to dissipate. I love our floor, its power to delude me into believing this place is traditionally rustic.

Familiar voices from above take me out of reverie; the rest of the family stomps downstairs, single file, into the great room, their faces puffy-sleepy. The boys beeline for the train set and soon embark on their daily program of continuous improvement and strategic re-engineering. Before long, the kettle is whistling again; Alison is in the kitchen, grinding up organic espresso beans for the French press.

"Daddy, next summer, me and Theo are going to dig a subway under our house over to Granddad's," Jackson says excitedly.

Theo is pulling a train along the floor, his soundtrack being a tuneful approximation of railway clatter. *A-dook, a-dook, a-dook.*

"The thing is, Jackson, you know we've just planted seeds to cover all the dirt and stones left over from construction."

"Dad-dee." Two syllables of disagreement. "We're going to dig under the ground, not on the ground!"

A-dook, a-dook, a-dook, a-dook.

The train stops at my feet. "Hi, Daddy."

I pick the little guy up, and as I do Rudy leaps off me and sullenly heads over to the kitchen island to seek attention from Alison.

"Have you checked the weather, honey?" Alison says.

"Haven't been downstairs yet."

"Could you get on the computer?" She lives by the proclamations of the Environment Canada website. "But no email, okay?" This said as if I'm Theo on the verge of tossing the cat into the bath.

Once I'm at the laptop in my basement office, time seems to pass out of mind. My homepage is one of the country's bigger newspapers, and I check in on things happening in the Middle East, Iran, North Korea. I fret about losses incurred by my favourite sports teams. As I'm doing that, I hit the email button and the alerts chime with Pavlovian consequence: stuff arrives from across the planet. Business. Friends. Junk mail. And soon I'm transported to everywhere I'm not, through the phone and the web and the things I'm reading and worrying about, and as this departure occurs, I begin to perceive my surroundings differently than when the sunrise served notice. It's as out-of-body as it gets.

Alison shouts down for me, and I shout back that I'm on the way. How long have I been gone? Ten minutes, possibly twenty? Alison sends out another request for my presence, in a higher pitch. I put the laptop back to sleep, glancing outside for a last look at the sea. As a calming influence, the sea speaks to me even when I'm not listening. For days last winter there was a thin white line on the water on the outer reaches of the bay. It never occurred to me to ask what that line might be, until a neighbour said, Did you notice that the ice along the shore moved out to sea? Is that right, I replied, a rhetorical lilt in my voice, in the spirit of what I understood to be the local dialect. Is that right?

"Dad-dee." Alison calling. Singsong impatience.

I enter the great room as her one-second smile, and the clatter of kitchen implements, send a clear message for me to get into the flow. I recap the situation, time-wise: we have nineteen minutes (and counting) to get the boys out the door, otherwise we'll be late. I've forgotten to check the weather, but it's too late for that now. It looks sunny out and that's good enough for me.

When we were justifying our sabbatical plans for Nova Scotia, there was a fair bit of optimism on my part that we'd be more laid-back here, with far less pressure on the schedule. Part of every day is like that, because the climate and surroundings have a way of slowing you down. A snowstorm can trap you for days. A hurricane, and there were several last fall, predictably brings out the insomniac in me, as I worry whether the house will hold up (it has). However, there are mornings that feel so Toronto-like.

The phone rings. Granddad, next door, reporting a bald eagle atop the beaver hutch near the pond. I dutifully turn to the windows. All I see, even with binoculars, is an unmoving blob of blurry black, because it's an eagle, obviously, not a launching space shuttle. I hang up after promising him some tech support in downloading images of the eagle to his laptop, although his digital camera doesn't have a telephoto lens so the pictures will look pretty much like unmoving blobs of blurry black.

My mobile phone chimes, the Toronto number, forwarded; nothing but static. Wireless phone calls mostly die in Foggy Cove. Business. Of course it is. I'm on the hook for the creative of a direct-mail campaign. Due today. I haven't given it any thought. I'll work up ideas on the drive into Lunenburg, refine them in my notebook while the boys are swimming, then come home and write up an email.

I turn back to the household drama. Alison has transcended to a daunting level of multi-tasking, assembling snacks, feeding the cat, wiping Theo's nose and pointing me to bathing suits on the floor near the door. I'm sure I'll find three mismatched socks but only one shoe, and that the second I try to lead the boys toward their bathing suits, they'll complain about the swimming lessons that they always hate beforehand, although it's impossible to get them out of the pool afterwards. But they allow themselves to be processed into their outfits without argument, which is a relief, and we're out the door, still within the window of possibility of arriving on time. So, good. All my anxieties die out in a single exhalation that loosens everything tight inside my chest. Behind me on the porch I hear Alison issuing instructions to the boys in a voice with so much love in it that I have to tune her out; the ferocious vigilance of her concern obliterates everything else.

As we get into the car, the waving between everyone starts—

Granddad on the front deck next door.

Grandmummy at the window.

Time teases me with its elasticity, the forever quality of a moment that's over an instant after it begins. I wish I could bottle the flow of love that floods around me. I don't want to lose anything to spillage.

—

Summer is a honeymoon of possibilities for everyone. On many days the boys become one with the sand, rolling around on the beach naked, revelling in the skin as sense organ, as the better part of intelligence. There are meals on the deck: grilled chicken or flank steak, the sweetest baby greens from Wanda's farm, dressed in lemon, olive oil, garlic and sea salt, munched down with a handy glass of sauvignon blanc (preceded by a cold beer while I stand heroically inert, observing protein searing on the barbecue). There are evening walks on the beaches at low tide, sauntering through a pink mist reflecting the sheen of dune sand and sunset light. The wind has shifted for the summer now, coming more consistently from the south in sultry breezes off the land; as a result, the fog banks are less Gothically present, reduced to a minor special effect in the drama of coastal weather. Friends and family arrive after long journeys involving airplanes and rental vehicles; they present the usual pathologies of urban stress and distraction, and we're always careful with them on their first walks along the high bluff, looking for any sign of disorientation or panic. Everywhere across Nova Scotia the tourist crowds are beginning to swell, and with them come the dreams of buying land or a cottage or a farm. Hardly a day goes by when we don't see one of the prospective sanctuary-seekers stumbling across a virgin hay-field or sheep pasture, only half listening to the real-estate agent, already visualizing the framed views to the horizon, the smell of hardwood in the fireplace, the chatter of a lover or pet in the background, everyone delirious in their remove, as we so often are on days when Foggy Cove is, inescapably, protection from everything we're trying to escape.

Alison and I sit on the couch after the evening chores, the boys in bed but not yet asleep, although the intervals are

increasing between their calls for more water, or adjust-
ments to the night light, or assurances that Daddy is on
high alert for monsters and bad men.

Both our laptops are open, sharing the wireless Internet
connection, our faces bathed in grey-blue as we connect to
websites and e-commerce systems and email servers far away.

The wind causes the windows to flex and the stud walls
to creak.

"When are you going to Toronto again?" Alison asks.
She's fretfully clicking through a website devoted to knock-
offs of fashionable shoes, the selling proposition being that
the sexiest and most expensive numbers from Manolo
Blahnik and Jimmy Choo can be bought for the price of a
burger and fries, as long as you have the courage to divulge
your credit card number to an outfit that ships from Macau
or Shanghai.

"I told you, I have to see if they organize the meeting. A
bunch of stuff needs to fall into place. There are scenarios to
work through."

"Makes it difficult to plan."

"I'm trying to narrow it down."

"What scenarios?"

What am I supposed to do? Rehabilitate, on my own, the
scheduling culture of my corporate clients?

"Do you think these shoes and handbags look real?" she
says. "It says here you can hardly tell the difference."

"Sure, they're real."

She doesn't like my tone. She clicks with more intensity
now. Seeking out larger images of the thumbnails.

"The big brands create these websites and actually own
the knock-off companies," she says. "That's what they say."

"It's entirely possible. Globalization and branding. Creates
unique challenges for any company in the fashion business."

"Toronto, Larry."

"What about it?"

"Are you even listening to me?"

Fine, then. "What shall we talk about?"

She gives me a baleful look.

"It just gets lonely out here sometimes," she says.

She wants to move back to Toronto this fall. I want to stay in Nova Scotia, sell the Toronto condo and buy one in Halifax and spend our weekends, summers and holidays out here. We can't talk about any of this without arguing, so we don't talk at all, which is fine with us for now.

"I'm going to the basement to pay the bills," I say.

"Can you take the laundry?"

"I can't think with the washing machine on."

"You're paying bills. Not thinking."

"True."

"Should I order the Manolos?"

"Should you?"

"They look like Manolos."

"They look like a digitally enhanced photo."

"They're sexy."

"It would appear."

"Which credit card should I use?"

"Maybe this isn't such a good idea."

"It's not as if I can wear them to the Wal-Mart anyway."

I yawn—annoying her.

"We can go back to Toronto anytime," I say apologetically.

"It's just hard sometimes. Lonely out here."

"But there are beautiful moments."

"Yes."

"The boys, the grandparents. It's once in a lifetime."

"Yes."

I close my browser window and laptop with finality and get up to leave, certain that I've read all Google-derived items (as sorted by date and relevance) on the recent activities of my musical hero, Daniel Lanois, now in his fifties, who has something of an Acadian background, born in Quebec to French-Canadian parents, but mainly a steel-town kid who grew up in Hamilton. His records blend folk, psychedelic rock and gospel, featuring guitars in the wild spirit of Jimi Hendrix and Neil Young.

In the basement, at my desk, I start with e-bill payments and soon move on to unanswered email. Not much visible outside beyond lights in the village across the wetlands. Now and then I stare at my greasy reflection in the window, as if to reassure myself that I'm actually here. For the most part I've tunnelled into a simulated world, a man disembodied, turned into bytes and bits that take me far from local time and place, away from the slow movement of moonlight and small rodents across the property. A man borderless and timeless.

I have Lanois on the iPod.

> *Mes mains sont noires à couchon*
> *Mes mains sont noires à couchon*
> *Trente jours, et trente nuits*
> *On travaille au tabac, hostie!*

In his songs there's a gumbo of narrative and musical echoes that speak to my cultural background: the raw tales of transient men picking tobacco like my uncles had after the fishing season, or who had taken up the rum and then wife-beating (in that order) after being laid off at the mill, or who had ridden the rails into the night until the trains ran no more. He sings of sad migrations: people rich in spirit, perhaps, but forced to drift here and there for paying work. The scenery is very Canadian, the turbulence and disappointments of those caught in shifts between the agrarian and the industrialized life, the mangling of dreams between leaving the farm and joining the assembly line. But this is also premeditated music, constructed with nuance, sutured on editing consoles. Lanois is a genius as a studio producer. He makes stories sound old and new at the same time. He brings the lost voices in my head alive, creating the authenticity of the beach singalongs I remember from my summers in PEI, my cousins and buddies and their guitars and harmonicas, beer, girls in jean shorts, kisses that tasted of apricot brandy, faces flushed in the reflections of bonfire light.

How far away I am from those adolescent moments, no matter how similar the scenery is. Even as we're trying to hide out here in Foggy Cove with our boys, pretending to be nowhere and out of touch, the world of everywhere taunts us. At night, we aren't exhausted from wood chopping or maple syrup making or oxen feeding. We're tired from banner advertising, pop-up screens, cookie alerts. *You are entering a non-secure site. Do you wish to proceed?* Click. A contemporary and common dilemma, no matter where you live or what you do. I once loved the idea of being instantly connected anytime and anywhere to anyone. What nonsense! Do we understand the experiment we're performing on ourselves? How many damaged souls and zombie perspectives have I seen revealed in the march of thumbs across tiny web-friendly keyboards, or the self-important voices polluting the ether of airport corridors as they commune with the cyborgian receivers coiled in their ears? But who am I to cast the first stone. The pathology of being connected tingles within me, a well-cultivated obsession to monitor unfolding crises and nurture relationships in a global field of information that is in constant flux, all available at my fingertips.

A day isn't a day out here unless I plug my fears and protective instincts—what others might call free-floating anxiety or latent paranoia or voyeuristic compulsions—into something more frightening and incomprehensible than my actual life in this house in this community. Maybe the only way I can fully experience the luxury of being snug and secure is to fabricate a fictional enemy from whom I'm escaping. Maybe a home, in part, is defined by a need to be protected from external threats. And if that threat doesn't exist, then we invent one. Maybe we're never really happy unless we're frightening ourselves half to death?

Last winter, on a sunny day in the biting cold, we went for an afternoon walk on the frozen lagoon below the house. We were led—Alison, Jackson and I—by Granddad. Before we set foot on the pond, Stan slashed repeatedly into the surface with an axe.

"You could drive a truck across this," he said, squinting at me.

"Okay, let's get the truck and make doubly sure."

The ice was concrete-block thick in the spot where we were right then, I thought, but not where we might be in ten seconds. And what if we were hit, as we had never been hit before, with the tsunami equivalent of a temperature thaw, or an earthquake, causing the ice to crumble before we could reach land, all of ten or fifteen steps away?

"What a beautiful day," Alison said breathlessly as we tentatively walked out onto the ice. She wore a grey tam, blond hair spilling out of it, her face alive with the cold.

"That patch over there," I said. "It looks a little thin to me."

Stan strolled over to the spot, jumped on it, repeatedly.

As we walked about, and as Jackson slid along, rolling on the ice in a stupor of total enjoyment, a human seal, I kept the disaster management systems in my head crunching data, grading the shades of ice into categories of safeness:

smooth, opaque grey being totally safe, marbled blue-grey less so. I didn't know how to fairly assess the thick ice on the pond edge; it felt much like peering into blocks of plastic, the surface etched in geometric patterns. I debated whether this variation was safer than opaque grey, but it felt less so, because I could see down too far, into plant life, the lagoon bottom that, granted, wasn't deeper than my forearm here, so the question of ranking ice safety was moot. The ice was nearly uniformly opaque grey everywhere that counted.

I wasn't raised to be afraid of everything. I'd taken risks in my life, some good, others not so wise, and others plainly stupid. But as I'd grown into a husband, a parent, I'd moved into paranoid response territory. Was everyone else like this? Certainly Alison, despite recreational rebellion in her early twenties, was cautious. How had my parents ever managed me, at six, going off to play street hockey by myself in distant neighbourhoods, or, at sixteen, doing wheelies on motorized dirt bikes, or, at twenty, taking off for trips to New York at a time when the city was a murderous sewer?

How did I become a risk-averse ninny?

Fear is something we all share these days, unless we're sociopathic or beyond pedestrian considerations of mortality, like people who have lingered too painfully on death's doorstep and want to check out, or those who are only alive hang-gliding through forest fires or tiger-wrestling or shark-observing or dangling off mountain tops. In general, fear rules. Because the world is violent, unforgiving, uncertain, and nature is a monster in its own right. Locusts, poisonous snakes and weekend traffic in summer. Snow and depression in winter. Wild beasts will kill you unless you kill them first (mission accomplished, pretty much). Other humans will kill or blog you unless you shut them out, unless you create walls or moats around the city, raise their taxes, confiscate their Swiss bank accounts, deploy bunker bombs.

Fear is one word but so many things: the connective tissue of anxiety, suspicion, the dialogue and confrontation between you and what is not you: the other. Fear can be elusively difficult to diagnose sometimes. But it's the dark matter, the intriguing vector, in the distance between two points, the invisible but very real content of separation, the spectre of conflict between us and everything that should concern us: the terrorist, the criminal, the rabid animals, the collection agency, the government, the gossip next door. Fear is the tingling in the chest, the numbness in the fingers, a black shard in the field of vision, a wrinkle across the brow, a demon or ghost we've buried inside, or heard about yesterday by email or ten seconds ago by instant message. Fear is the motive for sanctuary.

My mind, as yours does, I'd bet, often floods with mythically unsettling imagery, surreal tragedies on the home front, the planes filled with hijacked people, silver wings of death banking into Wall Street and Pentagon infrastructure. A shiver runs through many of us now when we hear phrases that used to be innocuous: *God is great. Let's roll.* Maybe the short period between the death of the Cold War and the birth of the War on Terror—the halcyon days, perhaps, of unprecedented safety from an incinerating threat, at least in my part of the world—is over for good. Maybe it's bunker mentality from now on, retinal scans at the borders and check-in counters, drug testing in the urinals, the vibe of paramilitary readiness on the streets, in suburban shopping malls, within the digital pathways, in every videocam in every lobby and on every roof, and maybe even grafted to our bodies. How far off can that be?

Why do we—so safe, so comfortable—feed on disasters, some real, but others fictions fed by unsubstantiated or exaggerated fears? I suspect that throughout history, whatever history happens to be, and regardless of who is doing the telling, people who are fortunate enough to lead safe lives in civilizing circumstances have always looked to the sky or the horizon, uneasily in thrall to the feeling the world is going to hell in a handbasket.

Our neighbours are already arriving for the party at Stan and Vivian's. But I have a ritual to perform before I can join them.

On the granite counter, the black creatures inch toward me, or so I imagine, an assembly of claws and antennae. One suddenly flaps itself upside down, its tail coiling and uncoiling until it falls off the edge, but I'm there to catch it. The claws seek my wrist, ineffectually, because of the rubber bands. Lobsters. Seven lobsters.

The giant pot starts to shudder on the stove: boiling water.

Boiling lobsters alive is something I've done without anxiety from childhood. I still cook lobster for family and friends because no one else will, although most will greedily eat the result. But in recent years, other people's revulsion at the killing has had an impact on me. At first I couldn't understand their anxieties and disgust, until I imagined what I'd feel at a slaughterhouse. I've never killed animals for meat, except snared rabbits. And I can't imagine I ever will. All this is to say I finally started to view lobsters as living beings. As a result, I can no longer go through with the killing unless I talk to the lobsters first as they froth and inch about on the counter. I talk to each one before the killing starts because I'm still a carnivore, not vegetarian, but maybe one day I will be, if I keep reminding myself that, as unsympathetically alien as lobsters look, as low on the food chain as they may be, their eyes flicker when you touch them.

I never remember afterwards what I said. The ritual is the point.

After I dump the lobsters into the boiling water, there's nothing to do for fourteen minutes but drink beer and let other thoughts come to me.

Twenty years ago, give or take, in PEI. Christmas at my aunt's house, on the ocean, a mile or two from the main harbour. My father and I had driven in from Montreal. The morning after we arrived, we set snares in the deep snow of the woods along the flank of the property. A day later, we came upon the large rabbit struggling in the snare. Blood on his white coat. I thought his leg was injured. I searched for a large rock, anything to put him out of the pain we'd caused. But by the time I'd found one and returned, my father, a man who'd grown up here, whose youth had featured the violent undoing of animals, rabbits, rats, every kind of fish, even cats, was standing there alone, tears in his eyes, the rabbit gone, a faint trail of escape into the bush, spotted in blood.

A perfect coastal evening.

A full moon rising, a giant orange circle, a parfait of light so diverse in its shading that it's acceptable to wonder whether food colouring has been brushed on. The moon is still low enough to infuse the sea with a pewter glare. No visible surf, no frothy highlights. The surface of the sea rises and falls rhythmically as underwater waves roll to shore. It's as if the sea is on the verge of boiling from a titanic argument unfolding in the depths.

In the comfy basement at the grandparents' house, we shuck oysters and drink beer, bullshitting one another: me, Stan and Willie Cornwall. The lobsters I've cooked are stacked in a metal tub by the door, giving off steam. I'm a fast shucker, fearless in jamming the knife in the crack between the oyster shells. It takes experience and skill not to slice one's hand open. This is a manly exercise, a credibility enhancer if you can shuck a plateful without having to head to the clinic for stitches.

"Ah, paradise," I utter, after slurping down my tenth raw oyster slathered in a pseudo-Cajun hot sauce bought at the superstore.

"The best Malpeques I've ever had," Stan replies. He disapproves of the hot sauce. Considers it impure.

"It's not like we can, you know, verify the quality," I suggest.

"Nah," Willie said jovially, "a bad oyster you can smell a mile away."

"They're right out of the water," Stan says. "The fellow put them on the bus from Charlottetown yesterday."

"Did you pay by credit card?" I asked. "Over the Internet?"

"No, no. This was a small operation, a retired fellow in the country. He said to mail a cheque. He wanted to make sure we liked them."

"Whether we like them?" I reply, incredulous. "What if we didn't?"

"How much for the whole box?" Willie asks.

Stan mentions a unit cost one-fifth the price of a quality restaurant oyster in the city. When he heads upstairs to help Alison out with the boys, Willie goes to work on me as I keep shucking and eating.

"The pressure on real-estate development, it's huge here," he says. "I don't think we can trust this—or any government—to honour the commitment to keep the protected zone intact. All it takes is a minister's decree and the marsh turns into a suburb."

"Come on, Willie. After all the drama of getting the protected beach designation? Is the government that stupid? People will go crazy."

"You see all those viewplanes we take for granted," he said, gesturing at the ocean through the window. "I'm telling you, this place could look like Cape Hatteras in ten years. Houses everywhere."

"Yeah, I guess."

I tell Willie that I can't summon a proper degree of outrage, given that many on our hill here, including him, me and Stan, have all built new homes, dug septics and drilled wells within two golf shots of the main beach.

"Those would be very long shots," Willie says.

"Depends on who's doing the hitting."

I slurp down three oysters in a row. A third of a beer per oyster.

I came out here to avoid stress and complications, and it's becoming apparent now that there's neighbourly encouragement—and gentle pressure—for me to get involved in the conservancy and put my skills, such as they are, to effective use. As a propagandist in the corporate world, I know how to write speeches, backgrounders, executive reports and studies configured to distort arguments in the favour of my clients. Here I can apply all that experience to an organization committed to making my new home safe and beautiful, forever.

"Let me think about all this," I say to Willie when he finally comes out with it and directly asks me to help out. I'm working up to a wishy-washy way of saying no.

Jackson and Theo come pounding down the stairs, Stan behind them.

Jackson rushes to me, blue eyes bulging. "Daddy, there's four deer under the apple tree! A mummy and three babies!"

Theo repeats him word for word.

After the party, Stan and I are in the basement, cleaning up the oyster shells. He asks me how my family is doing.

"I spoke to them all today. They're doing well."

"Your aunts?"

"Fran is doing great. May's still got some problems with the nerves in her hands. But better." My father's sisters.

"And Donna? Are you visiting her this summer?"

"Her and James are going up to Montreal for a week. A little romantic thing. A getaway." My sister and her long-time partner.

I'd had little contact with my mother's family after she died in 1982, and that chapter closed, pretty much, when my last maternal grandparent, Ethel, died a few years back. It was sad, but my mother's kin weren't family in any meaningful sense any more. Once in a while I still see a cousin or uncle on my trips to the Island, and enjoy a pleasant exchange with them, maybe an hour of reminiscing, but that's all. However, my sister, my only sibling, and my father's surviving sisters, I consider them all close family. We're overdue for a visit. But Alison and I have yet to get our minds around trip planning, and this bugs me.

"We'll get down to PEI before the summer is out," I tell Stan before we go upstairs again.

Dessert is a tense negotiation.

The kids have been snacking all day, and it shows. The combination of massive sugar intake and overwiredness from the lobster party causes effects often associated with concussion—blushing faces, unfocused eyes, mental distraction. They're totally attention deficit except in relation to dessert, laid out in multiple dishes on the table: shortbread cookies, blueberry pie and premium chocolate-chip ice cream. Alison thinks she can limit them to small portions. She even unprofitably dangles the idea of fruit as a sugar substitute. Neither grandparent has much sympathy. Meanwhile, the boys leap into the breach with double-sized portions of everything.

The next hour, in summary:

At the doorway, the boys refuse to go home and demand a sleepover, saying Mummy and Daddy are very mean and not very nice, not like other parents of good boys and girls. They assert over and over that it's only fair and normal to be up two hours past their bedtimes, completely out of control, exhausted, in tears.

"Jackson!" Alison says, trying to be the voice of patience but missing the mark by an octave, a quiver of exhaustion in her voice. "We don't want to overstay our welcome, do we?"

"No, Mummy," Jackson says, trying to break from her embrace.

"No," Theo says, somewhat automatically.

Jackson asks, "What does 'overstay your welcome' mean?"

"I don't want to go home," Theo says, sobbing now.

"But you're exhausted, little boy," I plead.

"He's not *zosted*," Jackson says.

"I'm not zosted, Daddy," Theo adds, sobbing harder still.

On the steps to our house, Alison complains about the lack of discipline next door, the need for a firmer hand, no, we're not going through this again, no, no, no, and what are we doing out here, in the middle of nowhere, Larry, I have no support, and you just stand there and tell me it makes sense to move out here for good.

After the kids go to bed, there's a lengthy phone call between Alison and Stan, the family diplomats. I hear ideas being tossed around about having dinner earlier, fewer desserts at the table. All the stuff you say on the phone but never actually do.

Finally, my wife, on the couch, graceful even when all bunnied out for bed, as she likes to say, a fatigued languor as she stretches, yawns.

We're all zosted.

—

A few days later I head out for a walk down the path through the wetlands, toward the beach. At sea level, the colours are much more alive than up at the house. Maybe it's just the rising sun that fluffs the scene, but, whatever it is, the grey sky is suffused with a mauve wash.

Everything's different at sea level, a beach in front of you, a pond behind you, surrounded by an amphitheatre of hills covered in green spruce. It's not as if I can physically feel the planet spin, but the vantage point, with everything *above* me—houses, roads, trees, dunes, the sky—makes me want to believe I'm moving with the momentum of bigger forces. I like the notion that solitary excursions like these make me more sensitive to things, just like the deer around here. They're sensitive—to weather that kills them, to the gale force winds we're expecting later. The deer are likely long gone to a protected hutch, deep in the woods, minus the corpse of the doe that I see floating at the edge of the pond.

As I reach our property on the way home, I startle a buck in the field. He exhales his annoyance: loud nasal whooshes as he bounds away or, rather, *high-tails* it into the woods.

During the walk I replayed the conversation with my sister, who called last night with the news that she and James had got married in Montreal. The event had been planned and celebrated with friends. Friends who had been friends of my father—the witnesses in the civic ceremony, guests at the dinner party afterwards. I'm happy for her but upset we weren't invited.

After my mother's death, the surviving members of the family destructed as a unit. My father avoided conflict, was childlike. My sister was wild and directionless until she settled into her life on the Island. I was shiftless with ambition, unreliable as a brother and son, trying to escape the sharecropper sensibility and reinvent myself as a man of the world.

Only slowly did we put the family back together. Over time. Decades. Humpty-Dumpty-together. But so many families must be like ours, everyone intimately lost and more confused as the years pass. And now what? I want to analyze this situation to the nines but know I'll only be marshalling facts and arguments to attack Donna. Distressing.

As is my habit, when my workout ends, I stretch on the parking pad. And as I do so, I think about what I love most about Foggy Cove, aside from it being a home base for our family. I love visualizing the shape of cliffs lost to shoreline erosion, the ghosts of wharves, nothing left but a few wooden footings, poking above the surface at low tide, evocative of the crazy human urge to build on the water. I love things once there and no longer. I'm big on absence, fragments of history.

To me, Foggy Cove is something almost gone, a phantom spirit, now existing mostly as a simulation, a rural life minus the rural, a fading collective memory. The place isn't dead yet; it still has tourism, heritage preservation, the dreams of seasonal citizens. What pleasure is there in watching something die?

The hooting of an owl.

The voices of Foggy Cove—the dying voices—speak to me in my yearning to know who built and lived in the old houses. I feel the same about the dilapidated barns that, at a certain point in their deconstruction, simply become organic. I seek out what are likely apocryphal or highly reworked stories—the myths from the village past—which I hoard and burnish myself in the retelling.

Like the one about the schooner in a hurricane being lifted over the dune beach and ending up in the lagoon.

Or how the villagers, a hundred years ago, wove a fence through the wetlands, an act of grassroots engineering done, apparently, so that sand and soil would remain stuck to the ropes and wood instead of floating away with the receding tides, thus creating the dune beach we have today.

Lovely stories. Any truth to them? It doesn't matter to me.

A summer storm, horizontal rain, ferocious winds, the eddying of stray currents funnelling between house and retaining wall, keenly felt in the drag around my raincoat when I step out to retrieve the wheelbarrow after it cartwheels into the field.

Because our house has so many windows, we're gloriously involved. Each time I lean close enough to see my breath on the panes, it's like being in an airplane taxied up to the de-icing vehicle; I am giddily aware of being safe, technologically so, although there are moments when my body involuntarily flinches from the weather outside.

The boys are up in the loft, launching balsa aircraft made from kits purchased in bulk in town. The planes have robust military designs and heraldry but survive only two hours, at most, of internal flight scheduling; new planes have to be assembled frequently.

"What happens when they destroy the last plane?" I ask Alison.

"Read them a book."

"They don't want to read. They're dive-bombing us."

"What about a DVD?" Alison suggests. "*Mary Poppins.*"

"Mary *what?*"

"Well. At least it isn't violent."

"Couldn't you have gotten something animated? That fish who searches the sea for his mummy?"

"*Finding Nemo.* I think Jackson would find that too scary."

"I think you find it too scary."

"Ha ha."

A plane swoops under the table, nails the cat.

Jackson yells, "Mummy, can me and Theo go over to Granddad and Grandmummy's to say hi?"

Alison looks at me; I look back.

"How are we doing on babysitting chits?" I ask hopefully.

"Let me call and find out."

"I'll get the rain jackets out and take them over."

"Good idea."

When Alison and I are alone, I break the news that I want to do something for the conservancy.

"With what free time? We're already too stretched."

"Look around you, sweetie. This could all be developed one day. Mansions right below us. More houses on the beach will create, like, this funnel effect. Like when you put your feet into the sand near the water. The water races past your heels faster, takes the sand with it. With more houses on the beach, the dunes will get destroyed a lot faster when the wind whips around the houses on the beach and blows away the sand."

"Can't you wait until you're actually *retired* to do this?"

"By then it might be all gone. You should read the reports!"

"Oh, Larry. Always so dramatic."

One report, commissioned by the conservancy, says that our beach is moving landward at the rate of about half a metre per year. Sea levels are rising, and doing so faster along the Nova Scotia coast than anywhere else on the continent. Our peninsula, for scientific reasons I don't pretend to understand, is sinking, albeit very slowly. Also, there is the consequence of thermal expansion, the increase in the volume of water because of changes in the global climate. The world is getting hotter, causing water molecules to expand and take up more space. So global warming, fine. Some predictions place the sea rise on our coastline as high as one metre by the end of the current century.

> Beaches and barrier island systems located along the Atlantic coast of Nova Scotia are affected by these high rates of sea-level rise. Even modest increases of sea-level position can transfer into substantial horizontal changes in the position of the coastline . . . thus, increases of sea-level position . . . can be expected to induce episodic shifts in the position of the beach and barrier profiles, causing these systems to migrate landward. . . .

Substantial horizontal changes, episodic shifts. What are we talking about? A submerged village, maybe; storm surges that breach the dunes more frequently and forcefully, destroying the beloved beach and wetlands, maybe even taking out roads, critter habitat, homes, and eventually turning some peninsulas into islands or submerging them entirely. And this could happen all along Nova Scotia, including in Foggy Cove? We'll all be generally okay in my lifetime, the report suggests, unless we're hit by the once-in-two-hundred-years hurricane, such as the storm in the 1750s, the winds in excess of 220 kilometres per hour, which completely destroyed the beach system farther south, near Port Mouton, turning the closed freshwater lagoon there into an open saltwater bay. But even if the worst storm doesn't come, will the beach I know today still be there for my sons? Or their children?

Last spring, at low tide, Stan went hiking around Wreck Point, the outer seaward edge of the land mass. He saw what looked to be tree stumps that were usually covered by water. There had been forests out there once.

I'm always looking for signs of dune erosion. I study storm forecasts and often find myself, in howling winds, down at the beach to watch high tides crash ashore. I listen to stories that come my way about the last time the sea broke through the wetlands and turned Wreck Point—for a short period—into an island. I monitor, observe, worry. I obsess with both plausible and crackpot perspectives on rising sea levels, erosion rates, the potential for destruction by forces operating on time horizons much longer than a mortgage amortization.

Today our home is buffered from the sea by wetlands and our position on the hill. But my children's children—if either one, in fact, produces children—could have open sea before them: beachfront on the doorstep. And waves licking at the foundations of this house.

Along the endless green hill that forms the spine of our village as it weaves toward the sea, a large meadow slopes to the marsh behind the dune beach. In all the summers I've been coming here, this meadow has been grazed by sheep. It's eye-catching in a postcard-tranquil way. It's what you'd expect in the opening scene of a movie about the country boy leaving home for the big city, his momma waving goodbye on the porch, his dog barking as the old truck trundles away. It's a meadow that makes me wish I'd grown up doing chores on it to earn my allowance and my father's approval. In some moments I let myself believe that I've been admiring its beauty since my childhood.

More than once I've heard someone refer to the meadow as *the empty field*. Perhaps in some spreadsheet-analyzed sense it is, because there isn't a home on it just yet. But that may change soon. Early this summer a big For Sale sign was planted there.

The meadow's beautiful emptiness is at risk right now. The few remaining ghosts of the old farming and fishing life have fewer places to hide these days, so I fantasize that this is where they've been invisibly evacuated, horrified by the expense to which some people will go, including myself, to put up a shingled building.

Forty years ago, all this land was practically worthless. It was where the cows and sheep were kept. Barefoot children walked the bluff's edge in summer, throwing rocks at seagulls or picking raspberries in accordance with a grandmother's strict edict not to come home without a full pail or else to bed with no dinner. Maybe teenagers came up here to fool around or get drunk. The only fences along the cow paths and cliffs were those built to keep the animals in, not keep the walkers out. You could even say the hill was communal property back then. Visually, it certainly was: a vista that belonged to everyone. Today all this land is worth millions, and my favourite meadow is for sale—for big money—in the international, web-connected vacation property market.

On one of my walks past the field, I get a wild idea: Why not assemble a group of property owners in the village, acquire the meadow and institutionalize it as a no-build green zone?

Let's create a *village green,* or a *commons.*

I like the word commons. Land owned by the community, in common, where we can keep farm animals, have a conversation about the weather or the sad state of the roads after the winter, or simply roam about in goal-free silence. That sounds good to me. I don't know whether it's worth the risk of antagonizing neighbours or unmooring our own finances to buy property on which there's no prospect at all of financial return. But the meadow speaks to me, flaunting its availability.

—

Alison loses it.

"Are you nuts? Where are we going to get the money?"

"We can borrow it. The line of credit."

"Larry!"

"It's for our children's future."

"What about their college fund?"

Late afternoon, hot, windless, the sea fiercely blue in its waveless repose. The lagoon is the same blue, but even calmer: black squiggles on the surface, like an oil slick . . . but what is it, really? A current flowing? A reflection from above? But it is so beautiful, this black-on-blueness.

I'm sitting on the lip of the lower deck, outside my office. A Czech beer, cold, imbibed in long swigs.

Inside a large purple bin filled with hot water, Jackson and Theo are having a bath outdoors after a brotherly escapade—a brush-fire of minor disobedience—involving a romp through the muddy spur lines of the path over the bluff.

Jackson jumps out to instruct Theo on how to leap from the deck into the bin, yelling "cannonball, cannonball, cannonball!" Then how to hold his breath for a million zillion seconds.

The seconds passing are each rungs on a ladder. I'm climbing and clinging at each step, afraid to look down but looking down all the same.

Falling in my mind.

It's not entirely healthy—this village green idea, my willingness to part with money we don't have. Alison is right. But I can't stop thinking of the meadow. It's talking to me. I'm courting it. I want to possess it.

—

Jackson doing his lawn-mower bit:

Ear protectors and plastic goggles doubling the size of his head. Pushing a chair through the great room. His lips producing a seriously annoying two-stroke engine sound. Saliva down his chin. Blue eyes appearing triple their actual size.

Theo with my ear protector unit on his head. He appears to have coconuts growing out of his ears. Pushing his toy wheelbarrow.

"Daddy, can you hear me?" he shouts.

Breakfast conversation.

"Look, Jackson, a spider, on the window," Alison says.

"Kill it, Mummy," Jackson says.

"Jackson! They don't hurt anybody."

"Oh."

Alison loping into the surf, the boys behind her. I've got the digital camera, clicking away at my family from the beach. I capture my wife's smile (and legs, let it be said) in a tiny silicon brain in my hand. Her laughter isn't captured, though, but somehow using the video function on the camera seems idiotic. I lounge in the sand near the high-tide mark. As the afternoon fun exhausts itself, we meander home over the bluff. I take turns carrying the boys on my back. I realize I've had this throat tickle for a lot longer than a normal cold. When I wake up the next morning, I can't get out of bed, my back in spasm, my throat raw from continuously clearing it in the night of something that doesn't appear to be there.

We treat the back first. The physiotherapist in Bridgewater drives the needles in. Acupuncture. Then she does a few releases, her thumbs pushing into lower back muscles. But her specialty isn't deep and painful tissue massage, which is what I need: a treatment that brings me to the edge of fainting, and requires me to breathe very slowly to take the edge off the spectacular discomfort of having someone's strong hands pushing into my internal organs through my hips. And that someone, my regular therapist, lives in Toronto. I start popping ibuprofen, hoping the spasm will let go on its own. Without a therapist, this can take weeks.

Now for the throat.

Smilla started out as a medical doctor in Copenhagen and evolved into a licensed naturopath when she emigrated to Canada; this enabled her to keep working as a healer without repeating years at med school or a hospital residency to get the doctor's licence she already has. She's tall, athletic, with a face you might describe as warmly regal. A caring person, but very frank in some way I stereotypically associate with Nordic sensibility, and thankfully lacking in touchy-feeliness.

During my appointment she hooks me up to a machine designed to measure my internal energy, my *chi* levels, by circulating electronic frequencies through my body to test for food sensitivities, allergies, all kinds of bad stuff—environmental toxins, viruses and so on.

"You're totally stressed out," she says. "This is the main problem."

"Am I going to die?"

"Ah, silly. No, not now, Larry. Not for a long time, God willing. I recommend you have blood work done every couple of years. You should do that when you get back to Toronto."

"But this tickle in my throat?"

"It's likely an intolerance. You say you've been working in the basement without a dehumidifier? After all the rains in the spring? Maybe there is mould in the basement. And there is, of course, mould outside. Spores on everything. This is very hard on the immune system, if you are at—what is this new term?—*the tipping point.* Your system can only handle so much, and then it reacts. It sends you a signal."

"That makes sense."

"Or it could be a combination of factors. Mould, the environment, the travel and stress. Diet. Pollen. A protein your immune system isn't properly processing. So you need to boost your immune system."

"Okay, great. What can you give me for this?"

"We will come to that, Larry. But perhaps you need to make changes in other parts of your life. You're doing too much."

"So you don't think I have something incurable?"

"You need rest."

"I have young kids. There's a lot going on. Decisions to make."

"And to do a complete detox."

"A what?"

"The testing shows a lot of potential trouble areas."

"Like what?"

Dairy, wheat, tomatoes, onions, yeast, beer, mould. And on and on. It seems I'm intolerant to nearly everything tasty.

"Well, it seems I'm okay on the red wine," I say, relieved to see on the results that it's apparently not an immune stressor for me.

"No alcohol. You should give your liver a rest and allow it to focus on processing other toxins in your system. Not just the alcohol."

"But what about the two glasses of wine a day?"

She shakes her head.

"But both my parents died of heart disease, and my father didn't drink at all. Isn't wine, like, a health measure for a guy my age?"

"Are you concerned you can't give up red wine for even a month?"

"No, not at all."

"Do you drink every day?"

"A health measure. Pleasurably done."

"If you can't go a day without alcohol, perhaps there is something there. Another problem. Possibly this is something, no?"

"Now hold on, Smilla," I say. "People do a lot of things every day they shouldn't. Not just red wine. They watch TV. They eat butter and meat. They work long hours and take abuse from idiotic, workaholic bosses. They live in polluted cities and breathe in, like, a pack of cigarettes every time they step out of the house. They use cellphones and sit in front of computers with no human contact."

"I have this supplement . . . it can reduce alcohol cravings."

"Really? Well, why not? Just in case."

"Okay, then."

"So when can I go back to the red wine?"

"One glass every three days for the next month."

"And after that?"

"Well."

"Am I going to be in the penalty box forever?"

"We make choices, Larry. And the penalty box—if you feel like that, that is not a good thing. That itself is a stressor."

"Exactly. So you know where I'm coming from."

I leave Smilla's office with a bagful of dietary supplements and homeopathic remedies to orchestrate my life during a month of detoxification. When I get back home and report to Alison, she says, trying to suppress a smile, "So, Nova Scotia has made you sick."

We don't speak normally to each other for hours.

What starts out as a solo acquisitive impulse to buy the meadow soon turns into the inefficient art of neighbourly coalition-building to organize a bid. Willie and Barb Cornwall sign on, as do two other couples, Dave and Lily Kingston, and Tracy Enys and Isaac Joffe.

Dave and Lily—long-time property owners on the hill—have just moved here after selling the Ontario farm where they lived for thirty years. He's a retired math teacher and she a retired nurse. They're fond of the Kenyan proverb that they append to their emails: "The world is not given to you by your parents. It is loaned to you by your children." So, good. We've got people who look at conscientious action creatively.

Tracy Enys and Isaac Joffe, both in their late forties, were among the first home-builders on the hill. She's gamine and boisterous, good at disguising her intellectual side, or not flaunting it at those less so. She worked in adult literacy for years and now seems footloose, ready for a change. Isaac is friendly yet intense, a bearded, olive-skinned guy in great shape, a collector of exotic whiskys and bourbons. He owns a freight brokerage in Toronto and spends pretty much every waking moment here either mowing the coastal trail or doing maintenance on their house.

I'm the self-appointed kamikaze pilot of the venture. Alison really does think I've lost it. But there are no tantrums from either of us.

Our strategy is grassroots to a fault. We approach one

landowner at a time. We discover that the concept of a village green isn't universally understood and means something different to pretty much everyone.

Twice I make the error of sermonizing to our prospects, as if I alone were an endless source of visionary insights, even suggesting that wind power might be one of the communal activities we could undertake in the meadow. I get confused looks. When it's suggested that a better strategy is to buy the lot and leave it untouched, I get petulant. Why shouldn't we do something, I suggest, to build a stronger community, put up a barn for meetings or parties, or create garden plots for everyone? Why not *develop* the meadow in a gentle way that brings people together?

Despite some bungling of mine, a few people express an audacious willingness, potentially, to part with a sum equal to the price of a new car to buy the meadow and take it off the market. We figure we'll need ten households to drum up the money. At least two more households are open to the acquisition. But then our luck goes bad. One of the two new prospects bows out, owing mainly to fears of neighbourly conflict. I may have put them off with the discussion about wind power. We get a fair number of no-votes from others we talk to. We're only about halfway there after we've talked to nearly everyone who's here for the summer.

I see a small, dead bird between a wall stud.

"What do they say about a bird in the house?" I ask. "Bad luck?"

"This is a barn, not a house," Tracy replies. We're in her barn loft for a meeting to consider our options on the empty meadow purchase.

"Well, it's unavoidable, folks," Willie says. We're all sitting around a spruce table near the windowed gable. "We don't have a majority of the households actually with us. We've got four out of ten homes."

"But there are another ten or more landowners who haven't built," Dave says, unwilling to give up. A dapper and reserved man until he starts to talk; then you realize he's a dreamer in love with wild schemes. "Should we approach those people? If so, how?"

"We can't do this stuff by phone or email," I say.

The conversation spins and lurches; the energy retreats from solutions and schemes. When the meeting breaks up, the project is dead.

After the others leave, I stick around to talk to Tracy. We walk across her property over to two Adirondack chairs on the crest of the bluff. The view extends south along a crescent dune beach that ends in a headland now under the control of the conservancy. It will remain undeveloped and houseless forever, a paradise for hikers and everything they touch and see.

"Maybe it's all for the better," I say as we settle into the chairs. "It was starting to get complicated." There's a big part of me relieved by our failure. Now I don't have to worry about spending money we don't have.

"Well, the irony is, the only way we can keep this place beautifully marginal is to start acting like bankers and developers ourselves," she says. "I didn't come out here for that."

It's a rare day up here, sunny and windless. The bay is so glassy calm and sensitive to disruption that when the minke whale breaches, Tracy and I shout at the same time. The sighting cheers us up.

"This is a marginal place," I say. "A marginal part of a marginal coastline in a country itself on the margins of the continent. Where else would you really want to be, eh? People thought we were nuts for buying this place."

"Most people don't like the insecurity of the edge," Tracy says. "But some are drawn to it. It can, of course, be destructive. But if we are conscious of the contradictions of the edge, and the chaos that's naturally here, we can learn to live comfortably."

"That's what we have: contradictions. We think we're doing some kind of protection of the land, but how much of it is about protecting something for its own sake, and how much is about making this place more the gated community it's already in danger of becoming? We think we want a sanctuary, but perhaps it's a gated community we're really trying to create. Something obscenely safe."

"Jung believed that if we hold on to the opposites within us, an unexpected third way will open up . . . this involves a creative process that demands that we let go of some old ideas about who we are and trust in the process of embracing our contradictions."

"Jesus, Tracy. I could never get through Jung."

"Maybe it's because he's such a terrible writer!"

We cackle over that.

I say, "To me it's like connecting two polarities to create a current. You have competing ideas—or contradictory elements of an idea—at the poles. And when you connect them, you get something a lot like life at its best, the energy and light of it."

"This is a marginal place," she says with some finality.

"Yup, you got it," I say, uncertain where to go next.

"How we view the natural environment, as friend or foe, is the crucial issue."

"It's the story of this country. All countries. All places."

"This environment isn't as natural as we think. The common bounty—it's what? It's not just the ocean views, the bluffs, the sandy beaches, the wildlife in the marsh. It's the human history and what people have done in years past by creating pastures, orchards, hedgerows, walking paths, stone walls, even the road winding through the village. Even the road. And these things need to be tended to."

"And once people discover this place, man, they'll do everything they can to keep the others out. Like us, I guess. Don't you think?"

"You're swirling toward the negative, Larry."

"Fair enough."

"No matter who does what, or when, let's recognize that roads fall into the sea. Pasture land becomes overgrown with alder, bayberry and wild rose. The wind knocks down trees. Houses get swept away in hurricanes and floods. Yet we've chosen to be out here. We build our buildings and bring our dreams here. We think there's a permanency to what we do. At best there's resiliency."

"And some people freak out. They want the sea to be calm and blue all the time. They want the fog to drift in only when they have a desire to snuggle up by the fireplace. Others lose their minds for different reasons."

"How so?"

I laugh. "Maybe they see themselves too closely in all their weird contradictions. And maybe that's not what they want at all."

My back is beginning to throb. I don't know what it's telling me, except it's time to go home for a large meal of dietary supplements.

I clear my throat.

"That cold not gone away yet?" Tracy says as I stand to go.

"It's an intolerance, maybe dietary, maybe environmental."

"And your back?"

I shrug. "This thing you talked about, the Jung thing. I've always liked the idea that contradictions or opposing forces can be put to good use. If you know the playing field, and if you keep throwing possibilities onto the pitch, something good can come from the conflict."

"We have to trust in the people we have around us."

That night I go online and research the supplements I'm taking, then, confused by all the technical and marketing bullshit, I call a friend in Montreal who does PR for pharmaceutical companies.

"These supplements—are they, like, vitamins?" I ask.

"Well, they're more than that," Arnold says. "What are you taking?"

I tell him.

"Look, these things aren't just vitamins. Some of them are drugs, only marketed differently to get around the law. They're legally called supplements, but don't kid yourself, they're synthesized to work like drugs. They may work, in some cases, or it may be a placebo effect. But I don't think anybody knows how all these supplements can affect you if you're swallowing them all day long."

"The garlic pill can't be all bad."

"No, but you eat a full clove of raw garlic on an empty stomach and you'll quickly find out the effect can be dramatic. It's strong stuff. Maybe good for you, sure. Maybe. But some people can react very badly."

After I get off the phone, Alison, who has been eavesdropping, says, "Just remember, Arnold works for the drug companies."

"I'm eating thirty pills a day."

"Well."

"Do you really believe that scientific research is just a vast conspiracy by the drug companies?"

I'm in a good mood: I'm allowed a glass of red wine tonight.

—

I spend the next three days in bed with a back spasm.

On the fourth day I chuck the pills. The whole lot of them. I also decide I've had enough time in bed moaning.

It's a beautiful day. The boys want to go to the beach.

I struggle downstairs, each step a nightmare. I say to Alison, "I don't care if I die getting there, but I'm getting us to the beach and I'm going for a walk."

Easier said than done.

The boys and Alison walk over the hill with the beach toys.

At some distance behind them, I'm dragging my left leg like some Igor in a horror movie. With each step I dig my thumbs as deeply as I can into the knotted mess of muscles, hoping to unlock the spasm as if I were merely unknotting Jackson's laces. The odds of releasing the spasm are remote. The therapists say you can't heal yourself; you need someone else torturing you.

Then the spasm lets go.

A pinging sensation. For a long second I believe something else is happening, something much worse than the pain I already have.

I'm still hobbling, and it will take a few more torture sessions on the table with a variety of therapists, but the spasming is over.

Another hot afternoon. I'm ferrying the kids' toys from the sandbox to the house and watering new hayseed where it hasn't yet taken over the septic field. I see Deirdre Salisbury hiking up from the marsh along the path beside our property line.

For more than thirty years, Deirdre and her husband, Luke Knowlton, have been coming here to retreat from their lives in Halifax, where both were doctors before they retired maybe five years ago, maybe longer. Over the years they acquired a lot of property in the area, which Luke fenced in for the purpose of operating, for his weekend amusement, various sheep farms. We bought our land from them.

As Deirdre approaches she waves, chugging along at a vigorous, determined clip. A fierce but friendly twinkle in her eyes, as usual. Before she climbs past and disappears over the hill toward the beach, I walk toward her. Deirdre and Luke, in their late sixties, are a sweet blend of urban sophistication and down-home friendliness. Now that their three children are grown and living in distant cities, they're spending more time here, having sold off much of their property and donated large hunks of it to the conservancy.

I unburden myself to Deirdre of the failed project to buy the meadow and create a village green. She finds the idea interesting.

A day later Luke shows up. Everyone's outdoors, soaking up the afternoon sun in the rueful spirit of late August, when each pause from a chore is an occasion to wonder why summers have to be so short and winters so bloody long. We hear Luke mowing a neighbour's field with his tractor. He seems to be gunning the tractor past my place more often than is strictly necessary. I step out from the firewood stack into the field, into his viewplane, as the tractor again comes into view.

It's me he wants.

As I walk toward him, he turns off the engine, tips his cowboy hat back on his brow. A wiry, compact man with arms that look like they can still wield a heavy maul the way some people twirl pens, Luke is the hands-on type—with a gentle manner. My guess is that he's equally at home wrestling with the egos of surgeons as the head of cardiology as he is rounding up sheep in the marsh.

"Hi, Luke. How she's going today?"

"I like your fence, Larry."

"You do?" It's like having Michael Jordan saying he likes your jumpshot or your short game. Luke is the king of the fence-builders around here. Over the decades, he's pretty much stitched the whole place for his sheep.

"Yep," he says, then comes to the advice. "I was watching you across the way this summer, pounding in the posts. You might think of doing that kind of work in the spring."

"Why?"

"The soil tends to be a little softer when you use the maul."

"Right."

"Hard on the back, too."

"Right."

"Deirdre was telling me about you and your buddies looking for land for this village green idea," he says.

"Yeah. I was just mentioning it—"

"We have this property," he says, cutting me off. "On the back side of the hill. With views going every which way."

He's talking about a long, wide strip of mown green, a staggeringly beautiful location on the bluff. The views go 360 degrees from a high elevation. He names a price that's one-tenth the market value.

"Luke, you're kidding me."

"Well, Larry, right now the property is landlocked. It'll take years, if ever, to get the adjacent lot owners to let you put a road there. But no one is ever gonna stop you from walking to your land."

"This is unbelievable."

"Deirdre and I like what you folks are doing. We've done some of that, but it's time for others to step in here with some new ideas."

—

For weeks now I've been blocking out the fact that Donna and I haven't been talking, and that this is largely the result of an email I sent to her expressing disappointment at not being invited to her wedding.

I said more or less that my heart was broken, and I not so gently hinted that we had different ideas about family. The anger is real, but I've hit back hard.

In the moments when I consider what I've done, I feel terrible. Even so, I'm good at packaging away the guilt into internal places where I don't have to feel it. I know how to compartmentalize. I believe this skill, if it can be called one, owes much to the collateral damage of my work, which often creates an involuntary spasm of mental distancing that makes me feel like I'm standing outside my body. Sometimes when I take a break after a conference call to Toronto or New York, or after I've read incoming email from London or Bucharest or Aspen or Winnipeg, I walk outside, taking in the horizon view with a heavy heart, realizing that it's hard work to reassemble my mind after dispensing chunks of it over the technologies that supposedly allow me to connect to wherever and whomever I wanted. It's a bitch sometimes to immerse myself intuitively in *any* moment, regardless of where I am or with whom; very tough to do the right thing in the right spirit. It's easy for important things to get lost. So time goes by, and the breach with Donna worsens.

Enough time has passed now that I know she won't pick up the phone. When I decide to call, James answers.

"She doesn't want to talk to you."

"That's not too healthy."

"I know it's not healthy."

James is about as good a man as I know: a lobster fisherman, just turned fifty, burly, a wonderful father to his two grown children, generous, high-spirited, now a grandfather. This is his second marriage. We've spent many nights drinking beer and trading stories from the old days. But he's angry with me too.

I cut him off before he gets going.

"James, I didn't call to fight."

"Easy for you to say."

I fend off the impulse to let it rip.

"I'll get her to call you in a couple of days," he says to end the call.

The call doesn't come.

Not so puzzling. It's a mix of fear, confusion, revenge. Or so I think: I hurt her, she'll hurt me back.

Eventually the email comes, the start of an exchange.

We've always spoken different languages in addressing conflict. I prefer the long-winded, archaeological approach, going back over old ground, exploring the sources of discontent or disillusionment that have built up between us over the years . . . or how else explain not being invited to the wedding? She's having none of that from me. She wants no part of a mutual inquisition. About the wedding, she says, she and James did what they wanted, and that's that, and she didn't want to hurt me, but she'd do the same thing again. I'm advised to *accept her as she is.* How do you argue with that? You don't. You put it back together.

Alison and I are walking the Knowlton/Salisbury property, one of the few remaining areas of the bluff not developed. Still wild. Very wild. Up and down the slope of the lot we go, wandering through a field of freshly cut hay. An amazing place. The views. The borders of it. Everything inside of it: ours. This feeling of imminent possession, ownership.

"What are we going to do with it?" Alison asks.

"Nothing for now—except close the deal. Pay for it."

Thirteen households came forward to pony up a share of the cost of buying the lot. That's a big leap from the original group of four investors we had for the so-called empty meadow. Many have responded with effusive emails that this kind of initiative will make our community a much better place.

"I think it's time we went home," I say.

"Really?" She searches my face for irony or sarcasm.

"We have unfinished business in Toronto."

"It's a good city."

I let that pass. The head-on approach with Alison always fails.

"We're not going to be able to figure out things from here," I say. "Not if you feel under siege."

"It's too isolated here in winter with young children."

I deflect that too, and keep walking.

"We're not saving the world by buying this lot," I say. "But the act of rescuing it? I can live with that, *easily*. We bought it fair and square. I'd like to think our boys will be having their college grad parties here. Getting married here one day. I don't know. Maybe their kids will be cutting trails here, or throwing my ashes off the cliff."

Sentimental suits me today, and she lets that pass.

"We need to send tuition to the Waldorf school," she says.

"I sent the cheque to Toronto yesterday."

"Oh."

In the fragmented sectors of my consciousness, things come together for me as we walk down toward the beach.

The empty meadow is still there, waiting for a buyer. I still fantasize that we'll get it and make it ours, somehow.

—

I'm up with the sun, before everybody else.

There's time for a walk around Wreck Point. It'll be my last day in Nova Scotia for a while. I leave this afternoon by car, two days before the rest of the family gets on a plane. I'll be on the road for two days.

A beautiful morning.

As I hike around Wreck Point at low tide, I pause on a reef of broken shale and bleached boulders, facing the open ocean. I squint into the sun on the horizon, telling myself that there's no way I'll ever tire of this experience. I'll go round and round this point for years, decades, for as long as my legs and my heart can carry me.

I want this year in Nova Scotia to go on forever. But the move here under the guise of a sabbatical didn't bring about a new beginning. So my departure feels like failure. I don't feel established anywhere, and while this condition has followed me through life, I feel bad that I've inflicted it on my family. At some point Alison and I have to settle down and raise our family without me acting on the juvenile premise that the grass is always greener elsewhere.

Still, who is to say what makes for a proper life?

Later in the day, when I get into the car after loading it with luggage, only the younger of our two boys is on the front step with Alison to wave goodbye. Jackson's next door at the grandparents, having a nap. He's wiped out from a flu bug. It's a sleepy afternoon. I'm grateful to get away without a big scene. Alison knows I'm disappointed to be going back, and keeps the conversation light.

I send out all the right signals. I'll be fine.

After I buckle in, the moment I've dreaded: me, in the car, heading out on the road, alone, embarking on a drive halfway across the country.

I've got an iPod loaded with my favourite tunes, a charged cellphone, a wallet. Loneliness surges in me as the picture-perfect view of the village recedes in the rear-view. Right now I want sanctuary to mean relief from that feeling. But I know where I'm going and why, and I accept the responsibility of arriving safely so that I can welcome Alison and the boys off the airplane. It's a comforting thought as the car follows the curving road, away from the village of my dreams.

ACADIAN IN EXILE, PART III

I EXPECT FAR TOO MUCH of Foggy Cove.

Early in my experience here, before we even built our house, I was in love with the romantic notion that moving to the village would be the happy ending in my Acadian exile tale, as if my feelings of rootlessness—of the provisional existence, partially the result of my ancestral or family inheritance—could be extinguished simply by pouring a foundation and nailing a satellite dish to the roof. Like I have done so many times over many years, I gathered up all my turbulent longings for home, for belonging, and threw them all at Foggy Cove, expecting it to solve everything. I have since lowered my overwrought expectations and these days appreciate Foggy Cove for what it actually is: a beautiful coastal village, transforming fast into an international tourist community, an exclusive, insular world by any standard of wealth. Nothing wrong with that.

Is it enough for me? I don't know.

I'm not personally leading the charge to return Foggy Cove to isolated rural status again or to its long-lost agrarian lifestyle. I'm one of the urban colonizers driving up real-estate values, potentially creating the conditions for the psychology of the gated community to take root.

I started out believing that our village green project was undoubtedly a progressive idea: a strategy to counter forces that could push Foggy Cove into becoming a gated community. My hope, naive as it seems, was that we would inspire other collaborations among our neighbours to help us share important communal assets—land, trails, the road—for the common good. Those collaborations are, in fact, now occurring; a group of residents, mostly newcomers aided by seasonal residents, has taken inspiration from our success with the Knowlton/Salisbury property, organizing a fundraising drive in partnership with the conservancy to buy more land under the banner of conservation. The group has plans to pitch its story to financial heavy hitters—high net-worth individuals—while also scouring the country for foundation and government funding. The ultimate goal is to preserve as much of the wildness of the area as possible so that future generations—regardless of whether they own land or live in Foggy Cove—can walk the beaches and coastal paths and enjoy the beauty as a public right, not as a privilege granted by the rich folks out of noblesse oblige.

It's a great idea, but I hope it's not cynical to state the obvious: our buying up properties to stop real-estate development will reduce the raw land for sale and create a more parklike setting overall, perhaps increasing the value of properties owned by people already in Foggy Cove. Using a financial analogy, this is akin to a corporation buying its common shares in the open market to reduce the number of outstanding shares. This creates a smaller equity base against which to distribute earnings; more money goes to those who still own shares. In investment jargon, this is called a share buyback.

Of course I support the conservation efforts. Expanding our village green concept and creating walking paths to link the commons land into a trail system will be a good kick in the balls to the trend toward excessive privatization, including neurotic conceptions of personal privacy. After all, this is a seaside community, all the houses out in the open, not a monastery or corporate retreat hidden on ten thousand acres, patrolled by guys in stretch-fabric uniforms and GPS implants in their heads.

I'm under no illusions; a village green can easily become a private fiefdom within a gated community.

It all depends on who's on the scene.

Gated community values have been around since humans started erecting structures to shelter themselves from whatever they considered enemies or dangers to communal wealth, stability or prestige. Walled cities, castles, ancient citadels and the like, these all technically qualify as gated communities. The gated community as modern cultural symbol is a different matter. "Gated" definitely implies a barrier, a means to keep people out unless invited in. "Gated" says exclusive, homogeneous, private, privileged, monthly fees; if your retina or bank card or licence plate doesn't scan into the system, the lasers will maim you. "Community" implies inclusiveness, a bonding, togetherness, fraternity, equality. In the marriage of these two words, something's not right: "gated community" sounds like the freakish outcome of an advertising brainstorming session facilitated by a creative director prone to extreme mood swings.

I can't predict the future of Foggy Cove. But the benefits of putting up gates and Private Road signs and hiring security guards can't outweigh the consequences. If gates do go up one day to keep people off our hill, my belief is that this situation will say more about perceived threats than actual ones; it will be a sign of something gone wrong in our minds.

—

In the Martin Scorsese film *Goodfellas*, the mobster main character played by Ray Liotta eventually rolls on his associates and testifies in order to escape imprisonment on a drug charge; he's supposedly given safe haven in a witness protection program. In one of the final scenes, the Liotta character opens the front door of his home in a new suburb, barefoot, in a bathrobe, just like any dad, scanning the street as he bends down to pick up the morning newspaper. There's no mistaking the message: he's escaped punishment but living in a prison all the same.

One person's safe haven is another's gated community.

In that statement, there's a warning I take seriously about being smug in criticizing what others require to feel safe.

A poignant dimension of sanctuary is the idea of safe haven: the history of what we now call humanitarian intervention.

In part, this is a tale of societies attempting to become more civilized by overcoming their inhumane tendencies, which, paradoxically, are completely human in that the problem hasn't been licked and may very well never be. Wars, terrorism, civil breakdown, criminal violence and persecution in endlessly creative forms still affect large geographic areas of the planet.

Innovation in safe haven is all around us, always has been.

Consider the black slaves of America escaping to Canada along the Underground Railway. A handful of Jews in Europe saved by Oskar Schindler with his list and Raoul Wallenberg with his passports. The boat people granted refugee status after arriving on the shores of British Columbia or south Florida. Shelter generally for those affected by countless injustices, for gay people escaping homophobia and for women who reject patriarchal submission in matters of marriage, their profession, choice of clothing and the shape and indeed the function of their genitals. We can also safely denote safe haven as the umbrella term for such civilizing developments as the invention of the hospital, the orphanage, children's rights, the mental asylum, the hospice, the school.

In the ancient Hebrew world, there were cities of refuge, where criminals and the dispossessed could find protection from persecution. These safe havens were suburbs on the outskirts of town where you could go if you inadvertently slaughtered someone who screwed you in a business deal, or disrespected your sister in the courting ritual. Inside these cities of refuge, you would be protected from retribution from your victim's family, at least until you could prove self-defence. The practice of assigning an entire city to be a place of refuge continued in ancient Greece, when the term *asulon* was used. During the Hellenistic period, some Greek city states and religious temples were declared to be sanctuaries from warmongers, places where violent conquests or reprisals couldn't take place.

In classical Roman times, the Christian Church established itself as a safe haven to those fleeing persecution. This tradition turned into law in England in the fourth century. Over time English asylum law broadened to include sanctuary for accused criminals. In some cases, a person seeking sanctuary had to get inside the church before being safe from a violent pursuer. Sometimes, there was an area around the church that could extend for as much as a mile, the boundaries marked by stone crosses; once the fugitive made it into this area, safety was theoretically assured. The law also declared that sanctuary-seekers must give up all their weapons and confess their sins while under the protection of the church, and that they could stay for up to forty days. During this time, they had to make a choice: either surrender and stand trial, or be sent into exile. The church sanctuary system in England was abolished in 1623 because criminals were routinely abusing the privilege.

But the English didn't abandon safe haven as a concept; they mutated it. Like other emerging nation-states with international spheres of influence, they smartly stole the idea from church people and honed it as an enduring, often humane instrument of colonialist foreign policy: the practice of offering political asylum, continuing a long tradition of sovereign countries, city states and tribes that accept those persecuted by their geopolitical enemies. In the later 1500s, England took in Protestant Huguenots who were being hounded and openly murdered in France by the Catholic majority; that large migration went on for a century or more. The former colonial powers in the West— Britain, France, Germany—have accepted large numbers of people from colonies they'd lost or given up, sometimes peacefully, sometimes less so. Today it would be a challenge to find a prosperous Western democracy without a significant population of refugees-turned-residents from lands where it fought a war, defended a colony or instituted regime change wholesale.

In surveying the centuries of progress in the history of safe haven, it seems to me that innovations in refugee protection in the West, from the seventeenth century onwards, occur mainly through the stabilizing force of representative or quasi-democratic governments egged on by private donors and provoked by the morality in action—the leadership—of church people, missionaries and social progressives, including labour organizers. The grassroots, in other words, not always the powers that be. At the beginning of the twentieth century, church people and social progressives began collaborating in ways that created the precursors to the modern humanitarian agency, or what we now call the non-governmental organization, or NGO. Today there are more than 50,000 NGOs at the international level alone—including the UN and its many agencies—doing work in human rights, the environment and economic development. NGOs have mandates, memberships, funding, the ability to issue tax receipts and send speakers to conferences. But the idea of the loose association, the coalition of interests, the alliance of the moment, has also been known to have very positive effects on the lives of refugees. In the early 1980s, what became known as the American Sanctuary Movement took root in Arizona when a small group of clergy and church workers decided to protect illegal refugees coming over the border from El Salvador and Guatemala. There was nothing formal about it, just good old-fashioned moral conviction at work. Courage.

When you follow the voices of youthful idealism and political dissension, the trail often ends in safe haven. For American men avoiding the Vietnam draft in the 1960s, Canada was the pacifist homeland until the amnesty program kicked in. In countless countries since time immemorial, men who didn't want to fight or kill have always moved on, often into the safe anonymity of life in a cosmopolitan city. The men who really do want to fight and kill sometimes leave their native land to find like-minded souls and patronage in support of their cause. For the terrorist in training or the global jihadist, there's the stateless-warrior haven, a home in the failed state, such as Afghanistan, where Osama bin Laden built his training camps with Saudi money and plotted. In the early 1960s there were anti-Castro warriors—many of them refugees from Cuba—all over the United States. Louisiana and Texas were apparently amok with paramilitary groups, supported by Mob money, training in the deserts and bayous, preparing for the day that never came when they'd take back Cuba from the Communists and, naturally, enable the Mob to rebuild its casinos, brothels and money-laundering operations.

Regarding the aspiring mobster, there are a variety of criminal organizations offering sanctuary for men on the make who want to become *made*: the Mafia, Triads, Bloods, Crips, gangs galore in every metropolis. In turn, these groups offer safety to local businesses on their turf by demanding protection money. Those who get caught and convicted for extortion enter a different kind of sanctuary: a prison. Or if you're a rich and telegenic criminal, it's house arrest with an electronic ankle bracelet. For insider traders, safe haven ideally means a tax shelter on a remote banking island, far from the oversight of regulators back home. On the visionary edge of corporate capitalism, lobbyists are pursuing strategies to have corporations defined, in law, as human beings entitled to human rights and requiring protection from activist groups that expect them to make their business decisions informed by ethical considerations.

At the other end of the socio-economic spectrum, we have the neo-Luddites: people unimpressed by modern technology and consumerism, or, indeed, certain of its evils, the back-to-the-land cults functioning in dour isolation, acting as if the Industrial Revolution never happened, the engine never invented, never mind the computers that operate many engines today. We have the supporters of a global network of Waldorf schools, for whom safe haven increasingly means protecting school-aged children from media exposure, the prevalent toxin in the mental environment. In my experience, the parents most likely to enrol their children in Waldorf education are the media types themselves: those who are—or aspire to be—writers, filmmakers, actors. It's all I can do not to ask, What is it about the world we inhabit ourselves that's so dangerous to our kids?

Aside from addiction to the non-reality of media experiences?

Aside from fragmenting their little brains on the advertising that pays for our salaries and consulting fees?

Aside from . . .

Safe haven is also the wild dream of future protection, the frontiers of innovation as a response to our infinite capacity to create and then inflict pain on new classes of victims whom we may not, in our ignorance, think of as victims at all, at the moment.

Two hundred years ago, the prospect of creating laws or investing in shelters to protect women, homosexuals, the poor, nature, pets—while maybe not entirely wacky to everyone—would have raised eyebrows in many bourgeois salons and political backrooms.

It's always easier to look at history and say, gee, the ancestors were uncivilized, dumb, venal; it's much harder to look at ourselves with the same clear-eyed ferocity.

PART III

DIAGNOSIS

3.1

ACADIAN IN EXILE, PART IV

Migwash, Prince Edward Island, August 2006

A GUNSHOT EVERY MINUTE OR SO—

I'm walking the dirt road toward the shore. A sweltering morning, the air sweet with sunshine and fragrant greenery, which takes me back to my childhood, when I ran happy and wild in these fields and woods and along the beaches. The sea gurgles unseen in the distance; tame water compared to the open North Atlantic off Foggy Cove.

The old settlement is around the next bend, a fenced pasture surrounded by tall trees and thick bush except for an opening that leads to the marsh, providing a clear view across the lagoon to a houseless dune and beyond to the harbour and lobster boats. Here on this land, in 1799, two Gaudet families arrived with maybe a dozen more Acadians who were on the run from those who'd been deporting them for the past forty years, coming here to live with the Indians rather than go back to France or to swampy Louisiana.

Here lie the remains of an Acadian village, untouched except for a lame excuse for an archaeological dig—a few shallow test pits—that established the fact of the foundations, the history decomposed in the red clay. The Acadian buildings and grave markers were all made of wood and rotted fast. Fortunately, stratigraphic methods and the scientific analysis of soil layers, combined with old documents in the hands of local historians, have reconstructed the scene: a village of small homes, big families, a subsistence life, mixed farming on land and the sea. Very humble.

A few years back the village of Migwash—my parents' hometown—celebrated the arrival of the Acadians, organizing a two-hundredth anniversary party. The pasture was mown, signs erected and tourists enticed to visit. A trail was bushwhacked between the settlement and the back woods where some early settlers had built a log church and buried their dead. The celebrations sparked interest in genealogy among my cousins, who traced the family line back to the mid-1600s in Nova Scotia. But everything's overgrown again, the signs gone, the trail lost. History here has had its fifteen minutes of local fame.

I like to imagine that this forgotten world is my secret and mine alone. My ghost village.

Guns weren't going off here when I was a boy, only pellet guns we fired at birds and squirrels and occasionally at one another. But then there weren't commercial blueberry operations in these fields and the apparent need to scare off the seagulls scavenging for berries. How can you can live with a shotgun set to go off every several minutes? It may not be an actual shotgun; maybe it's another technological device that makes violent eruptions. It sounds like a gun. Feels like one. And it angers me. But this is genuine rural life, on the economic and geographic margins of everything. People need work and so they don't complain.

We're on the Island for a long weekend, a few kilometres from the northern tip of the island, visiting my sister and her husband and my father's three sisters, including May and Fran, who live here year-round, and Susan, who drove in from New Brunswick because it's been two years since she's seen our boys. It's the first time I've seen Donna and

James since we fell out over their wedding plans. We arrived to big hugs and kisses from everyone.

Aunt Fran said right away that I'm greying nicely at the temples, but since, in her eyes, I'll always be six years old, I know she was surprised that I look like I'm actually in my mid-forties.

Last night was like old times with Donna. Over a quiet dinner at her place, we gladly jumped back into being brother and sister. It was a sweet reconciliation. After the meal she proudly showed me the brochure for the paints she used to paint the interior of her house, the theme being the Group of Seven colours. She's resourceful, wily, inventive. And this is where she's invented or reinvented herself, at the heart of the family compound. Maybe *compound* isn't the right word. It's three homes for an extended family, including Donna and James's place. My aunt May bought four acres of oceanfront here in the mid-1970s with the life insurance money she got after her husband died. She retired here in the early 1980s and built a split-level. Her older sister, Fran, retired now after thirty years working for the credit bureau in Montreal, has a cottage that's very close to the cape. She winters in the seniors home in Migwash.

This morning I got up early, and now here I am, at the old settlement, a half-hour walk from where we're staying. Alison and the boys are likely just waking up. Everything is so still and quiet except for the periodic shotgun blasts. There's little dialogue going on here between the past and present except the one in my head. There are no ghosts here except my own. As I wander through a field of tall grass, each step sends a squadron of grasshoppers into flight, a ballet of locusts around me.

I sit down in the field, crushing stems, swatting insects.

From my knapsack I pull out my journal.

—

When I began this book I knew it would involve a journey. I just didn't know what kind until I realized that a search for sanctuary and the experience of it, when undertaken in good faith, inevitably leads one toward a meditation on the self. That isn't a remarkable conclusion. But since I'm speaking to an audience larger than myself, I accept that the privilege of expression carries a responsibility to strive for originality.

This book offers a case study in support of ideas I've been developing for several years now to describe the human condition as it manifests in my cultural circumstance. I didn't seek this project for that explicit reason, but that's what happened the deeper I got into it. To be clear, I'm the "case" under "study" here. In this experiment, I'm like the mad scientist who has only himself to torment as the subject for the strange new potion. While I don't think I've breathed life into an evil Mr. Hyde, I definitely have some Dr. Jekyll in me: the arrogance to give definition to elements of my psyche that were mostly invisible to me previously.

So what have I done?

I've long been tempted to join the ranks of conceptualizers and classifiers of mental pathology. My interest in theoretical psychology goes back to college and my first exposure to Freud, who exploited the language of science and the clinical manners of the empiricist to convey what artists, philosophers, mystics and prophets have always done without hiding behind the white lab coat: explain human motivations and actions.

The effectiveness of Freud's theories applied to healing the mentally ill has always been debatable, no more so than by his professional descendants, the generations of psychotherapists who followed him. I find his case studies hard going. You have to wade through pretty laborious writing that is trying hard to sound medical, scientific. The jargon is dense. No doubt students of medical history, or psychiatrists in training, see value in studying them. I confess that I sit back at a distance from his words, content to admire his audacity, his clever thievery in appropriating from philosophy and the literary arts, in the name of scientific objectivity, the authority to articulate a design—not of a biological structure or chemical reaction—but of human consciousness itself. I don't propose to take back from psychology the mantle of credibility in creating models of human behaviour. The horse left that paddock a long time ago. All the same, I yearn to understand myself and my world, which is why the language of psychological investigation appeals to me. This journal entry culminates in the self-diagnosis you're about to read.

I hope it resonates with you.

A while back I came across a newspaper article that commented on a trend toward the voluntary ingestion of the drug GHB among partygoers in their teens and twenties. GHB is infamously known as the date-rape medication of criminal choice, the pill that the date-raper slips into the drinks of his victim, rendering her (it's almost always her) pliant, semi-comatose. GHB has also been used as a truth serum in torture methods in the police state, and by mental health professionals in our culture. The article stated:

> Known as a "dissociative," GHB makes users feel they are outside their bodies. One woman who has used it as an aphrodisiac said the drug enhances sensations. "It felt like my sensations were expanding but my emotions were dulled," said the woman, who asked that her name be withheld.

—

Who needs GHB for that?

You just need to turn on the TV or drive around the city or through the suburbs, studying the billboards, malls and fast-food signage. We're bathed in artificially induced sensation around the clock—stuff designed to steal your soul from your body through your eyes and ears. Dissociation, the feeling of standing outside your body, is the fundamental characteristic of contemporary life, the alien psychological outcome of participating in a culture where the primary mode of community connection is media-based and where the speed of electronic communication (and jet travel) makes you wonder sometimes why you have a body at all.

Our senses are assaulted from all directions. So much change—so much noise, light, motion—and so little time to adapt.

People imbued with a civilizing impulse have always believed that the world changes faster and more disturbingly than they can cope with. We're not the first civilization to be disoriented by massive change. A sober assessment of history dispels any notion that we live in uniquely chaotic times. But our emotions are frequently immune to factual input: knowledge of long-ago battles rarely mitigates the intensity of our despair over the current state of affairs. The present tense, for so many of us, will always feel novel. It wouldn't surprise me to learn that some evolutionary scientists believe humans are genetically predisposed to end-of-the-world fears. After all, we're mortal creatures, and live tethered to time, experience its ravages; if our lives are destined to come to an end—why not the world? Why get all worked up to prevent the apocalypse?

We all know that feeling—but what's unique or original here?

It's related to the forces shaping our ethical and moral faculties.

Many of us perceive that our moral horizon is expanding beyond our ability to comprehend changes in the world. At the geopolitical level of awareness, every day we have a larger world of images and perceptions against which we need to orient our internal compass, especially if we accept responsibility for the actions taken by our proxies—for example, governments, armies, celebrities. Today we can't open our eyes or plug into a media outlet without being presented with dramas and situations that instantly demand us to rethink what we're accountable for and to whom. Because of this so-called globalization of perspective, we live with difficult challenges in processing our involvement—or, indeed, culpability—in world events, such as the news of a genocide one day in Darfur, a tsunami the next in Indonesia. The fact is, we're experiencing an expansion in macro-morality awareness.

And this leads to difficult questions. Who does our dirty work in the global hot spots? In Canada, we sent one of our generals, Roméo Dallaire, to oversee a UN peacekeeping mission in Rwanda and we, otherwise known as the world community, left him there without the soldiers, weapons or the mandate to do much more than witness a genocide unfold. As a Canadian citizen, and therefore indirectly the employer of Roméo Dallaire, I accept his failure as my own failure. And what have I done about that?

Ask yourself what really happens when we observe the actions and results of the armies and NGOs we send into conflict zones under various charters, or of the journalists and media cameras that expose rapacity under the plausible notion of rallying global outrage. All this is supposed to add up to our institutional participation or reaction. But it doesn't add up to much individual involvement or emotional connection for us, the observer, at home. We may take comfort that our political/media machinery is doing something good, but most of us get the news and return to our spreadsheets. Many of us, unsatisfied by the emotional yield of voyeurism, tune out except when something dramatic happens; since we're a mannered society, it's bad manners not to express shock at fundraisers to raise money for the victimized.

Our proxies deal with dozens of potential and real Rwandas every day. How do we get emotionally tied into that without losing our minds?

Next, on a more intimate level, ours is a culture of increasing sophistication. All around us are the means (and consultants) to colour our interior world with ever more refined levels of accountability. Practically every aspect of behaviour or pseudo-behaviour (bad thoughts, impulses) in our roles in the family, as individuals, as community members, is open to inspection. There's no place to hide or breathe unmolested from rigorous criticism. Our most secret shortcomings are subject to twelve-step programs, zero-tolerance legislation, anti-shyness drugs, help lines, victim support groups. And this is the expansion, the detailing of higher expectation, in the realm of micro-morality.

The dynamic range of consciousness—of ethics and morality—is expanding. More big things to live with. More smaller things.

Macro and micro. We're getting hit from both ends.

The outcome of all this—in my life—is the intense sensation of engagement with the world that somehow lacks authentic emotional resonance. Some days I feel stoned on something that gauzily puts distance between me and everything around me. I may be in happy possession of an enlarged scope of awareness but emotionally numb all the same, dissociated, fragmented, moving too fast for the right things to make an impact on me. There seems to be so much happening on so many fronts—so much bad news, so much change—it's no wonder that I occasionally feel paralyzed, cognitively decoupled, a ghost of who I should be, or want to be. One of the consequences, I suspect, is that we ricochet too easily into the grip of fear and paranoia, which in turn can inspire a premature or selfishly contrived search for sanctuary. Even the privileged few— especially us—default to the worst case that inspires us to retreat: the fraudulent belief that not only are the dangers we face multiplying, but they're getting closer to home and becoming more complex, virulently subversive. As overloaded and fearful creatures, it's easier for us to yearn for the neverland past—the gated community—where the world is simpler, easier to understand. We look at the present and future as riskier, dangerous and unstable. A place we should avoid.

Please don't tell me you don't know what I'm talking about.

In the spirit of these excessively diagnostic times, and in the language of disorder and pathology, let's define the symptoms:

> *Ghosting* is characterized by disembodied sensations and perceptual states, personality virtualization and addiction to relationships that are enabled by networking and screen technology. Ghosting sufferers report feelings of alienation that contribute to ego fragmentation and emotional distancing. By divesting so much of ourselves into virtual worlds—computers, email devices, televisions, movie screens, even books—

we're turning into ghosts, increasingly divorced from our bodies, or possibly we're becoming something weirder: cyborgs, an unholy hybrid of technology and tissue, living out of body much of the time.

Velocity is a condition of psychological impairment produced by accelerated modes of human interaction and high-speed conduct. The result is diminished capacity in social, family and occupational functioning arising from disorders such as jet lag disorientation, carpel tunnel perspective, windshield vision, multi-tasking tic and obsessive-compulsive connectivity psychosis (or "crackberry mania"). Symptoms include dissociation and depression. We're moving so fast and on so many planes at once that, ironically, it feels like we're standing still, going nowhere. There is no redemptive sense of journey. There's only the spirit in violent motion, in pressurized cabins high in the sky or along fibre-optic cables below ground, or riding paved slabs of landscape where you're unable to stop without applying inhumane force, where even a small accident has the potential for injury or death.

Subdivision is characterized by the obsessive segmentation of impulses, appetites and emotions, and results in psychic fragmentation. The disorder is prevalent in cultures like ours, where consumer values and corporate marketing strategies dominate the social context and psychological space, undermining integrated consciousness. Subdivision sufferers exhibit distorted percep-

tions of reality, exaggerations of inferential thinking, hallucinations and abnormal levels of fear.
We've torn ourselves apart and isolated ourselves
in so many inventive ways. We are less than the
sum of our parts. The world isn't interested in
the integrated you, or me, only the different
parts of us, their economic value determined by
how much we spend tending to them.

Mythogyny is a media disorder that describes
pathological self-fictionalizing. Mythogynistic
tendencies result in compulsive behaviours arising from the belief that one's life is a series of
interconnected, cinematic events: an audience-
worthy storyline featuring classic themes and
recognizable narrative structuring. We've been
telling lies about ourselves—or what some call
myths or fables—since the dawn of civilization.
This disorder has now reached epidemic proportions. We're all media-diseased, media-
addicted. What happens to a culture when basi-
cally everyone—not just the shamans, artists and
mystics—spend large portions of their daily time
involved in mythic self-invention? What happens is that, collectively, we become anchored
more in fantasy than in any nurturing connection to reality.

These symptoms do not represent a fully realized model
of human consciousness. They're shards of a belief system,
not the whole mirror, and a satirical indicator of my discomfort with media culture and consumerism, and my love
of jargon. They speak to me as a plausible explanation for
my actions and responses as a sanctuary-seeker.

I have nothing against jargon; new words come into the world when existing language can't properly explain something. Here I'll introduce one more to describe a disease that occurs when we display too many of the symptoms I've mentioned in this chapter.

> *Pseudophrenia* is an illness of perception I would define as a pseudo-connection to experience, a consequence of a long-term pattern of observing and commenting on the world at a televisual or mediated distance—not engaging it directly. Pseudophrenics such as myself create and contemplate their expanding moral/ethical horizon mainly on voyeuristic terms. We might feel bad about the genocides and honour crimes we hear about, and we might even feel "culpable," but we develop our opinions third- or fourth-hand. And when we do act, we make decisions and select options from within the cocoon of the voyeur's sensibility, without the benefit of direct experience, being necessarily dependent on proxies.

Give me examples, you say.

You talk about the global political situation as if you've spent your adult life as a CIA case officer or assistant to the UN Secretary-General, certain that, from your condo downtown, you can analyze the breaking news and gauge the stability of the men who have their fingers on the big red button.

You lack awareness that your views are similar to those you've read in the papers, seen on TV or scanned in the blogs.

You can't properly weigh the relative emotional importance in your life of a plane crash in Russia, a hurricane in New Orleans, the bullying that occurs where you send your kid to school, the tears your spouse sheds because she has trouble communicating with you at times.

You're clueless why you weep at images of 9/11 and the TV fundraiser for the victims but not at the funeral of your own mother.

You believe nothing is real unless it's made artificial first, presented on a screen by people whose professional competence, in the main, is limited to the packaging of the real into the artificial.

Let me say it again: I'm the case under study, not you.

Pseudophrenia is also accompanied by a diminished capacity for reflection that adds up to what I call attention-deficit morality. In part, this attention-deficit morality is the detrimental impact of the digital/electronic messaging culture we inflict on ourselves—for example, the reshaping of sensibility into consumer appetites. The belief that we are conceding a lot of mental sovereignty to the corporate marketing machine is by no means a marginal or bohemian view. It is a mainstream issue.

You feel desire for a billboard, or something approaching desire.

Seeing is believing.

Noise is safe. Silence, scary.

You just know, in your heart of hearts, that after the next car or house or restaurant meal you buy, the next vacation or sabbatical you take, the next song or computer virus you download, you'll never have to acquire or consume anything again and you will, finally, live within your means and be happy until the end of time.

You believe weapons of mass destruction should be launched, stealth planes deployed, sanctions enforced and surveillance increased when there's a clear and imminent danger to democracy and civilization, but you don't know what clear and imminent danger means.

You remember lots from your childhood but nothing from last year or last week. You remember your first telephone number and the address of the apartment where you were born but can't remember how many mobile phones you now have, or the passwords to your online connection and bank account—without writing them down, that is, which you shouldn't do.

You take on too much and can't seem to get anything done even when you're working flat out. You overcommit to everything.

You're not the person you were in high school or college. Or maybe you are, and maybe that's the problem. You're not sure, either way.

Pseudophrenics can also be identified by their token responsiveness to moral and ethical crises, the displacement of the impulse to be helpful, from the difficult and meaningful into the convenient and trivial.

You recycle and feel very good about it.

You connect the dots: cars, oil wars, global warming, carbon neutrality, sustainable development, clean energy.

You keep driving. You keep turning on the lights.

Pseudophrenia is also abetted by the values of over-professionalization/specialization that are rampant in Western culture. Increasingly, we are passive consumers of the wisdom of others, not active agents in creating our own wisdom. Is there any aspect of modern life where we're not expected to default to an expert . . . or many experts?

You worry about your dependence on Wikipedia and Google.

I want to be the expert on myself, but that's difficult.

All this talk about pseudophrenia is just another way of reminding myself that sometimes I feel lost.

When we're lost or disoriented, we still take action, of course. Some people walk in circles until they die. (They get self-destructive.) Some build fires and huddle down in a warming embrace with others who feel lost. (They make do.) Others chew the bark on trees, eat the worms in the ground and find their way through the snow and spruce and resolve that they'll never get lost again. (They get idealistic or fundamental.)

In general, this is the problem:

We see, not do. And are losing a sense of the difference.

We speculate, not experience. And don't know the difference.

We are audience first, actors second, citizens last. And don't know the difference.

We don't know our own minds any more.

As you get deeper into a sanctuary, whether it's the church down the street, the cult in the jungle, the movie in your head or the book in your hands, there's pressure to get on your knees, bow your head or turn to the next person and offer your hand in friendship. At a funeral or wedding, only the most socially inept atheist will not join the service, sing the hymns, genuflect during the homily. And even if this participation is only lip service, and done without reverence, when you're in the sanctuary, the ritual will have its way with you.

I don't need anyone else's wafers for my tongue. I'm not foaming at the mouth, throwing down my crutches and walking when my name is called from the pulpit. I want to listen and acknowledge. I want to burn through the superficiality. I don't want to speak to Someone as grandiose as God. I want to do the impossible: examine my beliefs in a new light.

What can I tell you about my search for sanctuary?

My motivations aren't exotic, informed by epic experiences.

I don't require solitude in the aftermath of a peacekeeping stint, having failed to mediate between genocidal opponents.

I don't seek God in the intervals between each swing of the axe over my firewood pile. I don't stare uneasily at the shoreline fearing that Satan will appear on the dainty spindrift of a surging sea.

I don't worry about my security team on the perimeter, whether one of them might turn on me, put a droplet of dioxin in my soup on the orders of a mysterious cabal for my having fixed an election, stolen a billionaire's concubine, traded blood diamonds, laundered petrodollars.

I wish I could defend my sanctuary quest on the grounds that something within me is astonishingly unique and precious, or tortured and sad. It would be so simple, then, to argue that moving to Foggy Cove is the only way I can go on.

For years I've used the word sanctuary to mean something quite narrow and specific. It was shorthand for being mortgage-free, for the prospect of permanently closing the blinds on the streetscape in favour of the tranquility of making tea on solitary mornings, enjoying the view over a garden of obsessively cultivated perennials. Sanctuary was about walking away, keeping things out, and occasionally advertising that impulse as a form of social currency. It was all about me.

Sanctuary-seeking, as I initially embraced it, temporarily turned me into a ghost of myself, a disconnected and disoriented man.

Sometimes our sanctuary impulses should be questioned and, in many instances, even considered morally objectionable. People are denied safe haven all over the world. How, then, can any one of us enthusiastically launch a personal quest for sanctuary without feeling immoral? There are many false sanctuaries out there to amplify our feelings of distance from ourselves, our loved ones, our responsibilities, the world itself.

In its redemptive forms, sanctuary reduces the effects of pseudophrenia and connects us authentically and indeed ethically to the world of experience. It can make us whole. It can orient us to action and focus our empathy where it can do the most good. Without sanctuary, how can we ever hope to develop the self-knowledge and self-possession we need to engage the world morally? How can we find our spiritual or moral centre unless we step away from the contemporary chaos and reflect?

I'm certainly not alone in my thinking. Billions appeal to the gods—for example, we go to church—for protection from the heathens and the right to kill them or sell their enemies military hardware. We believe having reverence and awe before our God gives meaning to our lives. Religion relieves some pseudophrenic symptoms at the same time as it stimulates others by encouraging people to embrace dogmas and thought patterns that require the suspension of belief in the observable ways of the world.

In the safe haven, we protect people and ourselves through planned intervention and acts of creative remove (political asylum, etc.). The history of this is rich. Even when these responses are toothless or token, as they were in Rwanda, they make us feel like we are doing something good until the facts prove otherwise. Some pseudophrenics go into total and permanent remission after a visit to a catastrophic locale, for example, an AIDS hospice, a refugee camp, a drug treatment facility. They decide to get involved, take action, give an authentic or meaningful portion of their lives over to some cause, charity or good works project. Some do not, and pseudophrenic insularity helps them deny their eyes and ears.

The form of sanctuary known as solitude can also help pseudophrenics become whole. Solitude is the process of stepping temporarily outside the chaos of reality in the quest for self-knowledge. The American state of California was practically built on this aspect of sanctuary. For the past fifty years, a critical mass of New Agers has spawned thousands of movements, institutes and holistic notions of enlightenment that many millions have embraced. Let us not pursue here too strenuously the observation that many of these movements are flagrant examples of collective pseudophrenic behaviour. But it must be said that solitude can cause people to become more solipsistic.

In the gated community where we seek to remove ourselves from the complexities of life or the world as it exists, we often do so to create a simplistic, secure, controlled environment—an escape. The last thing that a pseudophrenic needs is the illusion of control.

I believe in sanctuary—in all its forms, contradictions.

What does sanctuary mean to me?

Everything.

As a writer, I've constructed a mental retreat, a fortress in my head. It provides psychological remove, the luxury of solitude regardless of the noise and movements around me. It lets me consider my condition, the pros and cons, and articulate it in words of my choosing. It is a wonderful place, but, like the Churchill train, it can go through desolate territory where bad things happen. The creation of this vehicle on the tundra of my internal world didn't happen overnight. It took twenty-five years of guerilla warfare with the anti-solitude forces around me. In that sense, sanctuary is the luxury to contemplate and to create. So many are denied this luxury, sometimes just because they're fighting to stay alive, scavenging for food during the famine, creating the false wall to hide from the secret police.

As a man living in a privileged, wealthy society, I've used my wits, ambition and energy to build a barn by the sea. A personal sanctuary for the family. Physical. Real. Who wouldn't do it if they could? Who wouldn't give the finger to the challenge of paying the rent to someone else? To hell with that. I'm no one's serf. Every time I arrive in Foggy Cove after time away and see our house, my ego shouts, Look here, I made this happen. From nothing I've created a shrine to resourcefulness. Maybe this is sanctuary defined as consumer hubris, as acquisitiveness made real. But if I don't invent the structure of my life for myself, then someone else will surely do it for me on terms I may not like. I'm an auto-didact, self-made, and rather pleased that, in words I once heard from an acquaintance from the ruling class, I came up from nothing, despite my dyslexic response around sophisticated table settings and my clumsiness in the better wine cellars. Came up from nothing? People still talk like that. And if you don't build a fortress to protect yourself from that mentality, you're fucked.

Resourcefulness itself is my sanctuary, especially in formulating a response to the unprotected status of the human being in the cosmic scheme of things. I don't have religion to prepare or console me for the afterlife. But neither am I devoid of respect for the mystical impulse. I'm scared that everything ends once the lights go out in the ultimate sanctuary of my body. Very scared. My faith, such as I have one, goes beyond science and religion. I worship mystery: what we don't know and never will know about the universe and our place in it. That's my church, my sanctuary. Faith in the mysterious isn't the same as faith in the supernatural or goblins. One must be resourceful to live with faith in mystery without being lured into the clutches of one religion or another.

As a husband and father, I've fought, as most of us do, to protect my family, and to give them safe haven for as long as they need it. Alison and I have given our boys and each other as much love as we can. And some grief. Life isn't always a movie trailer for happiness. Sanctuary here is opportunity: a chance to see whether the illusion of being a good parent—and husband—can be maintained. There's nothing to stop me. It's up to me.

I won't deny the allure of the false sanctuary: ending the day in thrall to a glass of wine, laughing at the doorman's jokes in the gated community of our condo in Toronto; building a home high on our hill where I can avoid staring at the unfair world. But sanctuary would be a poor tool in the battle against pseudophrenia if I used it mainly as an exalted word to describe a bed and breakfast, cottage country, wine tour or design-buying experience. Surely sanctuary as a force in one's life, with its ancient, storied past, can survive the base reflexes and selfish preoccupations of any given era.

So let us consider sanctuary on the moral or ethical plane.

Questions:

How should we act in the hyper-connected planet?

When/how should we avoid the global swirl?

And when does sanctuary best function as a momentary respite—a time for reflection—that can lead to deeper forms of moral engagement?

In *The Art of Pilgrimage,* the author, Phil Cousineau, quotes mythologist Joseph Campbell on the benefits of spiritual pilgrimage. "The ultimate aim of the quest, if one is to return [home], must be neither release or ecstasy, but the wisdom and power to serve others."

Ideally, sanctuary viewed as a wisdom-seeking journey should involve a means of submerging in or gravitating to an experience (place, idea, situation) and then emerging wiser in order to engage the "power to serve others." That's a lovely idea, a justification for the endurance of sanctuary as a concept in human relations.

Do you have the power to serve others?

Do I?

—

We've just finished cooking the lobsters in the barn when we hear my aunt Susan cry out in the yard, a despondent yelp, then a stream of complaints in her Acadian French that I can barely follow. She's locked her keys inside the car, and tomorrow morning she has to be on the road home to New Brunswick. She's in her late seventies, and very hard of hearing. I peek outside but can't see much. This August evening has gone dark fast. I swig beer, looking over at James, who pauses from cracking open lobster tails with his bare hands—as easily as if they're peanuts.

Within minutes I've taken apart a metal clothes hanger and shimmied it into the space between the passenger door and the frame that James used his pliers to create. The door lock is nestled into a little plastic cocoon, and it'll be very hard to unlatch with the tools we have. A crowd gathers in the darkness, including several of my cousins—seriously macho guys—who have dropped in to say hello and partake in the lobster feed. Alison and the boys are hovering, and so are Donna and our three aunts. I hear new strategies being proposed in the background. My cousins want to step in and take control of the hanger.

I unlock the bastard.

I coast on ego for the rest of the evening—I may not be a rugged fisherman, but I did display a fairly manly skill in the presence of men who respect what James and I did together.

More people arrive, and it's obvious now a real party is taking shape. There's more lobster to cook and beer to drink. It's far past Jackson and Theo's bedtime but we let them play on, climbing in and out of the trucks and on firewood stacked in the barn. They run around the field until they're too tired to talk and fall down in the grass, like puppy dogs, panting, thirsty and minutes away from sleep.

After I help Alison put the boys to bed, I go back to Donna and James's place, a house that started off as a cute but small bungalow that has been tastefully and sizably transformed over the years with the new addition. There's plenty of room for a big party in the living room, but it stays pretty much in the kitchen, as it always does.

I've come back with a bottle of single-malt whisky. No one likes the taste much. James says it's like drinking boiled seaweed.

This is a sensible adult gathering, no drunken singing or guitars or hooping it up to disturb the aunts next door or Alison and the boys in the cottage, no drugs or party animals on the premises. The men sit around the kitchen table and drink. Donna and the women band together in the bedroom, where I expect that secrets are being revealed and gossip exchanged: who's pregnant, or has cancer, or is having a hard time with the patch and is smoking on the sly, behind her husband's back.

James is riffing on his days when he was the night watchman at the lobster factory.

"I'll tell you," he says. "One night Freddie Drag-Arse and Charlie Billy Goat and a bunch from the shore—didn't they show up with two geese they stole from Gerry's barn? Jesus. We sat there all night, plucked them clean, one feather at a time, feathers everywhere, and cooked twenty-five pounds of potatoes and ate the whole goddamn thing."

Freddie Drag-Arse.

Charlie Billy Goat.

"Another time I was sleeping there when Clifford Hang-On drove his truck right up the wharf and smashed about fifty of Nelson Cajoe's lobster traps, and woke me up so fast I nearly died," he continues. "Now there was a drunk man that night, I'll tell you. It took me and Melvin Bog-Face, who was in the truck with him, an hour to clean him up. And then we hid him in the freezer when the Mounties got here. Sitting there in his long johns for an hour, maybe longer. Imagine. Nearly froze him to death."

Clifford Hang-On.

Melvin Bog-Face.

In Migwash, where so many people have the same Acadian surnames—Gaudet, Arsenault, Gallant, Doucette, Pitre—many acquire interesting nicknames to distinguish them, usually as a consequence of doing something silly. It feels like a Native thing to me. And that would make sense; there was intermarriage among the early Acadians and the Mi'kmaq.

I had a friend here named Larry Gaudet. There are at least three Larry Gaudets in and around Migwash. In my teens, I was briefly known as Larry Montreal.

My sister walks into the room while James is improvising with his night watchman story. "You're a fine bunch," she says, pretending to be annoyed. She gives me a big smile, then looks at James.

"Remember the time Larry—"

Soon Donna is telling stories about the silly things I did around here as a teenager. She has us all laughing.

My sister is pretty much my mother in the flesh: looks like her, talks like her, has her fiery temper and intense sentimentality, is easily hurt. But Donna isn't my mother; she's my sister. And I know her inside out, a brother's illusion, perhaps. She's a proud girl with big brown skeptical eyes. As a teenager she was a diva in high heels, a terror on everyone, including her boyfriends, indifferent to school, secretive and manipulative—this she freely admits. She ran circles around me, despite being three years younger. Now she's an experienced wharf maven; she holds her own with all the fishermen, swears as creatively as they can, talking a mile a minute, a cigarette hanging from her lips with tough-chick ease, although she's trying to give up the smokes. From what I've seen, the men around here, especially the older and crankier retired types, love her greatly, They like her openness, and her differentness too. She's from here, but also an exile, an ex-Montrealer in the land of our parents. The local women are somewhat less appreciative of her charms, and some were fairly hostile after she got together with James. Migwash doesn't take kindly at all to outsiders, never has, never will. But Donna stood her ground and took on all comers. I love my sister's combativeness. Of course I want to wring her neck now and then, and I can imagine she feels the same about me. Such are the ways between us. I'm so pleased at how easily we've readopted the patter from years past, the mutual teasing, the older brother, the younger sister.

Donna and James. My lovely aunts. Alison and our boys. What they've given to me—so much.

This morning when we leave Prince Edward Island in the sunshine, Donna and I are efficient with the goodbye hugs. We don't draw it out and torture the others by shedding tears. We both have troublesome memories of my mother's histrionic departures after our family holidays here, crying for a full day before we got in the car and then remaining sullen for the drive to Montreal. But it is very difficult to say goodbye to my aunts. They're getting old, if not yet frail. These are strong women who survived terrible poverty growing up, and the almost literal decimation of their family, losing nine brothers and sisters out of fourteen. May and Fran made their own lives, developed points of views, squirrelled away enough savings to create their sanctuary here by the sea, in the village where they started out. But as we get in the car, I see in their eyes only fear that there'll not be another summer for them to play with our boys and to make them molasses cookies and meat pies. I believe there'll be another summer and another one after that, and that's what I tell them, promising to come back soon, maybe at Thanksgiving, or Christmas, or next summer, the sooner the better.

On the six-hour drive back to Foggy Cove, I spend long stretches ignoring the banter between Alison and the boys. Two or three times Alison says something like, "Larry, your son is talking to you." And then I awaken, join the conversation, before drifting into private thoughts again. I should be, as they say, more in the moment with my guys.

Maybe I've spent too many years behind a computer, lost in ideas and the fears they've generated in my head. How much time can you spend alone, thinking, without cannibalizing your better instincts? But something has changed in me for the better in the past year. Alison seems to think so. She tells me my fuse has lengthened. I still feel too blind in the ways of self-knowledge, lost.

I should count my blessings.

As we come over the hill into the village at sunset, it's another shock, which really shouldn't be one: fog. And the foghorn.

The drive had been sunny all day. We stopped for ice cream halfway home and then for dinner in a Halifax suburb. Sunny all the way on multi-lane highways and secondary roads twisting around coves and over coastal marsh. Sunny it was, and sunny it remains in my head, with Alison beside me and the boys behind us, as we drive into the mist together.

ACKNOWLEDGEMENTS

This book is mainly a collaboration with Anne Collins, my publisher and editor. Anne has the finest creative sensibility. She excavated the soul of this enterprise, gracefully retrieving it (and me) from the chaos of my unfocused ambitions, always with amazing solutions for the page and timely invitations for coffee to offer editorial counsel and her friendship. She has made me a better writer in part by helping me understand, finally, that readers have imaginations that need room to breathe and that they like to do some work themselves in creating the story.

Bruce Westwood of Westwood Creative Artists (WCA) is a valued collaborator in many ways. He suggested I drop everything and write this book and helped shaped the concept. He remains a patient and always entertaining mentor. I'm enriched by his creative spirit, business acumen and sense of humour—his kindness to me, really. I'm indebted to agent Natasha Daneman, also from WCA, who has been so supportive, always empathetic and insightful with her counsel. Carolyn Forde and Ashton Westwood from WCA were always helping me out in one way or another.

Thanks to everyone at Random House Canada for their work and support, including Kylie Barker, Pamela Murray and designer Leah Springate. Special thanks to the book's copyeditor, Heather Sangster.

Polly Moore was a sympathetic and diligent researcher. Friends helpful to the making of this book: Helen Reeves, Steve Manners, Johnny Pylypczak, Diti Katona, Peter Cavelti, Caroline Cavelti, Andy Wainwright, Brad Woods, Courtney Pratt, Nikola Nikola, Luigi Fraquelli, Tracy Westell, Mariëtte Roodenburg, Jennifer Barclay, Bruce MacCormack, Paul Devorer, Sam Hiyate, Nick Arvista, Elliot MacDonald, Tony Gallant, Isabel Carter, Bill and Janet Young, Mark and Juliet Turnbull, Jeff Kirby, Sybil Thuns. Much love to Stan and Vivian Smith for their support.

To all my friends and neighbours in Foggy Cove—whom I haven't named to protect their privacy and to disguise the real identity of our village—and especially to those who consented (and even requested) to become characters in the text, let me say that I gave it my best effort to shape a proper story about a world we all know is more or less inexpressibly beautiful. A big thanks to everyone involved in making Foggy Cove Commons a reality.

Thanks to the builder of our Foggy Cove house, my friend Richard Byers, a man of integrity, and to his skilled, conscientious crew, including Stephen Mossman, Lloyd Tanner, Fred Zinck, Ken Bell and Rob Fancy.

The Nova Scotia architect Brian MacKay-Lyons is a continuing inspiration (www.mlsarchitects.com). In the tense final days of the project, Brian gave me an undeserved but very welcomed ego boost by suggesting parallels between his creative ambitions and mine.

I guiltily acknowledge a stolen line (or two) from writer Ron Graham to describe the intent of the language laws in Quebec. A reading of James Laxer's excellent *The Acadians* enabled me to refer to the Acadian expulsion in no uncertain historical terms. The newspaper quotation I cited on page 251 comes from a *Globe and Mail* article, "Trendy partygoers quaff date-rape drug" by Jane Armstrong, published on December 14, 2004. I've tried to give credit where credit is due. Any errors in this regard will be corrected in future editions.

This book exists only because of the unconditional love and support of my wife, Alison Smith, and our boys, Theo and Jackson.